Children's Comprehension of Text

Research into Practice

K. Denise Muth
University of Georgia

Editor

International Reading Association
Newark, Delaware 19714

INTERNATIONAL READING ASSOCIATION

OFFICERS
1988-1989

President Patricia S. Koppman, PSK Associates, San Diego, California

Vice President Dale D. Johnson, Instructional Research and Development Institute, Brookline, Massachusetts

Vice President Elect Carl Braun, University of Calgary, Calgary, Alberta, Canada

Executive Director Ronald W. Mitchell, International Reading Association, Newark, Delaware

DIRECTORS

Term Expiring Spring 1989
  Marie C. DiBiasio, Rhode Island Department of Education, Providence, Rhode Island
  Hans U. Grundin, Language and Literacy Consultant, London, England
  Nancy W. Seminoff, Central Connecticut State University, New Britain, Connecticut

Term Expiring Spring 1990
  Jerome C. Harste, Indiana University, Bloomington, Indiana
  Jane M. Hornburger, Brooklyn College, CUNY, Brooklyn, New York
  Merrillyn Brooks Kloefkorn, Jefferson County Public Schools, Golden, Colorado

Term Expiring Spring 1991
  Vincent Greaney, St. Patrick's College, Dublin, Ireland
  Dolores B. Malcolm, St. Louis Public Schools, St. Louis, Missouri
  Ann McCallum, Fairfax County Public Schools, Annandale, Virginia

Copyright 1989 by the
International Reading Association, Inc.

Library of Congress Cataloging in Publication Data

Children's comprehension of text.

  Bibliography: p.
  1. Reading comprehension. 2. Reading (Elementary)
I. Muth, K. Denise.
LB1573.7.C46   1989   372.4   88-34806
ISBN 0-87207-744-6

Cover design: Boni Nash

Cover definition: T.L. Harris and R.E. Hodges (Eds.), *A Dictionary of Reading and Related Terms*. Newark, DE: International Reading Association, 1981.

Contents

Foreword   *v*

Introduction   *vi*

Part One   Narrative Text

1. Research on Stories: Implications for Teachers   2
   Jill Fitzgerald
2. Using Story Retelling to Develop Comprehension   37
   Lesley Mandel Morrow
3. Teaching Repetition as a Story Structure   59
   Gail E. Tompkins and Lea M. McGee
4. Teaching Narrative Text Structure: A Process Approach to Reading and Writing   79
   Christine J. Gordon
5. Using a Literary Framework to Teach Mysteries   103
   Charles W. Peters and Marilyn Carlsen

Part Two   Expository Text

6. Research on Expository Text: Implications for Teachers   140
   Wayne H. Slater and Michael F. Graves
7. Teaching Expository Text Structure in Reading and Writing   167
   Donald J. Richgels, Lea M. McGee, and Edith A. Slaton
8. The Teaching with Analogies Model   185
   Shawn M. Glynn
9. The Know, Want to Know, Learn Strategy   205
   Donna M. Ogle
10. Getting the Gist of Expository Text   224
    Ted Schuder, Suzanne F. Clewell, and Nan Jackson

Part Three Summary

11 The Comprehension Experience 244
   James H. Mosenthal

12 Questions and Concerns about Teaching Narrative and Expository Text 263
   Joan Nelson-Herber and Carolyn S. Johnston

Contributors

Marilyn Carlsen
Farmington, Michigan,
Public Schools

Suzanne F. Clewell
Montgomery County, Maryland,
Public Schools

Jill Fitzgerald
University of North Carolina

Shawn M. Glynn
University of Georgia

Christine J. Gordon
University of Calgary

Michael F. Graves
University of Minnesota

Nan Jackson
Harcourt Brace Jovanovich
Orlando, Florida

Carolyn S. Johnston
Glen Avenue Elementary School
Salisbury, Maryland

Lea M. McGee
Louisiana State University

Lesley Mandel Morrow
Rutgers University

James H. Mosenthal
Michigan State University

K. Denise Muth
University of Georgia

Joan Nelson-Herber
State University of New York
at Binghamton

Donna M. Ogle
National College of Education

Charles W. Peters
Oakland Schools, Pontiac, Michigan

Donald J. Richgels
Northern Illinois University

Ted Schuder
Montgomery County, Maryland,
Public Schools

Wayne H. Slater
University of Maryland

Edith A. Slaton
Southeastern Louisiana University

Gail E. Tompkins
University of Oklahoma

Foreword

Starting about 1980, the Annual Conventions of the International Reading Association began to reflect the growing concerns of researchers and practitioners about children's comprehension of text. Each year from 1980 to about 1987, this movement toward a richer understanding of basic processes and instructional practices of text comprehension gathered momentum. IRA's programs and journals have reflected this momentum. As we approach the close of this decade, it is fitting that IRA publish a volume summarizing and celebrating this text comprehension tradition. It is even more fitting that the publication contain essays, syntheses, and teaching suggestions from many of the individuals and groups who played an important role in establishing the momentum of the movement.

Readers will appreciate the flow of ideas in this volume. The structure is straightforward: Each of the first two parts, one for narrative text and one for expository text, begins with a thorough and readable review of the processes by which students understand text. Both of these chapters (Jill Fitzgerald wrote the narrative synthesis, and Wayne Slater and Michael Graves collaborated on the expository synthesis) provide the reader with excellent background for the informative and useful instructional chapters that follow. Part Three contains two "reflections." James Mosenthal invites us to consider the phenomenological experience of comprehension itself and reminds us that this experience, and not any preconceived set of skills or strategies, should guide our attempts to help students develop text comprehension expertise. Joan Nelson-Herber and Carolyn Johnston take the point of view of a reading professional in a school in asking and answering a wide range of questions of concern to anyone trying to implement a comprehension based curriculum.

On behalf of reading educators everywhere, I want to thank Denise Muth and her colleagues for putting together such a useful and fitting volume.

P. David Pearson
Center for the Study of Reading
University of Illinois at Urbana-Champaign

Introduction

The purpose of this book is to define and provide examples of narrative and expository text and to describe research based strategies for helping children comprehend these two types of text. Narrative and expository texts have different purposes and structures; therefore, different strategies are frequently necessary for teaching them.

The book is divided into three main sections: narrative text, expository text, and a summary. Both the narrative and expository sections begin with a chapter that reviews the current research in the area and then discusses instructional implications. These chapters are followed by four application chapters that describe instructional strategies for helping children comprehend narrative and expository text, respectively. The summary section consists of two chapters; one discusses the role instructional strategies play in the comprehension process, and the other addresses questions and concerns about the teaching of narrative and expository text.

In Chapter 1, Jill Fitzgerald defines narrative text in general, and stories in particular. She provides specific examples of the key features of stories and summarizes the current research findings on stories, focusing on the classroom implications of the research.

In Chapter 2, Lesley Morrow discusses the benefits of story retelling to enhance children's comprehension of stories and to develop their sense of story structure. She demonstrates how story retelling can be used both as an instructional strategy and as an assessment tool.

In Chapter 3, Gail Tompkins and Lea McGee present a strategy for teaching repetition as a story structure to enhance children's comprehension and production of stories. The authors provide a list of children's literature and basal reader stories that use repetition as a story structure.

Chapter 4 describes a process approach to teaching reading and writing of narrative text. Christine Gordon demonstrates how this process approach, which combines direct teacher explanation with collaborative learning, enhances children's knowledge of story structure.

In Chapter 5, Charles Peters and Marilyn Carlsen recommend an interactive approach for teaching mysteries. The authors demonstrate how to teach mysteries in the context of a literary framework.

In Chapter 6, Wayne Slater and Michael Graves define expository text and identify its key features and specific categories. They also summarize current research findings on expository text with a focus on classroom implications. As the research shows, knowledge of text structure is one of the most important variables in the comprehension of expository text. With this in mind, the first of the next four application chapters illustrates a strategy designed to teach students the basic expository text structures. However, as Slater and Graves point out, the expository texts that students encounter in their reading are not always well structured. Hence, the last three application chapters illustrate strategies that are designed to take students beyond the use of text structure.

In Chapter 7, Donald Richgels, Lea McGee, and Edith Slaton present their seven step approach for teaching children to recognize and use expository text structures in reading and writing. They also include criteria for selecting expository passages and examples that meet these criteria.

In Chapter 8, Shawn Glynn discusses the advantages of using analogical reasoning as a tool for understanding new concepts presented in expository text. He describes a strategy that uses analogies to capitalize on children's existing knowledge in order to make new concepts more comprehensible and memorable.

In Chapter 9, Donna Ogle discusses the importance of involving students in an interactive approach to reading expository text. She describes a strategy in which the teacher leads students in brainstorming before reading, generating questions during reading, and reflecting after reading.

In Chapter 10, Ted Schuder, Suzanne Clewell, and Nan Jackson present a strategy designed to teach children how to use the decision making process to get the gist or main idea of expository text. The strategy teaches children to form hypotheses, identify problems, and make strategy decisions before, during, and after reading expository text.

In Chapter 11, James Mosenthal reflects on the relationship between the comprehension process and strategies designed to aid comprehension. He points out that using strategies to reveal and teach the various features of narrative and expository text is not an end in itself. Strategies for comprehending text should be perceived as vehicles to understanding the author's purpose.

In Chapter 12, Joan Nelson-Herber and Carolyn Johnston answer questions that teachers and other reading personnel might have about teaching children comprehension of narrative and expository text.

This book provides teachers and other reading personnel with a synthesis of the recent research on children's comprehension of narrative and expository text and translates this research into practical strategies for classroom use. We hope that our book provides educators with a repertoire of research backed strategies designed to help children better comprehend these two types of text.

KDM

IRA DIRECTOR OF PUBLICATIONS   Jennifer A. Stevenson

IRA PUBLICATIONS COMMITTEE 1988-1989   John J. Pikulski, University of Delaware, *Chair* • Phyllis E. Brazee, University of Maine at Orono • Kent L. Brown Jr., *Highlights for Children* • Margaret K. Jensen, Madison Metropolitan School District, Madison, Wisconsin • Carole S. Johnson, Washington State University • Charles K. Kinzer, Vanderbilt University • Gloria M. McDonell, Fairfax County Schools, Fairfax, Virginia • Ronald W. Mitchell, IRA • Allan R. Neilsen, Mount St. Vincent University • Tom Nicholson, University of Waikato, New Zealand • Donna Ogle, National College of Education • Jennifer A. Stevenson, IRA • Anne C. Tarleton, Albuquerque Public Schools, Albuquerque, New Mexico

The International Reading Association attempts, through its publications, to provide a forum for a wide spectrum of opinions on reading. This policy permits divergent viewpoints without assuming the endorsement of the Association.

Part One
Narrative Text

1

Jill Fitzgerald

Research on Stories: Implications for Teachers

> This chapter reviews research on stories and begins by asking, "What makes a story?" Features of narratives and stories are discussed. The structural aspect of stories is detailed and results of research on stories are summarized, with special emphasis on findings of particular interest to teachers. The chapter concludes with comments on key issues to consider in classrooms and in future research.

In *Three by the Sea* (Marshall, 1981) Lolly, Spider, and Sam are having a picnic on the beach. After they eat, they look for something to do, and Lolly says, "Want to hear a story?" So, from her "reader," Lolly reads about a rat, a cat, and a dog who see each other. The boys don't like the tale and bet they can tell better ones. Sam's is about a rat who buys a cat for a pet, thinking they will be friends. After a bit of "small talk," the rat asks the cat what his favorite meal is. "I do not want to say," replies the cat, who then entices the rat to come with him to the beach, where they can be alone. Suspense builds over the next few pages, as the rat naively tries to guess the cat's favorite meal. Finally, after the cat gets the rat very close to him, he says, "What I like…is…CHEESE! I love cheese!" Rather than telling you Spider's story, I invite you to find the book and read it.

I've shared *Three by the Sea* with hundreds of teachers over the past few years. Generally, they agree that the first tale doesn't even seem to be a story, that Sam's story is better than Lolly's, and that Spider's story is best of all. Some interesting questions are raised: Why do we believe some texts are stories but others aren't? Why do we think some stories are better than others? This chapter addresses these questions and others, such as how teachers can help children to understand and write stories.

To set the stage for understanding stories, I present a way of classifying discourse as narrative, descriptive, or expository. Stories represent one of many types of narratives. In this context, key features of narratives are defined and accompanied by examples. The section ends with a summary of what makes a story. Since recent studies have focused on the structural feature of stories, story structure is explained in detail. The chapter closes with a summary of selected research on story features, focusing on findings that have implications for teaching and learning in language arts.

What Makes a Story?

It isn't easy to answer the question of what makes a story. Academicians from disciplines such as literary theory, rhetoric, anthropology, and psychology have studied written and oral texts for many years. While various disciplines give us widely different viewpoints about what makes a story, a perspective may be constructed to help provide a context for understanding the research on stories.

Discourse Classification

The sketchy view of discourse classification shown in Table 1 reflects the various features of stories and discourse that have been discussed in the research literature on stories. It is not intended to summarize or present a theory of discourse or narratives. Works by Brewer (1980), Chatman (1975, 1978), and others helped me organize my thinking about discourse types, and Table 1 represents an amalgam of their ideas, as well as my own (cf. Barthes, 1975; Brewer & Lichtenstein, 1982; Moffett, 1983; Pradl, 1982). Table 1 suggests that texts can be classified into three broad types (narrative, descriptive, and expository) and that every text has features that can be categorized as content, structure, style, force and affect, and transmission. In the following sections, I'll define the discourse types and discuss the five broad features of text, focusing specifically on narratives. Slater and Graves (this volume) focus on description and exposition.

Table 1
Discourse Classification

Discourse Types	Content	Structure	Style	Force and Affect	Transmission
Narrative					
Mystery Western Science Fiction Fairy Tale Short Story Biography Light Drama	Plot, Theme, Point, Social Interactions, Foreshadowing, Flashback, Repetition, Character, Setting, Problem or Conflict, Goal and Intention, Plan, Action and Event, Ending		E.g., "Once upon a time"	Entertainment Surprise Suspense Liking	Inside View Point of View
Literary Novel Short Story Serious Drama				Literary-Aesthetic Surprise Suspense Liking	

Dimensions of Discourse Type (column group header)

Fitzgerald

Table 1 (continued)
Discourse Classification

Newspaper	
Story	
History	Informational
Instructions	
Recipes	
Biography	
Message	
Novel	
Parable	Persuasive
Fable	
Advertisement	
Drama	
Descriptive	
Expository	

Discourse types. Brewer (1980, p. 223) defines a narrative as "discourse that attempts to embody in linguistic form a series of events that occur in time...[and that has] a causal or thematic coherence." He gives the following as an example of narrative text: "The boy saw a dandelion. He picked the dandelion. He gave the dandelion to his mother." Description "is discourse that attempts to embody in linguistic form a stationary perceptual scene." Exposition "is discourse that attempts to represent in linguistic form the underlying abstract logical processes...[such as] induction, classification, and comparison."

Features of text. Chatman (1975, p. 295) states that content in narratives is "the chain of events...and...existents (characters and settings), the objects and persons performing...."

Structure is in some ways a container, "the expression, the means by which the content is communicated [in narratives], the set of actual narrative 'statements' " (Chatman, 1975, p. 295). Langer also says, "The structure of a thing is the way it is put together....In every structure we may distinguish the *relation* or *relations,* and the items *related*" (Moffett, 1983, p. 1). So one way to think of structure of text is as the parts and the connections between the parts.

There are two levels of content and structure: one which may be characterized as the underlying story world reality, and one conveyed in the text. For example, the actual personality of the wolf in *Little Red Riding Hood* is the underlying content substance for the character, whereas the portrayal of the wolf by the words in the text may convey only aspects of what the wolf is really like.

Similarly, events may occur in one order in real time, but may be structured in a different order in a text. Brewer (1980, p. 230) gives a good example of how underlying structure can be different from the structure expressed in the written words. "A series of events such as *Man sees broken glass on road—Man tries to swerve car—Car runs over glass—Tire goes flat—Man jacks up car* can be expressed in completely reverse order by a narrative such as: *John was jacking up the car. He remembered the sickening thump-thump-sound as the tire went flat. Right before he ran over the glass he had tried to swerve the car. Now he certainly wished he had been paying more attention and had seen the glass in the road soon enough to have missed it."*

Style "...is the set of lexical and syntactic choices made by an author trying to express a particular underlying discourse content" (Brewer, 1980, p. 233). Use of dialect and phrases such as "once upon a time" and "that ever did live" are stylistic examples used in stories.

Force "...is an interaction of the communicative intent of the author and the perception of the reader" (p. 224). Each type of discourse (narrative, descriptive, and expository) may have four forces: informational, entertainment, persuasive, and literary-aesthetic (Brewer, 1980).

Affective factors refer to affects the text has on the reader such as feelings of interest, liking, surprise, and suspense.

Transmission refers to the actual formal expression of the text. Narrative transmission "...concerns the relation of time of story to time of the recounting of story" (Chatman, 1978, p. 22). Examples of aspects of narrative transmission are inside view, which means seeing inside a character, and point of view, which is the perspective provided by the narrator (Bruce, 1984).

Interrelatedness of text features. The vertical dimensions shown in Table 1 are not really as separable as the simple scheme suggests (Schiffrin, 1985). Content, structure, and affect often are especially difficult to disentangle (Glenn, 1980). For example, one way to talk about structure of a narrative is to say it usually includes these components: complication, exposition, and resolution. We can think of these parts as occurring in most narratives, *regardless* of the story content. But if we are required to read a narrative and then identify the words that embody the complication, the exposition, and the resolution, we must make the designations, at least partly, on the basis of the content of the text.

A number of features have been identified and studied which may occur in narrative discourse and which I think fall under both content and structure. (See entries in brackets in Table 1.) These features have labels that are used to refer to both the underlying substance, the meat of the text, and the rhetorical means of expressing that substance (cf. Chatman, 1975). Definitions for the features are:

Plot A particular configuration of goals, actions, and affective states (cf. Chatman, 1975, 1978; Lehnert, 1981, 1982; Propp, 1968)

Theme A concept or idea that serves to relate or unify large chunks of story information (Bisanz et al., 1978)

Point An aspect of content that generates interest (Wilensky, 1982, p. 373)

Social Interactions Mutual or reciprocal relations among individuals

Foreshadowing Representing beforehand

Flashback Interjection of events occurring earlier

Repetition Recurrence of events or words

Character Actor or existent (Chatman, 1975, 1978)

Setting Time, place, and/or props (Mandler & Johnson, 1977)

Problem or Conflict Obstruction of goal (Steinberg & Bruce, 1980)

Goal and Intention Desire, wish, want

Plan Method for achieving ends

Action and Event Happening

Ending Long range consequence of action (Mandler & Johnson, 1977)

Another reason it is difficult to disentangle the vertical dimensions shown in Table 1 is that authors often make dimensions such as structure and content interact to convey a special meaning and/or to elicit particular feelings from the reader. In the classic folktale *Goldilocks and the Three Bears,* for example, we see Goldilocks as a character with "special" tastes (for example, she favors the "just right" softness of a bed). Her "special" tastes are emphasized through the structural device of repetition of events (she also favors the "just right" temperature of the porridge and the "just right" size of a chair). We also see Goldilocks as extremely vulnerable. She's lost and in a place where she shouldn't be, and her vulnerability as well as the reader's anxiety over her safety are heightened because the author keeps repeating a scene while slightly modifying its substance. The author uses this structure to develop Goldilocks' personality and to elicit empathy, giving us a good illustration of the interconnectedness of structure, content, and affect.

Classification of narratives. Brewer (1980) classifies narrative discourse according to structure and force, resulting in twenty narrative forms such as history, instructions, mystery novel, fairy tale, short story, advertisement, and "serious" drama. (See Table 1 for the full list.) Notice that the terms narrative and story are not synonymous (stories are a special class of narratives) and that there are several types of stories.

A note of caution about discourse classification. Classification of discourse isn't as simple as the schematic in Table 1 would suggest. For one thing, texts often combine genres. For example, texts that we might call stories often contain streams of text that easily could be classified as descriptive and may have embedded expository passages that explain factual information. Slater and Graves (this volume) demonstrate how expository text can contain streams of narration. Similarly, content does not always distinguish narrative, descriptive, and expository text. Sometimes the same content can be rewritten as any of the three types of discourse. Brewer (1980) describes other difficulties with such classification schemes.

Summary: What Makes a Story?

Although it is difficult to say precisely what makes a story, there are some features that are commonly discussed in the literature. A story is a particular form of a narrative which sometimes has content that differs from the type of content found in other discourse types. It has a structure or structures distinct from description and exposition. It has plots, characters who interact socially, and themes; it can have inside view, vary in point of view, and have foreshadowing. It contains a problem or a conflict or both, revolves around characters' goals, and has some sort of action and resolution, with various elements related temporally and causally. A story is often characterized by stylistic words and phrases such as "Once upon a time," has an entertainment or literary aesthetic force, and often evokes affective feelings such as interest, surprise, and suspense.

Structure: One Dimension of a Story

Over the past decade, educational and psychological researchers have renewed their interests in how people understand and remember stories. However, most of the research has narrowly focused on one dimension of discourse, such as structure, and on only a few of the many narrative types, most notably on stories growing out of a folktale or fairy tale tradition. Because so much of the research has centered on structure, it is important here that we take a closer look at the way many recent researchers have characterized story structure.

Story structure is sometimes characterized as story schema, or "an idealized internal [mental] representation of the parts of a typical story and the relationships among those parts" (Mandler & Johnson, 1977, p. 111). One of the most popular ways to identify story structure or schema is through a story grammar, which identifies the important elements in a story and the way the elements are related to one another.

Four major story grammars, derived from an oral folktale or fairy tale tradition, have been used in research. These were developed by Mandler and Johnson (1977); Johnson & Mandler (1980), Rumelhart (1978), Stein and Glenn (1979), and Thorndyke (1977). The four grammars have many features in common. Here's a brief description of how the Mandler and Johnson grammar describes story structure.

Mandler and Johnson posit six major story elements: *Setting* (introduction of the protagonist or main character of the first Episode, which may include statements about locale, time, or props); *Beginning* (a precipitating event); *Reaction* (the protagonist's internal response to the precipitating event and formation of a Goal); *Attempt* (effort to attain the Goal); *Outcome* (success or failure of the Attempt); and *Ending* (long range consequence of the action, final response of a character, or an emphatic statement).

Some key stylistic phrases often signal certain story parts. "Once upon a time" frequently introduces a Setting. Beginnings are often signaled by "One day...." The protagonist's Reaction usually includes words such as "thought," "knew," or "felt." Goals tend to include words such as "wanted," "wished," or "desired." Sometimes Endings contain the phrase "happily ever after."

Actually, some of the six major story parts are subparts of higher order units. Figure 1 shows a diagram which can be used to represent the units and their relationships. At the highest level, a story consists of a Setting and one or more Episodes. The Episode is made up of a Beginning, which causes the Development (the unfolding of the protagonist's response to the precipitating event), which in turn causes the Ending. Within the Development, there can be two major chunks, called the Complex Reaction and Goal Path. The Complex Reaction consists of a Simple Reaction which causes a Goal. Gordon (this volume) discusses another interpretation of Reaction. The Goal Path consists of an Attempt which causes an Outcome.

Let's look at the story *Albert the Fish* (Stein & Glenn, 1977) shown in Figure 1 and locate the major story parts. The Setting introduces Albert and tells where he is. Next, Albert spies a big juicy worm; this is the Beginning, the precipitating event. The Development consists of Albert's Reaction (he "knew how delicious worms tasted"), Goal ("and wanted to eat that one"), his Attempt to get the worm, and the Outcome (the failure of his Attempt as he is caught by the fisherman). The Ending tells Albert's response to his predicament.

There are other ways in which story Developments may unfold. One example is when the protagonist's Simple Reaction to the Beginning is followed by nonplanful Action. Figure 2 shows a diagram for such a story: Once upon a time there were three lovely princesses (Setting). One day they went on a picnic (Beginning). The princesses were enjoying themselves so much that they forgot the time (Simple Reaction) and stayed too long (Action). When they got home, their father was angry with them (Ending). (This story is modified from Mandler & Johnson, 1977; Propp, 1968.)

Another classic example is called a Repeated Development. A Repeated Development occurs when an Attempt followed by an unsuccessful Outcome is repeated over and over. A character tries something, and it doesn't work. The character may try it again to no avail or may try something slightly different to no avail.

Goldilocks and the Three Bears has three Repeated Developments. As Table 2 shows, one happens when Goldilocks tries to eat but has to try three times before finding porridge that is the right

Figure 1
Identification of Story Categories in *Albert the Fish*

The Story

1. Once there was a big gray fish named Albert
2. who lived in a big icy pond near the edge of a forest.
3. One day, Albert was swimming around the pond
4. when he spotted a big juicy worm on top of the water.
5. Albert knew how delicious worms tasted
6. and wanted to eat that one for his dinner.
7. So he swam very close to the worm
8. and bit into him.
9. Suddenly, Albert was pulled through the water into a boat.
10. He had been caught by a fisherman.
11. Albert felt sad
12. and wished he had been more careful.

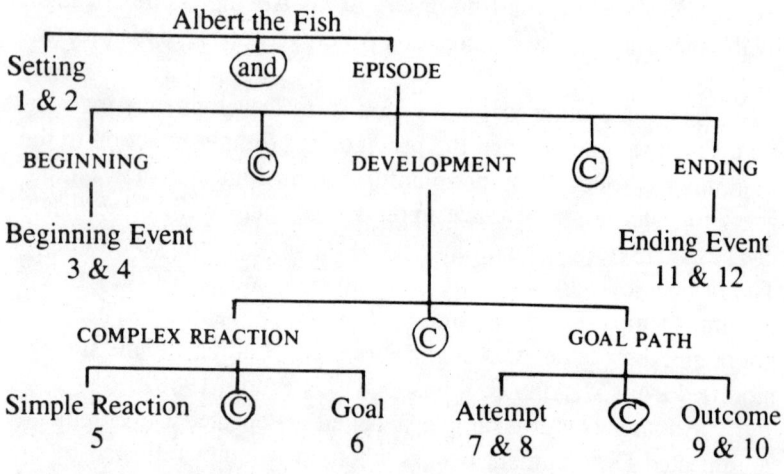

The Categories

C stands for Cause
From J.F. Whaley, "Story Grammars and Reading Instruction," *The Reading Teacher*, 1981, *34*, 764.

Figure 2
An Alternative Story Development

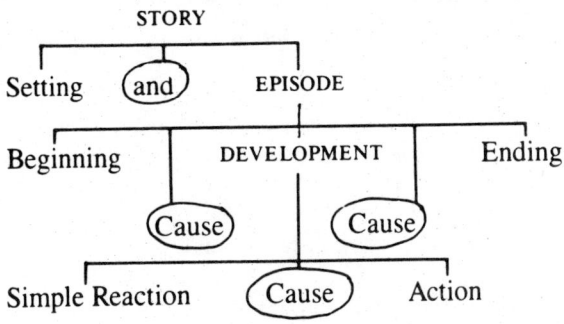

From J.F. Whaley, "Story Grammars and Reading Instruction," *The Reading Teacher*, 1981, *34*, 764.

temperature. Similar Repeated Developments occur when she wants to rest in a chair and lie on a bed. Many folktales and fairy tales use a repetition structure of this sort. (Tompkins and McGee, this volume, provide a detailed list of children's books and basal reader stories which use repetition.)

Stories also may have more than one Episode. Many seemingly simple stories are actually structured in relatively complex ways. One kind of structural complexity occurs when whole Episodes are embedded in Outcomes or Endings. Table 2 shows that *Goldilocks and the Three Bears* has four Episodes, with three of them embedded in Endings to previous Episodes.

Finally, the grammar is a way of representing stories "on the average." Not all stories explicitly include each of the story components described by the grammar. The Reaction and Goal often are omitted in the written text, but are usually inferred (Mandler & Johnson, 1977; Whaley, 1981b). Certain parts can be explicitly omitted if there are redundancies in the text which permit easy inferences about the omissions (Johnson & Mandler, 1980).

Table 2
Identification of Story Components for Main Events in *Goldilocks and the Three Bears*

Setting	Goldilocks is lost in the woods.
EPISODE 1	
Beginning	She sees a house.
Simple Reaction	Goldilocks is relieved
Goal	and decides to see if someone in the house can help her.
Attempt	She goes into the house.
Outcome	No one is home to help her.

Everything that follows is an Ending to EPISODE 1.

EPISODE 2	
Beginning	She sees porridge on a table,
Simple Reaction	realizes she is hungry,
Goal	and decides to eat some.
Attempt	She tastes some porridge from the first bowl,
Outcome	but it is too hot.
Attempt	She tastes some porridge from the second bowl,
Outcome	but it is too cold.
Attempt	She tastes some porridge from the third bowl,
Outcome	and it is just right, so she eats it all up.

Everything that follows is an Ending to EPISODE 2.

EPISODE 3	
Beginning	Next Goldilocks sees some chairs,
Simple Reaction	feels tired after eating,
Goal	and decides to relax.
Attempt	She sits in the first chair,
Outcome	and finds it is too little.
Attempt	She sits in the second chair,
Outcome	which is too big.
Attempt	She sits in the third chair,
Outcome	which is just right.

Everything that follows is an Ending to EPISODE 3.

EPISODE 4	
Beginning	Finally, Goldilocks sees three beds.
Simple Reaction	She is very tired now
Goal	and decides to take a nap.
Attempt	She lies down on the first bed.
Outcome	It is too hard.
Attempt	She tries the second bed.
Outcome	It is too soft.
Attempt	She tries the last bed,
Outcome	and it is just right.

**Table 2 (continued)
Identification of Story Components for Main Events
in *Goldilocks and the Three Bears***

Ending	While she is sleeping, the three bears come home, discover someone has been eating their porridge, sitting in their chairs, and finally, sleeping in their beds. And Goldilocks escapes out the window.

From J.F. Whaley, "Story Grammars and Reading Instruction," *The Reading Teacher*, 1981, *34*, 767.

There are several limitations and criticisms of the story grammar characterization of story structure which teachers should consider carefully. Critics of story grammars have been outspoken, and counterarguments have been plentiful (Black & Wilensky, 1979; Brewer, 1985; deBeaugrande & Miller, 1980; Johnson-Laird, 1983; Lehnert, 1982; Mandler & Johnson, 1980; Schmitt & O'Brien, 1986; Weaver & Dickinson, 1982).

Some of the major criticisms follow. (1) Researchers who devised the story grammars say that the grammars describe only a limited set of stories, those derived from a fairy tale or folktale tradition (cf. Mandler, 1984). They cannot describe stories, for instance, in which characters have simultaneously competing goals. (2) Some critics believe that structure is not an essential dimension of stories (Black & Wilensky, 1979; Johnson-Laird, 1983), or that knowledge of content (Weaver & Dickinson, 1982) is more important to decisions about what makes stories. A few psychologists contend that the content of plot units, such as requests that are denied or honored, or fleeting success leads readers to determine what makes stories (Lehnert, 1982). (3) Some say story grammars best describe relatively short, simple stories (cf. Schmitt & O'Brien, 1986). (4) Debates have been drawn over which specific type of grammar (one called finite state or one called context free) best describes stories (Black & Wilensky, 1979; Johnson-Laird, 1983).

Results of Research on Stories

In this section, I will summarize results of research on stories, giving special emphasis to findings of particular interest to teachers. The review is based on all research I could locate that investigated some aspects of stories, excluding research that merely used stories as a medium to investigate something unrelated to text features or story understanding. Studies that used the more generic term, narrative, were included when the research also appeared relevant to story understanding. Because of space limitations, only selected references are cited in this chapter.

In the following review, results of studies are sorted along the dimensions of stories noted earlier in this chapter and in Table 1. It was sometimes difficult to decide whether results of some studies (e.g., results on conflict) should be classified under the structure or the content dimension. When the material pertained to the *substance* of an element (e.g., type of conflict— interpersonal, environmental, or internal), it was included under the content dimension, regardless of how the author(s) of the article labeled the feature. If it referred to a formal characteristic (e.g., evidence that some kind of conflict is seen as an important element of a story), it went under structure. Such a distinction may help to clarify results of research. However, it is important to balance the simplification achieved by the distinction with the knowledge that there is considerable entanglement between the dimensions of structure and content.

Also, most of the research has used reading and listening and, occasionally, oral story telling; research on story writing is rarer. Results which were particularly informative about writing are separated from other findings.

Knowledge about Key Features of Text

Story structure. A major finding of research on stories is that many people have tacit knowledge about story structure (Applebee, 1977, 1978; Bartlett, 1932; Mandler, 1978, 1987; Mandler & Johnson, 1977; Stein & Glenn, 1979; Thorndyke, 1977; Whaley, 1981a, 1981b). That is, many people believe that a story has certain parts and that the parts occur in a relatively stable order from story to story. They may not attach labels to the parts or be aware of their own beliefs that there are such parts, but certain kinds of tasks used in research help to show that people do have the beliefs or knowledge.

In the jargon of the day, considerable research supports the contention that many people have a story schema. This is an incredibly robust finding that has emerged across a variety of ages, from preschool through adulthood, and across a variety of research tasks. Only three studies were noted which did not support the notion of story schema (Baker, 1978; Denhiere, 1982; Mosenthal, 1979b).

An example of one way researchers set up studies to ascertain individuals' knowledge of structural features of stories follows.

1. The researcher postulates the form of the story structure, a structure such as the one Mandler and Johnson's (1977) grammar characterizes.
2. The researcher reasons that if people have a mental representation of such a structure, they should give certain information in response to particular tasks.
3. Subjects listen to or read stories in canonical and/or noncanonical forms.
4. After listening or reading, subjects recall the story in total, summarize the story, and/or rate the importance of various parts of the story.
5. The researcher compares observed with predicted responses. A match implies support for the researcher's hypothesis. For example, when stories having a canonical form are better recalled than stories missing some constituents or presented in a mixed up order, the hypothesis is supported. Also, when subjects distort old information or add new information to make it conform to an ideally structured story, the hypothesis is supported.

Research has consistently shown that some story parts are more salient than others. For example, results of studies using story grammars tend to show that settings, beginnings, attempts, and outcomes are very central to people's ideas of what belongs in stories, but complex reactions and endings are often omitted. Many of the studies cited revealed this pattern, and, with the exception of children with certain types of brain damage (Dennis, Lovett, & Wiegel-

Crump, 1981), the pattern holds for every type of population examined.

Also, with the exception of results in one study (Monaco & Harris, 1978) information that is "higher" or more important in the story structure (e.g., higher in a diagram like the one shown in Figure 1) tends to be better recalled (Bower, Black, & Turner, 1979; Rumelhart, 1978).

A few studies have shown that although people commonly expect stories to be structured in certain ways, there are subjective variations in expected structures; individuals' story schemas sometimes differ slightly from one another (Knight & Yekovich, 1981; Mosenthal, 1979a, 1979b; Pollard-Gott, McCloskey, & Todres, 1979).

Content. A few studies have supported the contention that individuals think stories contain certain kinds of content. For example, Steinberg and Bruce (1980) say conflict is essential to "storiness." The expectation for conflict may be considered a structural expectation. However, there is apparently an expectation for the content of such conflict. Steinberg and Bruce (1980) describe three types of conflict: environmental, in which attainment of a character's goal is hampered by nature, society, or fate; interpersonal, in which two or more characters have incompatible goals; and internal, in which a single character has two or more incompatible goals. Intermediate grade children tend to expect story characters to be confronted with obstacles in each of the three forms (Fitzgerald & Spiegel, 1983b; Fitzgerald, Spiegel, & Webb, 1985; Spiegel & Fitzgerald, 1982).

Similarly, resolution of the conflict can be seen as a structural feature, but expectations for certain kinds of resolution can be seen as expectations for content. Steinberg and Bruce (1980) suggest five types of resolution. The goal is achieved, partially achieved, willingly forsaken, changed, or not achieved and the failure is accepted. Intermediate grade children also tend to expect conflict resolution, but they mainly think stories have the achieve/fail type of resolution (Fitzgerald & Spiegel, 1983b; Fitzgerald, Spiegel, & Webb, 1985; Spiegel & Fitzgerald, 1982).

Conflict resolution sequences are similar to other researchers' descriptions of plots. Research using plot units (configurations of goals, actions, and affective states) also provides some evidence that individuals think stories have certain types of plots, such as competition between two characters to attain a goal, or escape/pursue plots (Abrahamson & Shannon, 1983; Just & Carpenter, 1987; Lehnert, 1981, 1982; Reiser, Black, & Lehnert, 1985).

In addition, certain types of content are seen as more salient in stories than are others. Specifically, information that is most central to the causal chain of events is likely to be gauged as more important (Black & Bern, 1981).

Other. Limited evidence suggests that people tend to expect or prefer that stories maintain a consistent point of view (Black, Turner, & Bower, 1979). Also, individuals tend to organize characters in relation to story themes (Bisanz et al., 1978).

Effects of Text Features

Story structure. Many studies indicate that people use knowledge of story structure to guide their expectations, understanding, recall, and production of text (cf. the research already cited under the section on knowledge of story structure; Bereiter & Scardamalia, 1982; Black & Bower, 1979, 1980; Fitzgerald & Teasley, 1986). When reading and listening, people apparently use a sort of structural outline of the major story categories in their minds to make predictions and hypotheses about forthcoming information; anticipate certain types of material; set up slots which can be filled with information while reading or listening; serve as a framework, which helps allocate attention to certain information; better understand time and sequence in stories; and cue recall of specific information. When writing, people can use knowledge of text patterns or structures (Lindemann, 1982) to aid in shaping discourse.

Only two studies were found which challenged the belief that individuals use knowledge of story structure while reading or listening or to store information gained from reading or listening, claiming that the knowledge is used only to retrieve information from memory (Alba & Hasher, 1983; Kardash, Royer, & Greene, 1987).

Some have speculated that knowledge of story structure might either enhance or inhibit creativity or constructive thought (Bereiter, 1985; Fitzgerald & Teasley, 1986; Spiro, 1980). On one hand, story structure might be seen as a fundamental feature of stories, and knowledge of such fundamentals may facilitate creativity by freeing individuals' attention for other aspects of text production, such as imaginative content. Also, knowledge of fundamentals may enable artists to go beyond the basics, to create new and unique arrangements of elements of their medium. On the other hand, strict adherence to a particular story structure could have a detrimental effect, resulting in formulaic stories.

Very little research has been conducted on the effect of knowledge of story structure on creativity. Only one study on story structure was located which also assessed creativity; story structure instruction neither positively nor negatively affected judgments of creativity of fourth graders' written stories (Fitzgerald & Teasley, 1986).

Structure and affect. Structure also impacts readers' affective states (Brewer, 1985; Brewer & Lichtenstein, 1981, 1982). Narratives with no initiating event evoke little suspense. On the other hand, narratives with an early initiating event which catches the reader's interest, followed by material designed to prolong the interest, create rising suspense which drops at the point of the outcome. Narratives such as mysteries which contain an early significant event with some missing information also engage the reader.

Content. Some have argued that content influences what is recalled more than structure does. For example, Nezworski, Stein, and Trabasso (1982) found that when semantic content was controlled, recall of various parts of stories was nearly equal. They took one idea and rewrote it as a different story part in each of several stories. People recalled the idea equally well, no matter where it was placed in the story.

Also, typicality of certain content can affect recognition and recall (Adams & Worden, 1986; Graesser & Nakamura, 1982; Mandler, 1984). The most unusual content (such as actions, aspects of personalities, and locations of action) tends to be best recognized and recalled. (See Hastie, 1981, for criticisms of research on typicality effects.)

Content and affect. Certain content features also interact with reader characteristics to produce affective states. For example, when elementary grade students thought characters were similar to themselves, they identified more with the characters, which produced a greater feeling of suspense (Jose & Brewer, 1984). Additionally, degree of character identification, suspense, and liking of outcome were related to how much the students liked the story.

Other evidence suggests that material embedded in unfamiliar themes can increase readers' inferences, and themes more closely tied to students' backgrounds can produce more personal analytical responses (Alvermann, 1987; National Assessment of Educational Progress, 1981; Purves, 1973).

Development of Key Features of Stories

Structure. There is considerable evidence that many children develop a sense of story structure at a very early age (perhaps as young as four), and knowledge of story structure becomes richer and more elaborate as children grow older (cf. Applebee, 1978; Botvin & Sutton-Smith, 1977; Denhiere & LeNy, 1980; Fitzgerald & Spiegel, 1983b; Harste, Woodward, & Burke, 1984; Leondar, 1977; Mandler & Johnson, 1977; Stein & Glenn, 1979; Yussen et al., 1980). Children's knowledge of structural properties of stories tends to increase considerably over the intermediate grades (cf. Mandler & Johnson, 1977; Whaley, 1981a, 1981b). Developmental findings are robust across various research tasks such as retelling stories, unscrambling them, telling stories orally and in writing, predicting next parts of stories, and filling in missing parts of stories.

The development of structural knowledge can be characterized in at least three ways. First, when text is disorganized, younger children's accuracy of recall deteriorates substantially in comparison to that of older individuals (Buss et al., 1983; Mandler, 1978), suggesting that younger children are less able to impose order on the text as a means of facilitating recall. Second, some children, particularly younger ones, may lack knowledge of specific story constituents (cf. Applebee, 1977). Third, some younger children may be unaware of appropriate temporal connections between particular story parts (cf. Stein & Glenn, 1982; Stein & Policastro, 1984). For example, when important information is deleted from text or when the temporal order is disrupted, younger children are less able than older ones to restructure the text into an appropriate temporal order (cf. Buss et al., 1983; Stein & Glenn, 1982).

Just how children acquire knowledge of story structure is not clear. Many children appear to learn features of stories from exposure to them through reading and listening (Eckhoff, 1984). Instruction may also affect development of such knowledge. As noted earlier, structural knowledge blossoms over the intermediate grades. During those grades, teachers begin to stress certain characteristics of stories, such as plot, theme, and character development. Such instruction could contribute to growth in children's knowledge about these elements of stories.

It is especially important to note that nearly all studies of the development of story feature knowledge reveal that although most people tend to acquire such knowledge, some do not (Buss et al., 1983; Chall & Jacobs, 1984; Fitzgerald & Teasley, 1986; National Assessment of Educational Progress, 1977).

Content. Limited research provides mixed findings about the development of children's knowledge of various types of story content. For example, children's beliefs about kinds of conflict and conflict resolution may not change much over the intermediate grades (Fitzgerald & Spiegel, 1983b; Fitzgerald, Spiegel, & Webb, 1985). On the other hand, between the ages of five and ten, children appear to include more and more explanatory content in stories they tell (Stenning & Michell, 1985). Between the ages of six and twelve, children have a growing understanding of friendship interactions which seems to arise more from differences in social knowledge than from difference in how such knowledge is mentally organized (Goldman, 1982).

Other. Knowledge of how to shape stories (when writing) to elicit readers' affective feelings may develop later than knowledge of the structural dimension. There is some evidence that when writing or rewriting, students between grades three and seven have difficulty planning compositions to elicit certain feelings, such as suspense (Bereiter & Scardamalia, 1984).

Universality of Story Features

Do people from different cultures expect stories to have similar structures? The answer seems to depend upon which cultures and which types of stories are examined. For example, using stories from Mandler & Johnson (1977), Mandler et al. (1980), argued that story schema is universal (because Liberian patterns of story category recall paralleled those of Americans). However, several other researchers have found clear cultural differences in story structures (Anderson & Barnitz, 1984; Brewer, 1985; Kintsch & Green, 1978; Matsuyama, 1983; McClure, Mason, & Williams, 1983). For example, Blacks, Hispanics, and Anglos may use somewhat different strategies for opening and closing stories (McClure, Mason & Williams, 1983), and Matsuyama (1983) found that 80 percent of the Japanese folktales she studied did not have main characters who were goal oriented, an important feature of an American's expectations for story structure.

Brewer (1985), perhaps, comes closest to addressing the potential complexity in sorting out the conditions under which story structure is cross cultural. In stories from the oral tradition, he says the following story conventions vary from culture to culture: openings, characters, events, epilogues, and closings. However, story structure features of repetition and parallel structure and the use of affect to produce enjoyment were more likely to be universal.

Modality Effects and Story Features

A limited amount of research suggests that children and adults tend to reveal similar patterns in knowledge and use of story features whether they are listening, reading, telling stories orally or in writing, or viewing pictures (Gold, 1983; Hildyard & Hidi, 1985; Smiley et al., 1977).

Features in Children's Books

Structure. Little research has been done on the structure of children's books, but there is some evidence that among trade books and leading basals, many lower level books don't have any conflict (Bruce, 1984; Steinberg & Bruce, 1980). Also, structure as defined by story grammars is not related to traditional indices of readability (Templeton, Cain, & Miller, 1981). Such a finding may support the argument that readability formulas do not fully capture aspects of text that contribute to comprehensibility.

Revising basal stories to make them conform to an idealized story structure does seem to help students' comprehension, recall of explicit information, recall of order of events, and accuracy of recall (Brennan, Bridge, & Winograd, 1986; Feldman, 1985).

Content. Various analyses have been done of content features of children's books. Among the most salient findings: (1) As basal level goes up, more stories have contents not closely related to readers' experiences (Sippola, 1982). (2) When conflict is present in trade books and leading basals, lower level books are characterized predominantly by environmental conflict (Bruce, 1984; Steinberg & Bruce, 1980). (3) Some kinds of actions and themes predominate in certain children's literature, such as standing trial, being stranded and then rescued, being involved in pretense or being misunderstood, or attempting to achieve the impossible (cf. Abrahamson & Shannon, 1983). (4) Basal readers may have less variability in type of plot than do preferred children's trade books, consisting mainly of entries that have no identifiable type of plot, that have a confrontation with a problem, or that have a quest or aspiration (cf. Morrow, 1984).

At least one investigator found that revising texts by making character relationships, scenarios, and goals more explicit increased third graders' understanding of stories and enhanced their interest, but did not affect reading rate or amount of important information included in students' retellings (Sundbye, 1987).

Other features. Limited evidence suggests that inside view is less used in lower level basals, and the most common point of view in children's books is "observer account" (Bruce, 1984; Steinberg & Bruce, 1980).

Relationship of Knowledge of Story Features to Reading Ability

Structure. With some exceptions (McConaughy, 1985; Weaver & Dickinson, 1982), research findings show that better readers tend to have more fully developed knowledge of story structure (Fitzgerald, 1984; McClure, Mason, & Williams, 1983; Smiley et al., 1977). Also, better readers tend to include conflict as a structural element in their stories more often than poorer readers (Spiegel & Fitzgerald, 1982).

Instruction

While there is considerable agreement that it is useful for children to acquire knowledge of story features, there is some debate about whether and how features should be taught. Some dispel the idea of teaching story features directly to students (Moffett, 1983; Schmitt & O'Brien, 1986), believing that children will naturally learn the features through their own experiences with stories. Since much of the research on stories has used story grammars and story structure, a main debate over pedagogy has to do with whether teachers should directly teach children about story parts as defined by current grammars.

Typical arguments against teaching children about story parts include: knowing about a particular story organization will not help children understand the many noncanonical stories they will encounter; most children will learn the story parts on their own; it is not necessarily true that children need to have a conscious awareness of story parts; and it puts too much emphasis on one dimension of storiness and deemphasizes content, thereby "stripping the text of context" (Schmitt & O'Brien, 1986).

Counterarguments include: teaching children about common story structures will help them understand and generate some, if not all, stories; many children do not fully learn about story structure on their own; some children who don't have tacit knowledge of story structure may need more direct instruction which brings such knowledge to a level of awareness; and the problem of placing too much emphasis on one dimension of storiness can be overcome if teachers simultaneously stress other dimensions of stories and their interrelatedness.

Although the issues are unresolved, some intervention research begins to suggest that certain kinds of instruction designed to enhance knowledge of story features can be effective.

Structure. Over the past few years, the amount of research has steadily increased on instruction designed to increase children's knowledge of story structure in order to facilitate comprehension, recall, and story production. A variety of instructional techniques have been reported to be successful (mostly from work with elementary grade students): asking students questions that pertain specifically to story grammar categories; directly teaching children about the story parts by defining, demonstrating, and eliciting examples of story parts and their relationships; having children do exercises such as sorting story parts into piles and unscrambling disordered stories; completing flowcharts (often called story maps) to highlight important information from each story part identified in a grammar; and having students retell stories using a guide which helps them identify the important story parts. Some of these instructional techniques will be illustrated in forthcoming chapters.

A number of studies using such techniques report significant general effects on children's knowledge of story structure and on listening or reading comprehension and recall. The studies also report significant effects on awareness of specific story category adjacencies, knowledge of causal relationships, ability to infer and integrate information when specific content is forgotten, and accuracy of recall (Buss et al., 1983; Buss, Ratliff, & Irion, 1985; Carnine & Kinder, 1985; Fitzgerald & Spiegel, 1983a; Gordon & Braun, 1982, 1983; Morrow, 1985, 1986; Singer & Donlan, 1982; Varnhagen & Goldman, 1986). In many of the studies, significant effects emerged even after a short training schedule of one to six lessons.

Significant effects of story structure instruction on intermediate grade childrens' writing also have been found, although studies on writing are rarer. Effects have been noted specifically for organization of stories and, in at least one case (Fitzgerald & Teasley, 1986), for overall quality of stories (Fitzgerald & Teasley, 1986; Fitzgerald, Spiegel, & Teasley, 1987; Gordon & Braun, 1982, 1983).

Although many reports have been positive, a few using reading or listening have not (Dreher & Singer, 1980; Reutzel, 1984; Sebesta, Calder, & Cleland, 1982), and at least one on writing has not (Edmonson, 1983). Several factors may account for the insignificant findings. For example, it is harder to find statistically significant effects when the number of students in a study is small, which was the case in at least one of the studies where no significant effects emerged.

Another explanation is that the effectiveness of story structure instruction probably hinges on the preinstruction level of knowledge of the students (cf. Buss, Ratliff, & Irion, 1985). Students who have little knowledge of story structure are more likely to benefit from instruction in it than students who already have a fairly elaborated sense of story structure. Not many of the instructional studies conducted so far have screened students before teaching them. It's possible, then, that students' level of knowledge prior to instruction contributed to variations in results across studies. Also, some studies did not control for the readability and/or canonical story structure of the materials used for instruction and testing. If materials were too difficult to read or not well formed, effectiveness of instruction might be affected.

Content. Instructional research on nonstructural features of text is rare. At least two recent studies, however, touched on instructional techniques designed to enhance children's knowledge of nonstructural features of text. One found that having children act out the content of a story theme through fantasy play enhanced their comprehension (Pellegrini & Galda, 1982); and another found that a questioning routine about characters' motives or a single question about motives followed by feedback about correctness led to better understanding of characters' motives (Carnine et al., 1982).

Ideas for teaching story features. Though not research pieces themselves, many articles have been written in recent years that suggest applications of story feature research to the classroom (Fitzgerald, Spiegel, & Teasley, 1987; Jett-Simpson, 1981; Mavrogenes, 1983; McConaughy, 1980; McGee & Tompkins, 1981; Spiegel & Fitzgerald, 1986; Whaley, 1981b).

Summary of the Major Findings: Research on Stories
Knowledge of key features of text
- Many people have tacit knowledge about how stories are organized.

- Although people expect stories to be structured in certain ways, there are subjective variations.
- People tend to consider certain story parts (settings, beginnings, attempts, and outcomes) as more central to stories than others (complex reactions and endings).
- More important information in the story structure tends to be recalled better.
- Individuals think stories contain certain kinds of content (e.g., interpersonal conflict and competition).
- Certain kinds of story content (such as information that is most central to the causal chain of events) tend to be seen as more salient than others.

Effects of text features
- People use knowledge of story structure to guide their expectations, understanding, recall, and production of text.
- There is little evidence to help us determine whether knowledge of story structure either enhances or inhibits creativity.
- Story structure impacts readers' affective states. For example, narratives with no initiating event evoke little suspense.
- Content can influence what is recalled. For example, unusual content tends to be recognized and recalled best.
- Certain content features in stories may interact with reader characteristics to produce affective states. For example, themes closely tied to students' backgrounds can produce more personal analytical responses.

Development of key features of stories
- Many children develop a sense of story structure as young as four years of age. Knowledge of story structure becomes richer and more elaborate as children grow older, with considerable enhancement over the intermediate grade years.
- Some individuals do not easily acquire a rich sense of story.

Universality of story features
- Research does not clearly indicate whether people from different cultures expect stories to have similar structures.

Modality effects and story features
- A limited amount of research indicates that knowledge and use of story features is robust across different modality situations such as listening and reading.

Features in children's books
- Limited evidence suggests that among trade books and leading basals, many lower level books don't conform to adults' structural expectations.

Relationship of knowledge of story features and reading ability
- There tends to be a positive relationship between knowledge of story features and reading ability.

Instruction
- There are debates about if and how story features should be taught.
- Instruction can increase children's knowledge of story structure which can affect comprehension and recall as well as composition production.

Conclusion

Stories are a central part of children's lives, inside and outside of school. The more we know about stories and about children's knowledge of them, the better prepared we may be to guide children's academic and personal success.

My interpretation of the research on stories leads to a commentary on several issues that may be significant to teachers. First, a summary of selected research findings suggests that teachers may want to explore ways of facilitating the development of children's knowledge of story features. It is possible that at least some children might benefit from teachers' efforts to facilitate their understanding of story features.

Second, there are a number of direct and indirect ways that story feature knowledge can be enhanced in the classroom. A direct approach might involve the teacher telling children about the story parts and their relationships, defining them for children, and then having children produce them. An indirect approach might involve the teacher reading a story to children and then asking questions designed to tap information from central story categories. Questions could include "Where did the story take place?" and "How did it turn out?" All sorts of instructional methods in structural knowledge have been supported by research (although again, there are some mixed findings). To date, there has been little comparison of such methods, so there is no research to suggest that one method is better than another. Currently, teachers' choices of methods will depend on personal views of promising instructional techniques.

Third, we need to be sensitive to crosscultural variations in story feature expectations, especially structural ones. Minorities and students speaking English as a second language may bring a different understanding of storiness to the classroom.

Fourth, some investigators believe that readers and listeners can understand and recall text easier when it matches the readers' or listeners' expectations (cf. Haberlandt, 1980) or when it elicits involvement or interest (Bruce, 1984). Though quantitatively small, the research reveals an emerging sense of basal stories (especially lower level ones) that do not conform well to readers' structural expectations, are limited in the range of types of content (such as conflict), fail to provide a variety of views, and tend to distance readers from texts through diminished inside views. Such texts are "unpromising...candidate(s) for engaging a reader" (Bruce, 1984, p. 168). Publishers might need to take a second look at the content and structure of basals, and teachers might help by providing students with special guidance as they read the stories.

My fifth and sixth points are perhaps the most significant of all. The stories I've been talking about fall into a narrow band of the world of possible types of stories, a world snuggled inside the larger domain of narratives, which are contained in only one of at least three categories of text. I believe that our instruction should reflect as many of the text worlds as possible; teaching about stories should not preclude teaching about other types of texts.

Finally, stories can be characterized by several dimensions: structure, content, style, force/affect, and transmission. Most of the research on stories has dwelt on the structural dimension. As Spiro (1980, p. 273) said, "Work in the schema-theoretic tradition has focused on the structure of knowledge that must be analyzed, rather than on the texture that must be felt." While the research on structure has yielded considerable insight into stories and people's knowledge about stories, much more research is needed on the other dimensions of stories and especially on the interactions among dimensions. Some interesting strides have already been taken toward exploring nonstructural aspects such as force and affect. In the meantime, as we attempt to bridge the worlds of research and practice, we should be especially careful to help children to see structure as only one of several salient characteristics of text and, significantly, to see structure not as an isolated characteristic, but as one way of conveying meaning, a way that is deeply entangled with other facets of text.

References

Abrahamson, R.F., and Shannon, P. A plot structure analysis of favorite picture books. *The Reading Teacher,* 1983, *37* (9), 44-48.

Adams, L.T., and Worden, P.E. Script development and memory organization in preschool and elementary school children. *Discourse Processes,* 1986, *9* (2), 149-166.

Alba, J.W., and Hasher, L. Is memory schematic? *Psychological Bulletin,* 1983, *93,* 203-231.

Alvermann, D.E. Learning from text. In D.E. Alvermann, D.W. Moore, and M.W. Conley (Eds.), *Research within reach. Secondary school reading: A research guided response to concerns of reading educators.* Newark, DE: International Reading Association, 1987, 38-51.

Andersson, B.V., and J.G. Barnitz. Cross-cultural schemata and reading comprehension instruction. *Journal of Reading,* 1984, *28* (2), 102-108.

Applebee, A.N. A sense of story. *Theory into Practice,* 1977, *16* (5), 342-347.

Applebee, A.N. *Child's concept of story: Ages 2-17.* Chicago: University of Chicago Press, 1978.

Baker, L. Processing temporal relationships in simple stories: Effects of input sequence. *Journal of Verbal Learning and Verbal Behavior,* 1978, *17,* 559-572.

Barthes, R. An introduction to the structural analysis of narrative. *New Literary History,* 1975, *6* (2), 237-272.

Bartlett, F.C. *Remembering.* Cambridge, England: Cambridge University Press, 1932.

Bereiter, C. Toward a solution of the learning paradox. *Review of Educational Research,* 1985, *55* (2), 201-226.

Bereiter, C., and Scardamalia, M. From conversation to composition: The role of instruction in a developmental process. In R. Glaser (Ed.), *Advances in instructional psychology,* volume 2. Hillsdale, NJ: Erlbaum, 1982.

Bereiter, C., and Scardamalia, M. Learning about writing from reading. *Written Communication,* 1984, *1* (2), 163-188.

Bisanz, G.L., LaPorte, R.E., Vesonder, G.T., and Voss, J.F. On the representation of prose: New dimensions. *Journal of Verbal Learning and Verbal Behavior,* 1978, *17* (3), 337-357.

Black, J.B., and H. Bern. Causal coherence and memory for events in narratives. *Journal of Verbal Learning and Verbal Behavior,* 1981, *20,* 267-275.

Black, J.B., and Bower, G.H. Episodes as narrative chunks in memory. *Journal of Verbal Learning and Verbal Behavior,* 1979, *18,* 309-318.

Black, J.B., and Bower, G.H. Story understanding as problem solving. *Poetics*, 1980, *9*, 223-250.

Black, J.B., Turner, T.J., and Bower, G.H. Point of view in narrative comprehension, memory, and production. *Journal of Verbal Learning and Verbal Behavior*, 1979, *18* (2), 187-198.

Black, J.B., and Wilensky, R. An evaluation of story grammars. *Cognitive Science*, 1979, *3*, 213-230.

Botvin, G.J., and Sutton-Smith, B. The development of structural complexity in children's fantasy narratives. *Developmental Psychology*, 1977, *13*, 377-388.

Bower, G.H., Black, J.B., and Turner, T.J. Scripts in memory for texts. *Cognitive Psychology*, 1979, *11*, 177-220.

Brennan, A.D., Bridge, C.A., and Winograd, P.N. The effects of structural variation on children's recall of basal stories. *Reading Research Quarterly*, 1986, *21* (1), 92-104.

Brewer, W.F. Literary theory, rhetoric, and stylistics: Implication for psychology. In R.J. Spiro, B.C. Bruce, and W.F. Brewer (Eds.), *Theoretical issues in reading comprehension*. Hillsdale, NJ: Erlbaum, 1980, 221-239.

Brewer, W.F. The story schema: Universal and culture-specific properties. In D.R. Olson, N. Torrance, and A. Hildyard (Eds.), *The nature and consequences of reading and writing*. Cambridge: Cambridge University Press, 1985, 167-194.

Brewer, W.F., and Lichtenstein, E.H. Event schemas, story schemas, and story grammars. In J. Long and A. Baddeley (Eds.), *Attention and performance*. Hillsdale, NJ: Erlbaum, 1981, 363-379.

Brewer, W.F., and Lichtenstein, E.H. Stories are to entertain: A structural-affect theory of stories. *Journal of Pragmatics*, 1982, *6*, 473-486.

Bruce, B. A new point of view on children's stories. In R.C. Anderson, J. Osborn, and R.J. Tierney (Eds.), *Learning to read in American schools: Basal readers and content texts*. Hillsdale, NJ: Erlbaum, 1984, 153-174.

Buss, R.R., Ratliff, J.L., and Irion, J.C. Effects of instruction on the use of story starters in composition of narrative discourse. In J.A. Niles and R.V. Lalik (Eds.), *Issues in literacy: A research perspective*. Rochester, NY: National Reading Conference, 1985, 55-58.

Buss, R.R., Yussen, S.R., Mathews, S.R., Miller, G.E., and Rembold, K.L. Development of children's use of a story schema to retrieve information. *Developmental Psychology*, 1983, *19* (1), 22-28.

Carnine, D., and Kinder, D. Teaching low performing students to apply generative and schema strategies to narrative and expository material. *Remedial and Special Education*, 1985, *6* (1), 20-30.

Carnine, D., Stevens, C., Clements, J., and Kameenui, E.J. Effects of facilitative questions and practice on intermediate students' understanding of character motives. *Journal of Reading Behavior*, 1982, *14* (2), 179-190.

Chall, J., and Jacobs, V.A. Writing and reading in the elementary grades: Developmental trends among low ses children. In J.M. Jensen (Ed.), *Composing and comprehending*. Urbana, IL: National Conference on Research in English and ERIC Clearinghouse on Reading and Communication Skills, 1984, 93-103.

Chatman, S. *Story and discourse*. Ithaca, NY: Cornell University Press, 1978.

Chatman, S. Toward a theory of narrative. *New Literary History*, 1975, *6* (2), 295-318.

deBeaugrande, R., and Miller, G.W. Processing models for children's story composition. *Poetics*, 1980, *9*, 181-201.

Denhiere, G. Do we really mean schemata? In J. Le Ny and W. Kintsch (Eds.), *Language and comprehension*. Amsterdam: North Holland, 1982, 219-237.

Denhiere, G., and Le Ny, J. Relative importance of meaningful units in comprehension and recall of narratives by children and adults. *Poetics*, 1980, *9*, 147-161.

Dennis, M., Lovett, M., and Wiegel-Crump, C.A. Written language acquisition after left or right hemislecortication in infancy. *Brain and Language*, 1981, *12*, 54-91.

Dreher, M.J., and Singer, H. Story grammar instruction unnecessary for intermediate grade students. *The Reading Teacher,* 1980, *34,* 261-268.

Eckhoff, B. How reading affects children's writing. In J.M. Jensen (Ed.), *Composing and comprehending.* Urbana, IL: National Conference on Research in English and ERIC Clearinghouse on Reading and Communication Skills, 1984, 105-114.

Edmonson, J.C. *The effect of story grammar instruction on the writing process.* Paper presented at the annual meeting of the National Reading Conference, Austin, Texas, December 1983.

Feldman, M.J. Evaluating preprimer basal readers using story grammar. *American Educational Research Journal,* 1985, *22* (4), 527-547.

Fitzgerald, J. The relationship between reading ability and expectations for story structures. *Discourse Processes,* 1984, *7,* 21-42.

Fitzgerald, J., and Spiegel, D.L. Enhancing children's reading comprehension through instruction in narrative structure. *Journal of Reading Behavior,* 1983a, *15* (2), 1-17.

Fitzgerald, J., and Spiegel, D.L. The development of knowledge of social intentions, plans, and resolutions as reflected in story productions and recall of scrambled stories. In J.A. Niles and L.A. Harris (Eds.), *Searches for meaning in reading/language processing and instruction.* Rochester, NY: National Reading Conference, 1983b, 192-198.

Fitzgerald, J., Spiegel, D.L., and Teasley, A.B. Story structure and writing. *Academic Therapy,* 1987, *22* (3), 255-262.

Fitzgerald, J., Spiegel, D.L., and Webb, T.B. Development of children's knowledge of story structure and content. *Journal of Educational Research,* 1985, *79* (2), 101-108.

Fitzgerald, J., and Teasley, A. Effects of instruction in narrative structure on children's writing. *Journal of Educational Psychology,* 1986, *78* (6), 424-433.

Gaines, R., Mandler, J.M., and Bryant, P. Immediate and delayed story recall by hearing and deaf children. *Journal of Speech and Hearing Research,* 1981, *24* (3), 116-122.

Glenn, C.G. Relationship between story content and structure. *Journal of Educational Psychology,* 1980, *72* (4), 550-560.

Gold, R. Recall of story schema categories by reading disabled adults: Effect of mode of presentation. *Perceptual and Motor Skills,* 1983, *56,* 387-396.

Goldman, S.R. Knowledge systems for realistic goals. *Discourse Processes,* 1982, *5* (1), 279-303.

Gordon, C.J., and Braun, C. Story schemata: Metatextual aid to reading and writing. In J.A. Niles and L.A. Harris (Eds.), *New inquiries in reading and instruction.* Rochester, NY: National Reading Conference, 1982, 262-268.

Gordon, C.J., and Braun, C. Using story schema as an aid to reading and writing. *The Reading Teacher,* 1983, *37* (2), 116-121.

Graesser, A.C., and Nakamura, G.V. The impact of a schema on comprehension and memory. In G.H. Bower (Ed.), *The psychology of learning and motivation,* volume 16. New York: Academic Press, 1982, 59-109.

Graybeal, C.M. Memory for stories in language impaired children. *Applied Psycholinguistics,* 1981, *2,* 269-283.

Haberlandt, K. Story grammar and reading time of story constituents. *Poetics,* 1980, *9,* 99-116.

Harste, J.C., Woodward, V.A., and Burke, C.L. *Language stories and literacy lessons.* Portsmouth, NH: Heinemann Educational Books, 1984.

Hastie, R. Schematic principles in human memory. In E.T. Higgins, C.P. Herman, and M.P. Zanna (Eds.), *Social cognition: The Ontario symposium,* volume 1. Hillsdale, NJ: Erlbaum, 1981, 95-102.

Hildyard, A., and Hidi, S. Oral-written differences in the production and recall of narratives. In D.R. Olson, N. Torrance, and A. Hildyard (Eds.), *Literacy, language, and learning: The nature and consequences of reading and writing.* Cambridge: Cambridge University Press, 1985, 285-306.

Jett-Simpson, M. Writing stories using model structure: The circle story. *Language Arts,* 1981, *58,* 293-300.

Johnson, N.S., and Mandler, J.M. A tale of two structures: Underlying and surface forms in stories. *Poetics,* 1980, *9,* 51-68.

Johnson-Laird, P.M. *Mental models.* Cambridge, MA: Harvard University Press, 1983.

Jose, B.E., and Brewer, W.F. The development of story liking: Character identification, suspense, and outcome resolution. *Developmental Psychology,* 1984, *20* (5), 911-924.

Just, M.A., and Carpenter, P.A. *The psychology of reading and language comprehension.* Boston, MA: Allyn & Bacon, 1987.

Kardash, C.A., Royer, J.M., and Greene, B. *Locus of schema effects on prose: Storage or retrieval.* Paper presented at the annual meeting of the American Educational Research Association, Washington, DC, April 1987.

Kintsch, W., and Greene, E. The role of culture specific schemata in the comprehension and recall of stories. *Discourse Processes,* 1978, *1* (1), 1-13.

Knight, D.L., and Yekovich, F.R. *Subjective story structure in deaf adults.* Paper presented at the annual meeting of the American Educational Research Association, Los Angeles, California, April 1981.

Lehnert, W.G. Plot units and narrative summarization. *Cognitive Science,* 1981, *5,* 293-331.

Lehnert, W.G. Plot units: A narrative summarization strategy. In W.G. Lehnert and M.R. Ringle (Eds.), *Strategies for natural language processing.* Hillsdale, NJ: Erlbaum, 1982, 375-412.

Leondar, B. Hatching plots: Genesis of storymaking. In D. Perkins and B. Leondar (Eds.), *The arts and cognition.* Baltimore: Johns Hopkins Press, 1977, 172-191.

Lindemann, E. *A rhetoric for writing teachers.* New York: Oxford University Press, 1982.

Mandel, R.G., and Johnson, N.S. A developmental analysis of story recall and comprehension in adulthood. *Journal of Verbal Learning and Verbal Behavior,* 1984, *2,* 643-659.

Mandler, J.M. A code in the node: The use of a story schema in retrieval. *Discourse Processes,* 1978, *1,* 14-35.

Mandler, J.M. On the psychological reality of story structure. *Discourse Processes,* 1987, *10* (1), 1-29.

Mandler, J.M. *Stories, scripts, and scenes: Aspects of schema theory.* Hillsdale, NJ: Erlbaum, 1984.

Mandler, J.M., and Johnson, N.S. On throwing out the baby with the bathwater: A reply to Black and Wilensky's evaluation of story grammars. *Cognitive Science,* 1980, *4,* 305-312.

Mandler, J.M., and Johnson, N.S. Remembrance of things parsed: Story structure and recall. *Cognitive Psychology,* 1977, *9,* 111-115.

Mandler, J.M., Scribner, S., Cole, M., and DeForest, M. Cross-cultural invariance in story recall. *Child Development,* 1980, *51,* 19-26.

Marshall, E. *Three by the sea.* New York: Dial Press, 1981.

Matsuyama, U.K. Can story grammar speak Japanese? *The Reading Teacher,* 1983, *36* (7), 666-669.

Mavrogenes, N.A. Teaching implications of the schemata theory of comprehension. *Reading World,* 1983, *22,* 295-305.

McClure, E., Mason, J., and Williams, J. Sociocultural variables in children's sequencing of stories. *Discourse Processes,* 1983, *6,* 131-143.

McConaughy, S.H. Good and poor readers' comprehension of story structure across different input and output modalities. *Reading Research Quarterly,* 1985, *20* (2), 219-232.

McConaughy, S.H. Using story structure in the classroom. *Language Arts,* 1980, *57,* 157-165.

McGee, L.M., and Tompkins, G.E. The videotape answer to independent reading comprehension activities. *The Reading Teacher,* 1981, *34* (4), 427-434.

Moffett, J. *Teaching the universe of discourse.* Boston: Houghton Mifflin, 1968, 1983.

Monoco, G.E., and Harris, R.J. The influence of narrative structure on memory. *Bulletin of the Psychonomic Society,* 1978, *11* (6), 393-396.

Morrow, L.M. Effects of structural guidance in story retelling on children's dictation of original stories. *Journal of Reading Behavior*, 1986, *18* (2), 135-152.
Morrow, L.M. Reading and retelling stories: Strategies for emergent readers. *The Reading Teacher*, 1985, *38* (9), 870-875.
Morrow, L.M. Reading stories to young children: Effects of story structure and traditional questioning strategies on comprehension. *Journal of Reading Behavior*, 1984, *16* (4), 273-288.
Mosenthal, P. Children's strategy preferences for resolving contradictory story information under two social conditions. *Journal of Experimental Child Psychology*, 1979a, *28*, 323-343.
Mosenthal, P. Three types of schemata in children's recall of cohesive and noncohesive text. *Journal of Experimental Child Psychology*, 1979b, *27*, 129-142.
National Assessment of Educational Progress. *Reading, thinking, and writing: Results for the 1979-1980 national assessment of reading and literature*. Denver, CO: Education Commission of the States, 1981.
National Assessment of Educational Progress. *Write/rewrite: An assessment of revision skills. Selected results from the second national assessment of writing*. Washington, DC: U.S. Government Printing Office, 1977. (ED 141 826)
Nezworski, M.T., Stein, N.L., and Trabasso, T. Story structure versus content effects on children's recall of evaluative inferences. *Journal of Verbal Learning and Verbal Behavior*, 1982, *21*, 196-206.
Pellegrini, A.D., and Galda, L. The effects of thematic fantasy play training on the development of children's story comprehension. *American Educational Research Journal*, 1982, *19* (3), 443-452.
Pollard-Gott, L., McCloskey, M., and Todres, A.K. Subjective story structure. *Discourse Processes*, 1979, *2*, 251-281.
Pradl, G.M. (Ed.). *Prospect and retrospect: Selective essays of James Britton*. Montclair, NJ: Boynton/Cook, 1982.
Propp, V. *Morphology of the folktale*, second edition. Translated by Scott. Baltimore, MD: Port City Press, 1968. (Originally published Leningrad, 1928.)
Purves, A.C. *International studies in evaluation II: Literature education in ten countries*. Stockholm, Sweden: Almquist and Wiksell, 1973.
Reiser, B.J., Black, J.B., and Lehnert, W.G. Thematic knowledge structures in the understanding and generation of narratives. *Discourse Processes*, 1985, *8*, 357-389.
Reutzel, D.R. Story mapping: An alternative approach to comprehension. *Reading World*, 1984, *24* (2), 11-25.
Rumelhart, D.E. Understanding and summarizing brief stories. In D. LaBerge and S.J. Samuels (Eds.), *Basic processes in reading: Perception and comprehension*. Hillsdale, NJ: Erlbaum, 1978, 265-303.
Schiffrin, D. Multiple constraints on discourse options: A quantitative analysis of causal sequences. *Discourse Processes*, 1985, *8*, 281-303.
Schmitt, M.C., and O'Brien, D. Story grammars: Some cautions about the translation of research into practice. *Reading Research and Instruction*, 1986, *26* (1), 1-8.
Sebesta, S.L., Calder, J.W., and Cleland, L.N. A story grammar for the classroom. *The Reading Teacher*, 1982, *36* (2), 180-184.
Singer, H., and Donlan, D. Active comprehension: Problem solving schema with question generation for comprehension of complex short stories. *Reading Research Quarterly*, 1982, *17* (2), 166-186.
Sippola, A.E. Story distance in basal readers. *The Reading Teacher*, 1982, *35*, 550-553.
Smiley, S.S., Oakley, D.D., Worthen, D., Campione, J.C., and Brown, D.L. Recall of thematically relevant materials by adolescent good and poor readers as a function of written versus oral presentation. *Journal of Educational Psychology*, 1977, *69*, 381-387.
Spiegel, D.L., and Fitzgerald, J. Conflict and conflict structures in stories told by children. In J.A. Niles and L.A. Harris (Eds.), *New inquiries in reading research and instruction*. Rochester, NY: National Reading Conference, 1982, 282-286.

Spiegel, D.L., and Fitzgerald, J. Improving reading comprehension through instruction about story parts. *The Reading Teacher,* 1986, *39* (7), 676-682.

Spiro, R.J. Constructive prose comprehension and recall. In R.J. Spiro, B.C. Bruce, and W.F. Brewer (Eds.), *Theoretical issues in reading comprehension.* Hillsdale, NJ: Erlbaum, 1980, 245-278.

Stein, N.L., and Glenn, C. An analysis of story comprehension in elementary school children. In R.O. Freedle (Ed.), *New directions in discourse processing,* volume 2. Norwood, NJ: Ablex, 1979, 53-120.

Stein, N.L., and Glenn, C. Children's concept of time: The development of a story schema. In W.J. Friedman (Ed.), *The developmental psychology of time.* New York: Academic Press, 1982, 255-282.

Stein, N.L., and Glenn, C. *The role of structural variation in children's recall of simple stories.* Paper presented at the annual meeting of the Society for Research in Child Development, New Orleans, 1977.

Stein, N.L., and Policastro, M. The concept of a story: A comparison between children's and teachers' viewpoints. In H. Mandl, N.L. Stein, and T. Trabasso (Eds.), *Learning and comprehension of text.* Hillsdale, NJ: Erlbaum 1984, 113-155.

Steinberg, C., and Bruce, B. Higher level features in children's stories: Rhetorical structure and conflict. In M.L. Kamil and A.J. Moe (Eds.), *Perspectives on reading research and instruction.* Washington, DC: National Reading Conference, 1980, 117-125.

Stenning, K., and Michell, L. Learning how to tell a good story: The development of content and language in children's telling of one tale. *Discourse Processes,* 1985, *8,* 261-279

Sundbye, N. Text explicitness and inferential questioning: Effects on story understanding and recall. *Reading Research Quarterly,* 1987, *22* (1), 82-98.

Templeton, S., Cain, C.T., and Miller, J.O. Reconceptualizing readability: The relationship between surface and underlying structure analyses in predicting the difficulty of basal reader stories. *Journal of Educational Research,* 1981, *74* (6), 382-387.

Thorndyke, P. Cognitive structures in comprehension and memory of narrative discourse. *Cognitive Psychology,* 1977, *9,* 97-110.

Varnhagen, C.K., and Goldman, S.R. Improving comprehension: Causal relations instruction for learning handicapped learners. *The Reading Teacher,* 1986, *39* (9), 896-904.

Weaver, P., and Dickinson, D.K. Scratching below the surface structure: Exploring the usefulness of story grammars. *Discourse Processes,* 1982, *5,* 225-243.

Whaley, J.F. Readers' expectations for story structure. *Reading Research Quarterly,* 1981a, *16,* 90-114.

Whaley, J.F. Story grammars and reading instruction. *The Reading Teacher,* 1981b, *34* (7), 762-771.

Wilensky, R. Points: A theory of the structure of stories in memory. In A.G. Lehnert and M.H. Ringle (Eds.), *Strategies for natural language processing.* Hillsdale, NJ: Erlbaum, 1982, 345-374.

Worden, P.E., Malmgren, I., and Gabourie, P. Memory for stories in learning disabled adults. *Journal of Learning Disabilities,* 1982, *15,* 145-152.

Yussen, S.R., Matthews, S.R., Buss, R.R., and Kane, P.T. Developmental change in judging important and critical elements of stories. *Developmental Psychology,* 1980, *16* (3), 213-219.

2   Lesley Mandel Morrow

Using Story Retelling to Develop Comprehension

> This chapter discusses the importance of children's active participation in literature experiences. The author focuses on story retelling as an active reconstructive experience that can foster the development of children's comprehension. The first part of the chapter discusses research and theoretical values for the use of this strategy. Emphasis is then placed on guiding children in how to retell stories, materials that will promote retelling in the classroom, instructional strategies that encourage retelling, and retelling as a tool for assessing comprehension.

Reading stories to children has long been recognized as beneficial by both educators and the general public. Teachers acknowledge the importance of classroom story times, and generations of parents have read stories to children as part of a bedtime ritual. Such popular practices and general perceptions have been reinforced by theoretical, correlational, case study, and anecdotal reports that identify direct relationships between reading stories to children and specific aspects of their literacy development.

In theoretical perspectives, Clay (1979) and Smith (1978) have suggested that reading to youngsters helps them learn about features of written language. They learn that written language is different from oral language, that print generates meaning, and that words on a page have sounds.

The relationship between reading to children and literacy development has been demonstrated. Studies have found that early readers (including children who learned to read before they entered school) and successful readers tend to have been read to frequently at home (Clark, 1984; Durkin, 1966, 1974; Mason & Blanton, 1971; Morrow, 1983; Sutton, 1964; Teale, 1978; Walker & Kuerbitz, 1979). Children's language development, specifically growth in syntactic complexity and vocabulary, is associated with early read aloud experiences (Burroughs, 1972; Chomsky, 1972; Irwin, 1960; Templin, 1957).

According to anecdotal reports and case studies by Baghban (1984), Doakes (1981), Hoffman (1982), and Rhodes (1979), children to whom stories are frequently read know how to handle books, can tell which is the front of the book, and know the appropriate direction for reading print. In classrooms where stories were read daily over a long period of time, children scored significantly better on measures of vocabulary, comprehension, and decoding ability than did children in classrooms where stories weren't read (Cohen, 1968; Feitelson, Kita, & Goldstein, 1986).

Recent investigations have attempted to show why reading stories to children is so valuable. Experimental research in school settings has tried to determine the types of activity that enhance literacy skills through storybook readings. Some of these studies have involved children in different forms of active participation after the storybook reading. Others who have focused on the influence of the teacher when reading to a whole class have found that the teacher's reading style affects children's comprehension of stories (Dunning & Mason, 1984; Green & Harker, 1982; Peterman, Dunning, & Mason, 1985).

We are in the early stages of learning more precisely how story reading helps to develop literacy, but important practices already have been indicated. Simply reading to children does not necessarily bring positive results. What happens before, during, and after the reading; how the child participates in the event; and the style in which the story is read all seem to play important roles in children's literacy development.

Children's interaction with adults in book reading experiences enhances their development of comprehension, oral language, and sense of story structure (Blank & Sheldon, 1971; Bower, 1975; Fitzgerald, Gordon, this volume). Brown's (1975) research suggests that the active involvement of children in story reconstruction facilitates comprehension of the story. Reconstruction was defined in Brown's study as thinking about individual story events and arranging pictures of the story in sequence. By mentally reconstructing events and arranging pictures, children built an internal representation of the story.

Pellegrini and Galda (1982) found that children's story comprehension and retelling ability improved with their active involvement and peer interaction in story reconstruction through role playing. Similarly, Amato and Ziegler (1973) found that retelling enables the child to play a large and active role in reconstructing stories and provides for interaction between the teller and the listener.

Support for Story Retelling

Story retelling appears to have potential for skill development. However, it has not been widely tested as an instructional technique. There have been studies of children's participation in strategies with characteristics similar to those of story retelling. Blank and Sheldon (1971) reported that both semantic recall and syntactic complexity in the language of four to six year olds were enhanced when subjects were asked to repeat sentences in a story during a story reading. Zimiles and Kuhns (1976) found that retelling improved story comprehension in six to eight year olds who were asked to retell a story after it was read to them. Posttests indicated that retelling stories shortly after listening to them facilitated recall.

Morrow (1984, 1985, 1986) carried out three different studies with kindergarten children to determine specific instructional benefits of story retelling. Children in experimental groups retold stories after listening to them. In their eight weekly sessions, guidance in retelling was offered when children needed assistance. Significant improvement was found for the experimental groups in oral language complexity, comprehension of story, sense of story structure during retelling, and inclusion of structural elements in dictations of original stories generated by the youngsters. Children who were considered to be low achievers also made significant gains in the areas tested.

In spite of the apparent benefits, a survey of nursery schools and kindergartens reveals that children rarely are given the opportunity to retell stories in school since teachers tend to view retelling as time consuming and difficult for children (Morrow, 1982). There is however, sufficient data documenting the educational value of retelling. Consequently, retelling stories in the classroom probably should be encouraged.

Engaging children in retelling a story reflects a holistic concept of reading comprehension. Retelling requires the reader or listener to integrate information by relating parts of the story to one another and to personalize information by relating it to one's own background of experience. As an activity, it contrasts with the piecemeal approach of traditional teacher posed questions which require students to respond with specific bits of information about the text (Morrow et al., 1986).

Rose, Cundick, and Higbee (1983) found that retelling or verbal rehearsal significantly increased the reading comprehension of elementary age learning disabled children. This finding is particularly important since reading deficits in learning disabled children have been found to be associated with production deficiencies in mnemonic strategies (Tarver, Hallahan, & Kauffman, 1976; Wong, Wong, & Foth, 1977).

Another study by Gambrell, Pfeiffer, and Wilson (1985) found that having fourth grade students engage in retelling resulted in superior performance in reading comprehension immediately following the silent reading of the test passage and on a delayed recall test two days later.

These studies suggest that verbal rehearsal of what has been read or listened to results in significant learning with respect to the comprehension and recall of discourse. The reader or listener learns something about the organization and retention of text information. Engaging in retelling during and following text processing (Gambrell, Pfeiffer, & Wilson, 1985) helps children to plan actively, to organize, and to deploy their processing capacities more effectively.

What Are Retellings?

Retellings are postreading or postlistening recalls in which readers or listeners tell what they remember either orally or in writing. This chapter focuses on oral retelling by children in kindergarten through third grade. According to Johnson (1983, p.54) "retelling is the most straightforward assessment...of the result of text-reader interaction."

Retelling indicates a reader's or listener's assimilation and reconstruction of text information, and it can reflect comprehension. Retelling allows readers or listeners to structure responses according to personal and individual interpretations of text. It is an active procedure that involves children in the reconstruction of text and also allows interaction between adults and children. Retelling encourages both integration and personalization of content, helping children see how parts of the text interrelate and how the text meshes with their own experiences.

Vygotsky's (1978) definition of higher mental functions as internalized social relationships further contributes to the discussion. Applying Vygotsky's theory, literacy appears to develop from children's social interactions with others in specific environments involving reading, writing, and oral language (see Ogle, this volume). The literacy activities and interactions mediated by adults determine children's ideas about skills acquired in literacy development (Teale & Sulzby, in press).

Holdaway's (1979) model of developmental teaching indicates that children benefit most when their earliest experiences with storybooks are mediated by adults who provide problem solving situations. Children are asked to respond (in this case, retell the story), and the adults offer information when necessary (in this case, guide the retelling). In such situations, children and adults interact to integrate, construct, reconstruct, and make relationships with printed text. One of the primary goals of retelling is the reconstruction of story meaning within the interactive process. The interaction during story retelling is interpsychological as adult and child reconstruct meaning together, and intrapsychological, as the child gains the ability to undertake the retelling task independently (Teale, 1984).

The Use of Story Retelling in the Classroom

Instructing and Guilding Children in Story Retelling

Retelling is not an easy procedure for students of any age,

especially if they have had no prior experience with it. Morrow (1985) found that children had difficulty retelling, but that practice added to both the quality of retellings and the ease with which students approached the task. Children should be told before reading or listening to material that they will be asked to retell it.

Further guidance depends on the purpose for retelling. If the immediate intent is to teach or test sequence, for instance, instruct the child to concentrate on what happenend first, second, and so on. If the goal is to teach or assess ability to integrate information and make references from text, instruct the child to refer to personal feelings or experiences related to the text.

When asking children to retell as a teaching technique to reconstruct story meaning, pre and postdiscussions of the story often help improve the retelling (Mitchell, 1984; Morrow, 1985). Follow-up practice sessions in retelling and discussion about the quality of the retelling are also recommended. Retellings can be taped and played back so that children can identify their own strengths and weaknesses.

Guidelines for retellings. The guidelines presented here for eliciting and guiding a child's retelling (Morrow, 1985) emphasize the inclusion of some of the features of story structure described in this volume by both Fitzgerald and Gordon: Setting (introduction of characters, time, and place), Theme (an initiating event that causes the main character to react and form a goal or face a problem), Plot Episodes (events in which the main character attempts to attain the goal or solve the problem), and Resolution (attainment of the goal or solution of the problem).

1. Ask the child to retell the story by saying, "A little while ago I read (name of story). Would you retell the story as if you were telling it to a friend who has never heard it before?" Young children might be provided with props from the story to help them retell the story. Sometimes children should retell to others who actually do not know the story.
2. Use the following prompts only if necessary:
    A. If the child has difficulty beginning, suggest starting with "Once upon a time," or "Once there was...."
    B. If the child stops retelling before the end of the story, encour-

age continuation by asking, "What comes next?" or "Then what happened?"
  c. If the child stops retelling and cannot continue with the prompts offered in B, ask a question that is relevant at that point in the story. For example, "What was Jenny's problem in the story?"
3. When a child is unable to retell the story, or if the retelling lacks sequence and detail, prompt the retelling step by step. For example:
  A. "Once upon a time," or "Once there was...."
  B. "Who was the story about?"
  C. "When did the story happen?" (For instance, day, night, summer, winter?)
  D. "Where did the story happen?"
  E. "What was the main character's problem in the story?"
  F. "How did he or she try to solve the problem? What did he or she do first (second, next)?"
  G. "How was the problem solved?"
  H. "How did the story end?"

The child's ability to retell will determine how much guidance and scaffolding is required. In this situation, scaffolding refers to adults supplying all the responses that the child cannot. Scaffolding allows children to discover what is expected of them to complete the task later (Applebee & Langer, 1983). Scaffolding offers the child as much help as needed, even if the teacher ends up retelling the whole story in early guidance sessions. As children begin to discover how to handle the retelling task themselves, scaffolding should diminish.

Sample retelling with teacher guidance. The sample story retelling session presented here features a six year old girl. She has had the benefit of a few story retelling sessions with the teacher and, therefore, has some knowledge of what is expected of her.

The story being retold is called *Under the Lemon Tree* (Hurd & Hurd, 1980). It is about a donkey who lives under a lemon tree near the other animals on a farm. He is quite happy there. Every night a fox comes to steal one of the animals. When this happens, the donkey hee haws loudly to scare the fox away. This causes the other animals to cluck, quack, and gobble, which wakes the farmer and his wife. When they look to see what all the fuss is about, the fox has already gone, and all they hear is the donkey.

After several nights, the farmer and his wife decide to have the donkey sleep far from the farm so he won't awaken them. That night the fox returns and steals a rooster. The animals begin to cluck, quack, and gobble. As the fox passes, the donkey hee haws, causing the fox to drop the rooster and run away. The farmer and his wife arrive on the scene in time to realize what has been happening. They are pleased with their noisy donkey and bring him back to sleep under the lemon tree near the other animals.

Sample Verbatim Transcription

Teacher: Gillian, would you retell the story I just read to you? Pretend that I have never heard it before, and try to include as many parts as you can remember, okay?

Gillian: Okay. I forget how to start.

Teacher: You can start with Once Upon a Time.

Gillian: Oh yeah. Let's see. Once upon a time there was a donkey and he was in a farm and he was close and he lived under a lemon tree. ummm, umm.

Teacher: What happened next?

Gillian: I don't know.

Teacher: Maybe I can help. Do you remember when the story starts? Was it morning or night?

Gillian: It was in the morning, and all the bees buzzed in the flowers under the lemon tree. He was next to the ducks, the chickens, and the roosters. (Gillian pauses a long time.) This is hard; I can't remember.

Teacher: I know it is. Maybe I can help. The next part starts to tell about how the donkey got into trouble; it tells about his problem. Do you remember? It happened at night.

Gillian: Yeah, now I remember. It was nighttime. The red fox came to get something to eat. The donkey went heehaw, heehaw. And then the chickens went, what sound does they make, gobble gobble? Oooh no (laughing at herself), cluck cluck. And the ducks went quack quack.

	And then the farmer and his wife waked up and looked out the window and saw nothing. They didn't know what came into their farm that night. They said, "How a noisy donkey. When it gets dark we will bring him far away." So when it get darker they brang the donkey over to a fig tree. And he stayed there. He couldn't go to sleep alone. I can't do anymore. I'm tired and I don't remember.
Teacher:	You're almost at the end, and you're doing so well. Let me help you finish. Now comes the part when the donkey's problem is solved. Remember the fox came back that night.
Gillian:	Yeah, let me finish. That night the red fox came into the farm again and tried again. The ducks went cluck cluck, and the turkeys went gobble gobble. I almost couldn't remember that one again. Then they said, "Is that noisy donkey back again? And they rushed to the window and saw the fox saying, "Come back here, thief." And the donkey went heehaw, heehaw and then the red fox heared it and put the little—the chicken down. And the farmer and his wife said, "What a noisy—what a noisy donkey we have. Noisier than the whole world." And they put, they picked up the chicken and put one hand around the donkey and they all went home together and that's the end, the end, the end.
Teacher:	That was wonderful, Gillian. Thank you for retelling the story.

Since Gillian has had some experience, minimal guidance by the teacher prompted her retellings. The teacher guided her through the story when necessary and began to retell when Gillian couldn't. She encouraged her to continue, modeled behavior for her, and offered positive reinforcement. For children who are less able, the teacher models retelling by doing much of the retelling until the child is able to take over.

Materials for retelling. Again, because story retelling is not an easy task for young children, books selected should have good plot structures (as described earlier) that make their story lines easy to follow and therefore easy to retell. Other elements can add to a story's predictability and thus aid initial experiences in retelling it, particularly repetitive phrases, rhyme, familiar sequences (use of numbers, letters), conversation, and general familiarity or popularity of a given story. Following is a short bibliography categorized into these areas and recommended for the purpose of retelling.

Books with Repetitive Phrases*

Eastman, P.D. *Are You My Mother?* New York: Random House, 1960.

Martin, B. *Brown Bear, Brown Bear, What Do You See?* New York: Holt, Rinehart & Winston, 1967.

Shaw, C.G. *It Looked Like Spilt Milk.* New York: Viking Press, 1947.

*See Tompkins and McGee, this volume, for a more detailed list.

Books with Rhyme

Bonnie, R. *I Know an Old Lady.* New York: Scholastic, 1961.

Brown, M. *Goodnight, Moon.* New York: Harper & Row, 1957.

Keats, E.J. *Over in the Meadow.* New York: Scholastic, 1971.

Books with Familiar Sequences

Baum, A., and Baum, J. *One Bright Monday Morning.* New York: Random House, 1962.

Carle, E. *The Very Hungry Caterpillar.* New York: Puffin, 1970.

Mack, S. *Ten Bears in My Bed.* New York: Pantheon, 1974.

Books with Conversation

Arno, E. *The Gingerbread Man.* New York: Scholastic, 1970.

Flack, M. *Ask Mr. Bear.* New York: Macmillan, 1971.

Zolotow, C. *Mister Rabbit and the Lovely Present.* New York: Harper & Row, 1962.

Popular and Familiar Stories

Galdone, P. *Goldilocks and The Three Bears.* New York: Seabury, 1972.

Galdone, P. *The Little Red Hen.* New York: Scholastic, 1975.

Slobodkina, E. *Caps for Sale.* Reading, MA: Addison Wesley, 1974.

Stories with Good Plot Structures

Keats, E.J. *Peter's Chair.* New York: Harper & Row, 1967.
Lionni, L. *Swimmy.* New York: Random House, 1973.
Potter, B. *The Tale of Peter Rabbit.* New York: Scholastic, 1902.

The Teacher's Role in Retelling Stories

    Teachers and parents play critical roles in influencing children's behaviors. Children who have grown up in rich literacy environments in which reading is valued have been found to be eager to read, and they have tended to be early readers as well as successful readers (Clark, 1984; Durkin, 1966). One obvious rationale for this is that children model the behavior of the adults around them. Like parents, teachers can model story retelling behavior for children.

    It should be noted that retelling stories is a form of storytelling. Therefore, when retelling stories, select books that have good plot structures as mentioned earlier. Choose stories that appeal to children and are easy to retell because of predictable elements—rhyme, catch phrases, and repetition. Be sure to know the story well so that you can retell it well. Retelling does not mean memorizing; it means telling the story in your own words. But if a story includes catch phrases crucial to the story, use them to encourage children to join in the retelling.

    Because your purpose for retelling stories to children is to provide them with a model to imitate, you will want to do it well. Be expressive while retelling the story, changing your voice and facial expressions to reflect dialogue spoken by different characters and to highlight special events. Storytelling is similar to a dramatic presentation. Retell slowly and with animation, but not so dramatically as to overshadow the story. As opposed to reading directly from a book, retelling enables you to shorten stories to accommodate the attention span of your audience. It also enables you to develop a personal relationship with the children, since you are able to look directly at them as you retell. Record or videotape your own retellings to observe and critique your technique.

Alternative Strategies for Children's Story Retelling

As stated earlier, retelling is not common in schools, partly because it is time consuming and difficult for children. There are, however, many ways to make retelling a practical technique for classroom use. For practice and to gain skill, children can retell stories to classmates and to younger children in the school. Children also can retell stories into a tape recorder to listen to themselves or to be listened to by the teacher and other children. A story can be retold with or without the help of the book, although with young children (preschool and kindergarten) it is recommended that early attempts be prompted with pictures from the book to provide some guidance.

Retelling can take many forms. The following techniques can make retelling enjoyable, whether used by teachers or by students and whether the audience is an individual or a group. After demonstrating these techniques yourself, encourage children to retell stories using these props (Morrow, 1981).

Flannel board. As a teacher, retell a story using a flannel board and flannel board characters, and place the materials in the classroom library corner. Then encourage the children to use the flannel board to retell the story during a recreational reading period. Stories that lend themselves to the use of a flannel board are those with a limited number of characters which appear throughout the story, such as *Ask Mr. Bear* (Flack, 1932), or *Caps for Sale* (Slobodkina, 1947).

Chalk talks. Chalk talks involve drawing the story while telling it. Chalk talks are most effective when done on a large chalkboard so that the story can be told in sequence, without interruption, from beginning to end. The same technique can be used on mural paper hung across a wall or with an easel and chart paper, with the storyteller using crayons or felt tip markers instead of chalk. Choose a story with simple illustrations and one in which only a few pictures need to be drawn. You do not have to be a great artist, as the art work is secondary. Some stories have been written as chalk talks, such as the series, *Harold and the Purple Crayon* (Johnson, 1955). Children are quite eager to try chalk talks once they have seen this method of retelling modeled.

Prop stories. Stories can be retold with props such as stuffed annimals, toys, or other articles that represent the characters and objects in a story. The props are shown at appropriate points during the storytelling. Three stuffed bears and a yellow haired doll, three bowls, and three chairs can be used to retell *Goldilocks and the Three Bears* (Galdone, 1972). A large inflated red balloon is the only prop needed for *The Red Balloon* (Lamorisse, 1956).

Puppet stories. Provide children with various types of puppets: hand puppets, stick puppets, finger puppets. Shy children tend to feel more secure retelling stories with puppets since they can let themselves believe that the puppets are telling the story. Stories with dialogue and a limited number of characters such as *The Three Little Pigs* (Galdone, 1970) or *The Three Billy Goats Gruff* (Brown, 1957) are best suited for retelling with puppets.

Sound stories. In this retelling technique, the audience and the storyteller provide appropriate sound effects for the story. The sounds can be made with voices or rhythm instruments. In preparing to retell such a story, first select the parts where sound effects are appropriate. Next, decide on the sound that will be made and who will make it. During the retelling, the students chime in with the sounds they have been assigned. Record the presentation and leave the tape in a library corner with the book. Children can retell the story that has been told by the teacher, using the sound effects created by the class. Some books good for retelling with sounds are *Noisy Book* (Brown, 1939), *Too Much Noise* (McGovern, 1967), and *Mr. Brown Can Moo. Can You?* (Seuss, 1970).

Advantages of alternate strategies. These techniques and props are quite effective in helping young children to retell stories. The techniques allow for independent retelling, consequently not taking whole class time. Because they are entertaining, they encourage retellings with friends in the classroom or even with children in other classrooms.

When children retell stories, they tend to use book language such as:

"One bad day a tuna fish, swift, fierce and very hungry, came darting through the waves." (Lionni, 1973)

"The wild things roared their terrible roars and gnashed their terrible teeth and rolled their terrible eyes and showed their terrible claws...." (Sendak, 1963)

Book language is different from oral language. As children become accustomed to book language, they become more able to comprehend the language of other books when they read them for the first time. They also increase their vocabularies and enhance the syntactic complexity of their own oral language by modeling the structures used by the authors.

Often during their retellings, children use repeated catch phrases from books such as Piper's (1954) *The Little Engine That Could* ("I think I can, I think I can, I think I can, I think I can...") or Dr. Seuss's (1940) *Horton Hatches the Egg* ("I meant what I said...and I said what I meant. An elephant's faithful...one hundred percent!") The young child who is not yet reading will often ask a teacher to "show me those words in the book. I want to see where it says that." Such responses represent a growing need and a desire to learn to read.

After using the materials provided in the classroom for retelling, children should be encouraged to create and tell their own felt stories, prop stories, chalk talks, and puppet stories. To develop a storytelling technique for use with an audience, children use, enhance, and demonstrate competence in basic comprehension skills. They learn to recognize and make use of the theme, sequence, basic facts, and organization of a story and to blend them together. Thus, retelling demonstrates the ability to comprehend literally.

Children also must be able to set the mood for the audience, anticipate outcomes in the oral presentation, imply through expression how the characters feel, and determine how the audience feels about the presentation. These requisites demonstrate the child's ability to comprehend interpretively.

In addition, the child must select a piece of literature, judge its worth and appeal, compare types of storytelling methods, and choose the best technique to tell the story. These decisions demonstrate critical thinking. (Resources for storytelling ideas are provided at the end of the bibliography.)

Retelling as an Assessment Tool

Story retellings can be used to measure both the product and the process of a child's comprehension of a story (Morrow et al., 1986). Through analysis of retelling, one can diagnose a child's ability for literal recall (remembering facts, details, cause and effect relationships, and sequencing of events). Retellings also can reveal a child's sense of story structure (see Fitzgerald, this volume). For example, does the child's transcribed retelling include statements of setting, theme, plot episodes, and resolution?

Through retelling, children also reveal their ability to make inferences as they organize, integrate, and classify information that is implied but not expressed in the story. They may generalize, interpret feelings, or relate ideas to their own experiences (Irwin & Mitchell, 1983; Lanier & Davis, 1972; McConaughy, 1980; Morrow, 1989). The holistic comprehension revealed through a child's retelling may give retelling an advantage over the more traditional piecemeal means of assessing comprehension by asking children specific questions (Morrow et al., 1986).

Guidelines for using retellings as an assessment tool. A child's story retellings can be assessed several times during a school year to evaluate change. If you are going to evaluate a retelling, let the child know that before you read the story. During the retelling, do not offer prompts as suggested earlier. You may, however, encourage children to offer their best by saying when they pause, "Can you think of anything else about the story?" or "You are doing very well. Can you continue?" Evaluation of young children's retellings often focuses on some of the more literal elements of comprehension, such as inclusion of structural elements and awareness of facts, details, and sequence. But review of retelling transcripts can also reveal interpretative and critical thinking, such as whether the child demonstrates a grasp of the underlying theme in the story.

To assess a child's retelling for a sense of story structure or inclusion of structural elements, the examiner should divide the events of the story into four categories: setting, theme, plot episodes, and resolution. The examiner then notes the number of ideas and events that the child accurately includes within each of the four structural categories, regardless of their order. A story guidesheet, outlining the parsed text, is used to help tabulate the ideas and events the child includes in the retelling.

The child receives credit for partial recall or for recounting the gist of a story event (Pellegrini & Galda, 1982; Thorndyke, 1977). Having checked off the child's inclusion of elements, the examiner observes sequence by comparing the order of events in the child's retelling with the original story. The analysis indicates not only which elements a child includes or omits and how well a child sequences, but also where help in areas of weakness might be necessary. A comparison of several retellings over a year will illustrate whether the child has progressed.

Sample retelling used for assessment. The following outline presents the events or parsed story for *Jenny Learns a Lesson* (Fujikawa, 1980), a story about a little girl who likes to play pretend games and invites her friends to do so. When her friends come to play, Jenny bosses them by telling everyone what to do. After several such episodes, her friends leave angry and do not return. Jenny is lonesome and realizes her problem. She apologizes to her friends, invites them back to play, and promises not to boss them. They agree to play, and this time all pretend as they wish. The parsed story is followed here by the transcription of a five year old child's retelling of the story, then an analysis of the retelling.

Parsed Story: *Jenny Learns a Lesson*

Setting
- a. Once upon a time there was a girl who liked to play pretend.
- b. Characters: Jenny (main character), Nicholas, Sam, Mei, Su, Shags the dog.

Theme
Every time Jenny played with her friends, she bossed them and insisted they do what she wanted them to.

Plot Episodes

First Episode Jenny decided to pretend to be a queen. She called her friends and they came to play. Jenny was bossy and told them all what to do. Her friends became angry and left.

Second Episode Jenny decided to play dancer, with the same results as in the first episode.

Third Episode Jenny decided to play pirate, again with the same results.

Fourth Episode Jenny decided to play she was a duchess, with the same results.

Fifth Episode Jenny's friends decided not to play with her again because she was so bossy. Many days passed, and Jenny became lonely. She went to her friends and apologized to them for being bossy.

Resolution

a. The friends play together, and each person does what he or she wants.

b. They all had a wonderful day and were so tired they fell asleep.

Sample Verbatim Transcription
Beth, age 5

Once upon a time there's a girl named Jenny and she called her friends over and they played queen and went to the palace. They had to, they had to do what she said and they didn't like it, so then they went home and said that was boring....It's not fun playing queen and doing what she says you have to. So they didn't play with her for seven days and she had...she had an idea that she was being selfish, so she went to find her friends and said, I'm sorry I was so mean. And said, let's play pirate, and they played pirate and they went onto the ropes. Then they played that she was a fancy lady playing house. And they have tea. And they played what they wanted and they were happy....The End.

Story Retelling Analysis

Child's Name_____Beth_____ Age _____5_____

Title of Story___Jenny Learns a Lesson_____Date_____

General directions: Place a 1 next to each element if the child includes it in his or her presentation. Credit gist as well as obvious recall, counting *boy, girl,* or *dog* under characters named, as well as *Nicholas, Mei, Su,* or *Shags*. Credit plurals (friends) as two.

Sense of story structure

Setting
- a. Begins story with an introduction ... 1
- b. Names main character ... 1
- c. Number of other characters named ... 2
- d. Actual number of other characters ... 4
- e. Score for other characters (c/d) 5
- f. Includes statement about time or place ... 1

Theme
Refers to main character's primary goal or problem to be solved ... 1

Plot Episodes
- a. Number of episodes recalled ... 4
- b. Number of episodes in story ... 5
- c. Score for plot episodes (a/b) 8

Resolution
- a. Names problem solution/goal attainment ... 1
- b. Ends story ... 1

Sequence
Retells story in structural order: setting, theme, plot episodes, resolution (score 2 for proper, 1 for partial, 0 for no sequence evident) ... 1

Highest score possible __10__   Child's score __8.3__

(Morrow, 1989)

Summary

Retelling helps us to understand, in part, the comprehension processes used by readers or listeners. Retelling requires the child to construct a personal text, making inferences based on original text as well as on prior knowledge. Research demonstrates that instruction and practice in retelling usually result in the development of comprehension, a sense of story structure, and oral complexity in a child's use of language (Gambrell, Pfeiffer, & Wilson, 1985; Morrow, 1984, 1985, 1986). Retelling is also a valuable assessment tool. Analysis of retelling can help a teacher identify problems not obvious when a student is asked simply to answer questions (Marshall, 1983).

Young children should receive instruction and guidance in retelling, and time should be provided for them to practice the technique in school. Retelling must not be thought of as a frill; it is a genuine strategy for skill development in several areas of literacy. Children's story retellings in the classroom, to teachers and to friends and in the variety of formats, should be encouraged.

Retelling has the potential to improve and develop the same skills it can assess, and it should be used for both purposes. As an instructional strategy and as an assessment tool, retelling helps teachers view reading as a process for conveying and recreating meaning.

References

Amato, T., and Ziegler, E. The effectiveness of creative dynamics and storytelling in a library setting. *Journal of Educational Research*, 1973, *67,* 161, 162-181.

Applebee, A.N., and Langer, J.A. Instructional scaffolding: Reading and writing as natural language activities. *Language Arts,* 1983, *60,* 168-175.

Baghban, M. *Our daughter learns to read and write: A case study from birth to three.* Newark, DE: International Reading Association, 1984.

Blank, M., and Sheldon, F. Story recall in kindergarten children: Effect of method of presentation on psycholinguistic performance. *Child Development,* 1971, *42,* 299-312.

Bower, G. Experiments on story understanding and recall. *Quarterly Journal of Experimental Psychology,* 1975, *28,* 511-534.

Brown, A. Recognition, reconstruction, and recall of narrative sequences of preoperational children. *Child Development,* 1975, *46,* 155-166.

Brown, M.W. *Noisy book.* New York: Harper & Row, 1939.

Brown, M. *The three billy goats gruff.* New York: Harcourt Brace Jovanovich, 1957.

Burroughs, M. *The stimulation of verbal behavior in culturally disadvantaged three year olds.* Unpublished doctoral dissertation, Michigan State University, 1972.

Chomsky, C. Stages in language development and reading exposure. *Harvard Educational Review,* 1972, *42,* 1-33.

Clark, M.M. Literacy at home and at school: Insights from a study of young fluent readers. In J. Goelman, A.A. Oberg, and F. Smith (Eds.), *Awakening to literacy.* London: Heinemann Educational Books, 1984.

Clay, M.M. *Reading: The patterning of complex behavior.* Auckland: Heinemann Educational Books, 1979.

Cohen, D. The effect of literature on vocabulary and reading achievement. *Elementary English,* 1968, *45,* 209-213, 217.

Doakes, D. *Book experiences and emergent reading behavior in preschool children.* Unpublished doctoral dissertation, University of Alberta, 1981.

Dunning, D., and Mason, J. *An investigation of kindergarten children's expressions of story character's intentions.* Paper presented at the Annual Meeting of the National Reading Conference, St. Petersburg, Florida, 1984.

Durkin, D. *Children who read early.* New York: Teachers College Press, 1966.

Durkin, D. A Six year study of children who learned to read in school at the age of four. *Reading Research Quarterly,* 1974, *10,* 9-61.

Feitelson, D., Kita, B., and Goldstein, Z. Effects of listening to series stories on first graders' comprehension and use of language. *Research in the Teaching of English,* 1986, *20,* 339-356.

Flack, M. *Ask Mr. Bear.* New York: Macmillan, 1932.

Fujikawa, G. *Jenny learns a lesson.* New York: Grosset & Dunlap, 1980.

Galdone, P. *The three little pigs.* New York: Seabury, 1970.

Galdone, P. *Goldilocks and the three bears.* New York: Seabury, 1972.

Gambrell, L., Pfeiffer, W., and Wilson, R. The effects of retelling upon reading comprehension and recall of text information. *Journal of Educational Research,* 1985, *78,* 216-220.

Green, J.L., and Harker, J.O. Reading to children: A communicative process. In J.A. Langer and M.T. Smith-Burke (Eds.), *Reader meets author/bridging the gap: A psycholinguistic and sociolinguistic perspective.* Newark, DE: International Reading Association, 1982, 196-221.

Hoffman, S.J. *Preschool reading related behaviors: A parent diary.* Unpublished doctoral dissertation, University of Pennsylvania, 1982.

Holdaway, D. *The foundation of literacy.* Sydney: Ashton Scholastic, 1979.

Hurd, E., and Hurd, C. *Under the lemon tree.* Boston: Little, Brown, 1980.

Irwin, O. Infant speech: Effects of systematic reading of stories. *Journal of Speech and Hearing Research,* 1960, *3,* 187-190.

Irwin, P.A., and Mitchell, J.N. A procedure for assessing the richness of retellings. *Journal of Reading,* 1983, *26,* 391-396.

Johnson C. *Harold and the purple crayon.* New York: Harper & Row, 1958.

Johnston, P.H. *Reading comprehension assessment: A cognitive basis.* Newark, DE: International Reading Association, 1983, 54-56.

Lamorisse, A. *The red balloon.* New York: Doubleday, 1956.

Lanier, R., and Davis, A. Developing comprehension through teacher made questions. *The Reading Teacher,* 1972, *26,* 153-157.

Lionni, L. *Swimmy.* New York: Random House, 1973.

Marshall, N. Using story grammar to assess reading comprehension. *The Reading Teacher,* 1983, 161-165.

Mason, G., and Blanton, W. Story content for beginning reading instruction. *Elementary English,* 1971, *48,* 793-796.

McConaughy, S. Using story structure in the classroom. *Language Arts,* 1980, *57,* 157-164.

Mitchell, J.N. *Advantages and disadvantages of retelling for reading assessment.* Paper presented at the International Reading Association Convention, Atlanta, Georgia, 1984.

McGovern, A. *Too much noise.* Boston: Houghton Mifflin, 1967.

Morrow, L.M. Effects of structural guidance in story retelling on children's dictation of original stories. *Journal of Reading Behavior,* 1986, *18,* 135-152.

Morrow, L.M. Effects of story retelling on young children's comprehension and sense of story structure. In J. Niles and L. Harris (Eds.), *Changing perspectives in research in reading/language processing and instruction.* Rochester, NY: National Reading Conference, 1984, 95-100.

Morrow, L.M. Home and school correlates of early interest in literature. *Journal of Educational Research,* 1983, *76,* 221-230.

Morrow, L.M. *Literacy development in the early years: Helping children read and write.* Englewood Cliffs, NJ: Prentice Hall, 1989.

Morrow, L.M. Relationships between literature programs, library corner designs, and children's use of literature. *Journal of Educational Research*, 1982, 75, 339-344.

Morrow, L.M. Retelling stories as a diagnostic tool. In S. Glazer, L. Searfoss, and L. Gentile (Eds.), *Reexamining reading diagnosis: New trends and procedures.* Newark, DE: International Reading Association, 1988.

Morrow, L.M. Retelling stories: A strategy for improving children's comprehension, concept of story structure and oral language complexity. *Elementary School Journal*, 1985, 85, 647-661.

Morrow, L.M. *Super tips for storytelling.* New York: Harcourt Brace Jovanovich, 1981.

Morrow, L., Gambrell, L., Kapinus, B., Koskinen, P., Marshall, N., and Mitchell, J. Retelling: A strategy for reading instruction and assessment. In J. Niles and R. Lalik (Eds.), *Solving problems in literacy: Learners, teachers, and researchers.* Rochester, NY: National Reading Conference, 1986.

Pellegrini, A., and Galda, L. The effects of thematic fantasy play training on the development of children's story comprehension. *American Educational Research Journal*, 1982, 19, 443-452.

Piper, W. *The little engine that could.* New York: Platt and Munk, 1954.

Peterman, C.L., Dunning, D., and Mason, J. *A storybook reading event: How a teacher's presentation affects kindergarten children's subsequent attempts to read from the text.* Paper presented at the Annual Meeting of the National Reading Conference, San Diego, California, 1985.

Rhodes, L.K. *Visible language acquisition: A case study.* Paper presented at the International Reading Association Convention, Atlanta, Georgia, 1979.

Rose, M.C., Cundick, B.P., and Higbee, K.L. Verbal rehearsal and visual imagery: Mnemonic aids for learning disabled children. *Journal of Learning Disabilities*, 1983, 16, 352-354.

Sendak, M. *Where the wild things are.* New York: Harper & Row, 1963.

Seuss, Dr. *Horton hatches the egg.* New York: Random House, 1940.

Seuss, Dr. *Mr. Brown can moo. Can you?* New York: Random House, 1970.

Slobodkina, E. *Caps for sale.* New York: Scholastic, 1947.

Smith, F. *Understanding reading,* second edition. New York: Holt, Rinehart & Winston, 1978.

Sutton, M.H. Readiness for reading at the kindergarten level. *The Reading Teacher*, 1964, 17, 234-240.

Tarver, S.G., Hallahan, D.P., and Kauffman, J.M. Verbal rehearsal and selective attention in children with learning disabilities: A developmental lag. *Journal of Experimental Child Psychology*, 1976, 22, 375-385.

Teale, W.H. Positive environments for learning to read: What studies of early readers tell us. *Language Arts*, 1978, 55, 922-932.

Teale, W.H. Reading to young children: Its significance for literacy development. In H. Goelman, A.A. Oberg, and F. Smith (Eds.), *Awakening to literacy.* London: Heinemann Educational Books, 1984.

Teale, W.H., and Sulzby, E. Literacy acquisition in early childhood: The roles of access and mediation in storybook reading. In D.A. Wagner (Ed.), *The future of literacy in a changing world.* New York: Pergamon Press, in press.

Templin, M. *Certain language skills in children.* Minneapolis, MN: University of Minnesota Press, 1957.

Thorndyke, P. Cognitive structures in comprehension and memory of narrative discourse. *Cognitive Psychology*, 1977, 9, 77-110.

Vygotsky, L.S. *Mind in society: The development of psychological processes.* Cambridge, MA: Harvard University Press, 1978.

Walker, G.H., and Kuerbitz, I.E. Reading to preschoolers as an aid to successful beginning reading. *Reading Improvement*, 1979, 16, 149-154.

Wong, B., Wong, R., and Foth, D. Recall and clustering of verbal materials among normal and poor readers. *Bulletin of the Psychonomic Society,* 1977, *10,* 375-378.

Zimilies, H., and Kuhns, M. *A developmental study in the retention of narrative material, final report.* Bank Street College of Education, Research Report 134. Washington, DC: NIE, 1976.

Resources for Storytelling

Bauer, Caroline. *Handbook for storytellers.* Chicago: American Library Association, 1977.

Champlin, C., and Renfro, N. *Storytelling with puppets.* Chicago: American Library Association, 1985.

Hunt T. *Puppetry and early childhood education.* Illustrated by N. Renfro. Austin, TX: Nancy Renfro Studios, 1981.

Sierra, J. *The flannel board storytelling book.* Bronx, NY: Wilson, 1987.

Wilmes, L., and Wilmes, D. *Felt board fun.* Illustrated by D. Dane. Elgin, II: Building Blocks Publishers, 1984.

3

Gail E. Tompkins
Lea M. McGee

Teaching Repetition as a Story Structure

> This chapter presents a strategy for teaching primary grade students to read and write stories using repetition, a literary device that authors use to create more complex and interesting plots in stories. Many traditional stories use repetition of events and words to make the story complex and heighten readers' interest. Reading educators explain that repetitive stories are a valuable instructional tool because of their predictability. The steps in the instructional strategy are as follows: introduce children to repetition, read repetitive stories, examine how repeated events and words are used in stories, and write repetitive stories. The authors conclude their chapter with a sample lesson on repetition for second graders.

Stories are an important part of childhood. Children love hearing bedtime stories, viewing television and movie dramas, and telling stories about real and imagined events. They learn much about being literate and about the world from their experiences with stories. Children learn what to expect in a story (Fitzgerald, this volume). They learn that stories have certain conventions such as formal openings (Once upon a time), and closings (and they lived happily ever after.), and that stories have characters which behave in predictable ways (e.g., witches do bad things and princesses are good). Children also learn that stories have predictable patterns of events (a princess is captured, a prince rescues her, and they marry). This predictable pattern of events is called story structure.

As Fitzgerald (this volume) explained, story structure has many important features, including plot. A plot is the series of actions a character undertakes to solve a problem. The turning point comes when the character either solves or fails to solve the problem. But most stories do not have a simple plot. Typically, the character must overcome many obstacles before the problem can be solved (deBeaugrande & Colby, 1979; Johnson & Mandler, 1980). Subplots involve the character's attempts to eliminate obstacles that stand in the way of obtaining the main goal or solving the problem in the story.

Frequently, the plots in the stories very young children create are not well developed (Applebee, 1978; Botvin & Sutton-Smith, 1977; Leondar, 1977). Their stories often include the introduction of a problem (Once there was this little girl and she was lost in a big forest...) and its immediate solution (then a good fairy godmother came and took her home to her Mommy. The end.) without the development of the plot in the middle of the story.

Children's knowledge of plot and other aspects of story structure develops rapidly as they learn to read and write during the primary grades. This knowledge plays an important role in students' ability to comprehend the stories they read (Johnson & Mandler, 1977; Stein & Glenn, 1979) and produce the stories they write (Golden, 1984).

Repetition: An Important Literary Device

Repetition of events and dialogue is one of the simplest literary devices authors use to create more complex and interesting plots. *The Three Little Pigs* (Galdone, 1970) is an example of a story with a complex plot consisting of repeated events, each creating an episode in the story. Each little pig builds a house which the wolf attempts to blow down. This event is repeated three times, and with each repetition, the building materials—straw, sticks, and bricks—become more sturdy. It is this variation that heightens readers' interest as they predict whether the wolf will be successful at blowing the house down.

Each time the wolf visits one of the pigs, he asks, "Little pig, little pig, let me come in," and the pig responds, "No, no! Not by the hair of my chinny chin chin." Then the wolf responds by threatening, "Then I'll huff, and I'll puff, and I'll blow your house in," and he attempts to blow the house down. This repeated dialogue makes the events more interesting and memorable.

Many traditional stories, such as *The Gingerbread Boy* (Galdone, 1975), have both repeated events and dialogue. In other stories, either the dialogue or the events are repeated. *The Mitten* (Tresselt, 1964) is an example of a story with repeated events. A little boy goes out to collect firewood on a cold, snowy day and loses one of his mittens. A mouse finds the mitten and decides it would make a warm house. Then a series of progressively larger animals—a frog, an owl, a rabbit, a fox, a wolf, a boar, and a bear—also squeeze into the mitten to escape the cold. Finally, a tiny black cricket tries to join the others in the overcrowded mitten. It bursts open and all the animals are tossed back into the snow.

In Wanda Gag's *Millions of Cats* (1928), the refrain "Hundreds of cats, Thousands of cats, Millions and billions and trillions of cats" is repeated, as is the haunting refrain "Give me my bone!" in *The Teeny-Tiny Woman* (Galdone, 1984). This repetition of words heightens interest and provides a literary device that children can use for retelling the story.

Another way repetition is used to create complex plots is through accumulation, adding new characters or new information to each repeated event. In *Henny Penny* (Galdone, 1968), the hen travels to tell the king that the sky is falling, and she meets a series of animals—Cocky Locky, Ducky Lucky, Goosey Loosey, Turkey Lurkey, and Foxy Loxy—who join her on the trip. The author develops the plot by introducing a new character with each repeated event.

In each of these patterns, repetition heightens interest and plays a vital role in the plot structure. It also helps readers predict the events and words (Tompkins & Webeler, 1983). Repetition can be equally important in writing stories. As writers introduce events and/or dialogue that will be repeated, they develop an organization to carry the story to its logical conclusion. Repetition provides young writers with a tool for expanding their stories and crafting more complex and interesting narratives.

Repetition: An Instructional Strategy

Many instructional strategies for teaching children about story structure have been developed and tested (Fitzgerald, this volume). Most of these strategies focus on teaching children about story parts directly or indirectly through questions focusing on the parts (Sadow, 1982; Speigel & Fitzgerald, 1986). While children learn that characters make many attempts at solving their problems (Whaley, 1981), few instructional strategies focus on helping children learn about the complexities of plot. Teaching children about repetition is one way of increasing their awareness of the complexity of stories.

Repetitive stories can be valuable instructional tools because of their predictability as well as their appeal to primary grade children (Bridge, 1986; McClure, 1985; Rhodes, 1981; Tompkins & Webeler, 1983). Following is a five step instructional strategy for teaching children about repetition in stories as a way of increasing their awareness of complex story structure. Children are introduced to repetition, read repetitive stories, examine how repeated events and words are used in the stories, compose a collaborative story, and then compose individual stories.

We have field-tested this instructional strategy with young children as they experiment with repetitive patterns and compose collaborative and individual stories. Students' excitement about reading and writing as they share favorite stories and their success in using repeated events and words in their own stories confirms the usefulness of this instructional strategy.

Teachers should adapt this strategy to meet the needs of their students. Some primary grade students, probably having already noticed that authors use repetition in their stories, use it themselves as they write. Other students may need to participate in only a few activities to activate an interest and awareness. None of the activities we suggest for predictable books should be used to constrain children's reading and writing to match exact repetitive sentences or syntactic patterns. Rather, we believe our activities provide a scaffold for children's active exploration of a literary device and story structure.

Step 1: Introduce Repetition

Introduce repetition by reading aloud a familiar repetitive story, such as *The Gingerbread Boy* (Galdone, 1975). After reading, discuss the story and the way the author made the story complex. Ask students if some events recurred, and invite them to recall these events. Next, ask if some words were repeated. Reread portions of the story and invite students to join in as the gingerbread boy's refrain is repeated. Explain that some authors repeat events and words to make their stories more interesting, and that these stories are called repetitive stories.

Next, present a chart describing the two types of repetition — repeated events and repeated words — as illustrated in Figure 1. Ask

**Figure 1
Repetition Chart**

REPETITION

Two things are repeated in repetition stories:

1. Events happen over and over.

2. Words are said over and over.

> Run, run as fast as you can. You can't catch me, I'm the gingerbread man.

Teaching Repetition as a Story Structure

students to help complete the chart by drawing pictures of the characters that the gingerbread boy runs past on his journey and placing under sentence 2 a picture of the gingerbread boy and dictating his refrain. Prepare the chart in advance by writing the title and sentences. Children personalize the chart with their drawings, which can be removed before use of the chart with another group of children.

Step 2: Share Repetitive Stories

Share additional stories that exemplify repetition, including some that incorporate both the repetition of events and words, as well as some that use only one type of repetition. Teachers may want to begin by sharing other stories with a similar journey motif, including *The Pancake* (Lobel, 1978) and *The Bun* (Brown, 1972). Select these stories from the following list of trade books and basal reader stories.

Repetition Stories in Trade Books

Brown, Marcia. *The Bun: A Tale from Russia.* New York: Harcourt Brace Jovanovich, 1972.

Brown, Margaret Wise. *Goodnight Moon.* New York: Harper & Row, 1947.

Brown Margaret Wise. *The Runaway Bunny.* New York: Harper & Row, 1942.

Brown, Ruth. *A Dark, Dark Tale.* New York: Dial, 1981.

Burningham, John. *Mr. Gumpy's Outing.* New York: Holt, 1975.

Carle, Eric. *Do You Want to Be My Friend?* New York: Crowell, 1971.

Carle, Eric. *The Grouchy Ladybug.* New York: Crowell, 1977.

Carle, Eric. *The Very Busy Spider.* New York: Philomel, 1984.

Carle, Eric. *The Very Hungry Caterpillar.* Cleveland, OH: Collins-World, 1969.

Cauley, Lorinda Bryan. *The Cock, the Mouse, and the Little Red Hen.* New York: Putnam, 1982.

Cauley, Lorinda Bryan. *Goldilocks and the Three Bears.* New York: Putnam, 1981.

Ets, Marie Hall. *Elephant in a Well.* New York: Viking, 1972.

Flack, Marjorie. *Ask Mr. Bear*. New York: Macmillan, 1958.
Gag, Wanda. *Millions of Cats*. New York: Coward-McCann, 1928.
Galdone, Joanna. *The Tailypo: A Ghost Story*. Boston: Houghton Mifflin, 1977.
Galdone, Paul. *The Gingerbread Boy*. New York: Seabury, 1975.
Galdone, Paul. *Henny Penny*. Boston: Houghton Mifflin, 1968.
Galdone, Paul. *The Little Red Hen*. New York: Seabury, 1973.
Galdone, Paul. *The Teeny-Tiny Woman*. Boston: Houghton Mifflin, 1984.
Galdone, Paul. *The Three Bears*. Boston: Houghton Mifflin, 1972.
Galdone, Paul. *The Three Billy Goats Gruff*. Boston: Houghton Mifflin, 1973.
Galdone, Paul. *The Three Little Pigs*. New York: Seabury, 1970.
Ginsburg, Mirra. *The Chick and the Duckling*. New York: Macmillan, 1972.
Hailey, Gail E. *A Story, A Story*. New York: Atheneum, 1970.
Hutchins, Pat. *Good-Night, Owl!* New York: Macmillan, 1972.
Hutchins, Pat. *Rosie's Walk*. New York: Macmillan, 1968.
Lobel, Anita. *The Pancake*. New York: Greenwillow, 1978.
Lobel, Arnold. *How the Rooster Saved the Day*. New York: Morrow, 1977.
Low, Joseph. *Mice Twice*. New York: Atheneum, 1981.
Martin, Bill. *Brown Bear, Brown Bear, What Do You See?* New York: Holt, 1983.
McGovern, Ann. *Too Much Noise*. New York: Scholastic, 1967.
Plume, Ilse. *The Bremen Town Musicians*. New York: Doubleday, 1980.
Tolstoy, Alexei. *The Great Big Enormous Turnip*. New York: Watts, 1968.
Tresselt, Alvin. *The Mitten*. New York: Lothrop, Lee and Shepard, 1964.
Viorst, Judith. *Alexander and the Terrible, Horrible, No Good, Very Bad Day*. New York: Atheneum, 1972.
Wescott, Nadine Bernard. *I Know an Old Lady Who Swallowed a Fly*. Boston: Little, Brown, 1980.
Zemach, Harve, and Zemach, Margot. *The Judge*. New York: Farrar, 1969.

Zemach, Margot. *It Could Always Be Worse.* New York: Farrar, 1976.
Zemach, Margot. *The Little Red Hen.* New York: Farrar, 1983.

Repetition Stories in Basal Readers (Grades 1-3)

Ginn (1985)

Level 3 *Fish and Not Fish*
"The Hen and the Bread" (pp. 56-63)

Level 5 *Birds Fly, Bears Don't*
"Three Kittens" (pp. 50-55)
"The Chick and the Duckling" (pp. 76-81)
"Rabbit and the Long One" (pp. 119-128)
"No Room!" (pp. 141-151)

Level 6 *Across the Fence*
"Help for the Hen" (pp. 8-15)
"The Surprise" (pp. 110-119)
"What Does a Pig Say?" (pp. 120-124)
"Chicken Forgets" (pp. 138-145)
"How Little Lamb Fooled Señor Coyote" (pp. 157-165)

Level 7 *Glad to Meet You*
"Nobody Listens to Andrew" (pp. 10-17)
"On the Way to Bremen" (pp. 163-167)

Level 8 *Give Me a Clue*
"The Wolf in the Wool Suit" (pp. 134-138)
"The Turnip" (pp. 164-171)
"The Robbers and the Fig Tree" (pp. 172-181)

HBJ Bookmark Reading Program (1983)

Level 1 *Sun Up*
"Little Dog" (pp. 67-72)

Level 4 *Sun and Shadow*
"The Big Carrot" (pp. 77-84)
"The Boy Who Called Wolf" (pp. 85-93)

Level 5 *Together We Go*

           "The Little Red Hen" (pp. 34-40)
           "The Clay House" (pp. 45-54)
           "The Bremen Band" (pp. 162-171)
Level 6   *World of Surprises*
           "No One Listens to Andrew" (pp. 20-24)
           "Timothy Turtle" (pp. 112-118)

Holt Basic Readers (1986)
Level 3   *Rhymes and Tales*
           "The Three Little Pigs" (pp. 42-49)
           "Goldilocks and the Three Bears" (pp. 56-63)
Level 5   *Pets and People*
           "Stop Gus!" (pp. 5-11)
Level 6   *Can You Imagine?*
           "A Good House" (pp. 5-12)
           "A Bear Like Me" (pp. 26-32)
           "Who Will Play?" (pp. 43-50)
           "The Big City" (pp. 52-61)
Level 7   *A Place for Me*
           "Too Much Noise" (pp. 104-117)
Level 8   *A Time for Friends*
           "That's What Friends Are For" (pp. 48-61)
           "The New Spring Hats" (pp. 108-120)
           "All the Lassies" (pp. 124-133)
           "Where Have You Been?" (pp. 217-229)
Level 10   *The Way of the World*
           "Such Is the Way of the World" (pp. 14-21)

Houghton Mifflin Reading (1986)
Level C   *Drums*
           "A Good Home" (pp. 3-10)
Level E   *Parades*
           "The Little Red Hen" (pp. 40-49)
           "The Hungry Fox" (pp. 114-126)
Level G   *Adventures*
           "The Rabbit and the Turnip" (pp. 165-173)

Scott, Foresman Reading (1985)
Level 2C *On Our Own*
"Are They People?" (pp. 34-37)
"Wishing" (pp. 43-47)
Level 3 *Hang On to Your Hats*
"The Three Goats" (pp. 200-206)
Level 4 *Kick Up Your Heels*
"The Mouse and the Winds" (pp. 130-134)
"Who Will Fill Up the Little House?" (pp. 137-145)
"The Turtle and the Rabbit" (pp. 189-197)
"Mr. Gumpy's Motor Car" (pp. 249-257)
Level 5 *Rainbow Shower*
"That's What Friends Are For" (pp. 67-77)
Level 7 *Hidden Wonders*
"You Look Ridiculous" (pp. 8-20)
"Jack and the Beanstalk" (pp. 102-110)

Depending on the versions of the stories available and children's reading levels, children may listen to some of the stories read aloud and may read other stories independently. When sharing stories, have students sample, predict, and confirm (Tompkins & Webeler, 1983). Focus children's attention on repetition by asking questions such as:

What do you think will happen next?
Why do you think that will happen?
What do you think (*character*) will say/ask next?
Why do you think (*character*) will say/ask that?

These questions show children that the repetitive structure of the text allows them to make predictions.

After reading the story, review the repetition chart in Figure 1 and ask children to identify the events and/or words that are repeated in each story. These pictures and words then can be removed and new ones added. Or, students may make their own charts, adding words and pictures to represent a favorite story.

Step 3: Examine Repetition in Stories

Children can examine repetition in stories through a variety of oral and written activities, including storytelling, informal drama, drawing, and writing. Exploration should be spontaneous, with teachers responding to children's language rather than directing children to repeat or practice exact sentence patterns (Wason-Ellam, 1988). The emphasis in these activities is on supporting children's meaning-making, not on the rote learning of the repetitive patterns. Five response activities in which students explore and extend their understanding of the repetitive elements of the story are described.

Retelling stories using puppets. Children can make simple finger puppets, line up the puppets in front of them, and one by one use the puppets to retell the story. The puppets provide a structure for children to follow in telling the story. In particular, children enjoy adapting stories and telling their own versions with new characters or new events. One second grader adapted *The Gingerbread Boy* to create "The Gingerbread Girl," in which a gingerbread girl cookie runs past a little old man and little old woman, a cow, a duck, a dog, a cat, and a cricket before meeting a gerbil that ate the gingerbread girl with relish.

Retelling stories using storylines. Hang a clothesline across one part of the classroom and identify it as a storyline. Distribute to students pictures illustrating the repeated events of one of the stories shared in the first two steps. As children join in retelling the story, clip the pictures to the storyline in sequence. Pictures for this activity can be drawn by students or cut from inexpensive editions of the book. Children also can create their own storyline stories by drawing pictures and telling stories to accompany their drawings.

Figure 2
Storyline

Retelling stories using informal drama. Invite children to re-enact a favorite repetitive story. Little preparation is needed other than to select characters and review the repeated events and repeated words. Children retell the story for their own enjoyment rather than to present a polished performance. They also can create their own stories with repetitive elements and share them with classmates through informal drama.

Story maps. Students draw story maps in which they list the repeated words and events in the story, as well as organize the plot into the beginning, middle, and end. A story map for *The Little Red Hen* (Zemach, 1983) is illustrated in Figure 3. Drawing a story map is a good comprehension check activity, and one that children can use in developing their own stories.

Retelling stories in writing. Have children choose a favorite repetitive story and write and illustrate their own version. Compile the pages and add a cover to make a story booklet. Children often

Figure 3
Story Map for *The Little Red Hen*

```
                    The Little Red Hen
           ┌──────────────┼──────────────┐
       Beginning       Middle            End
                    ┌─────┴─────┐
                Repeated    Repeated
                 Events      Words

Little Red Hen   She asked for help to    "Now who will    Little Red Hen
found some       1. plant the seeds       help me…?"       ate the bread
seeds.           2. harvest the wheat                      all by herself.
                 3. thresh the wheat      "Not I!"
                 4. grind into flour
                 5. bake the bread
```

draw pictures to retell the entire story first and then add text for each page. Some young children may want to dictate their stories, while others will use invented spelling to write independently. A six year old's retelling of *The Little Red Hen* is shown in Figure 4. On the first page, the child dictated the text, but on succeeding pages, the child did the writing. The child was very successful in writing the text because the story is so repetitive.

Figure 4
Retelling of *The Little Red Hen*

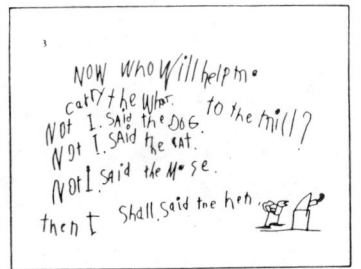

Teaching Repetition as a Story Structure

Step 4: Compose a Collaborative Story Using Repetition

Students may write a repetitive story together as a rehearsal before writing individual stories (Hoskisson & Tompkins, 1987). First, introduce the idea of writing a group composition in which the students suggest the ideas and the teacher serves as scribe to write the story. Next, plan the repetitive story with the students. It is often helpful to use a story map to record ideas as they are discussed. Draw a skeleton story map, like the one presented below, on the chalkboard or on a large sheet of poster paper. As children plan the story, add their ideas to create the story map.

Figure 5
Skeleton Story Map

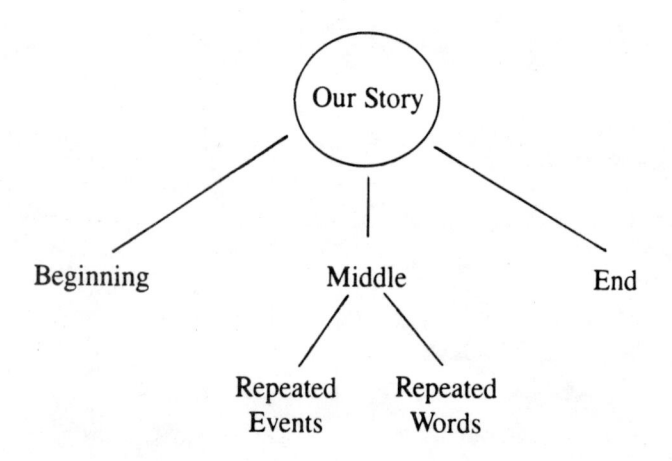

```
            Our Story
           /    |    \
          /     |     \
    Beginning Middle  End
              /    \
         Repeated  Repeated
          Events    Words
```

Use questions such as these to probe students' thinking as they plan the story:
    What will our story be about?
    Who will be the main character in our story?
    What will the main character do?
    What events will happen again and again?
    What words will be said over and over?

If students have difficulty thinking of an idea for the story, suggest that they write a new adventure for a familiar character (e.g., the gingerbread boy visits your town and tries to outrun students in your class or people in your community) or substitute a new set of characters for a familiar plot (e.g., vary the plot of *The Great Big Enormous Turnip*, Tolstoy, 1968 so that a dog needs help digging up a gigantic bone). In this way, children use the literary pattern as a scaffold for making a meaningful story.

After students develop a tentative plan on the story map (which often is revised as the story is written), they are ready to begin dictating the rough draft. First, review the beginning section of the story map and ask students to dictate the beginning of the story. Record students' dictation on the chalkboard. Try to record their dictation exactly, even if some ideas are jumbled. Reread the beginning section and ask students for any changes they want to make.

Second, review the middle section of the story map and ask students to dictate the middle part of the story. This part is the longest, and its many repetitions may seem tedious to write, but it is indispensable. Also, students seem to like this part best because they feel comfortable with its predictability. After recording the middle part, reread it and ask for changes.

Third, review the end section of the story map and record students' dictation about the ending of the story. Fourth, choose a title.

Once children have dictated the rough draft of their story, they need help making revisions. Sometimes it is helpful to wait a day or two before having the children reread and revise their story so they can get some distance from their composition. Children make suggestions about how to improve their story, including their use of repeated dialogue and events, so that their readers will understand and enjoy the story. For example, they may suggest adding descriptive words, resequencing events, or combining sentences.

Finally, the story is copied on a sheet of paper and copies are made for each student. They can illustrate their stories later, if they wish. Students also can collaborate to produce a big book version of their story to use for shared reading in their class and with other classes (Heald-Taylor, 1987).

A story map and class collaborative story composed by a group of second graders is presented in Figure 6. This story features a Cabbage Patch doll who is locked in a closet. She repeatedly calls for help, but everyone refuses to help her, saying "No way, Jose!" until a little mouse hears her. The children chose the mouse because they recalled that in some of the stories they had read, it was a mouse who solved the problem.

**Figure 6
Class Collaborative Story Map and Story**

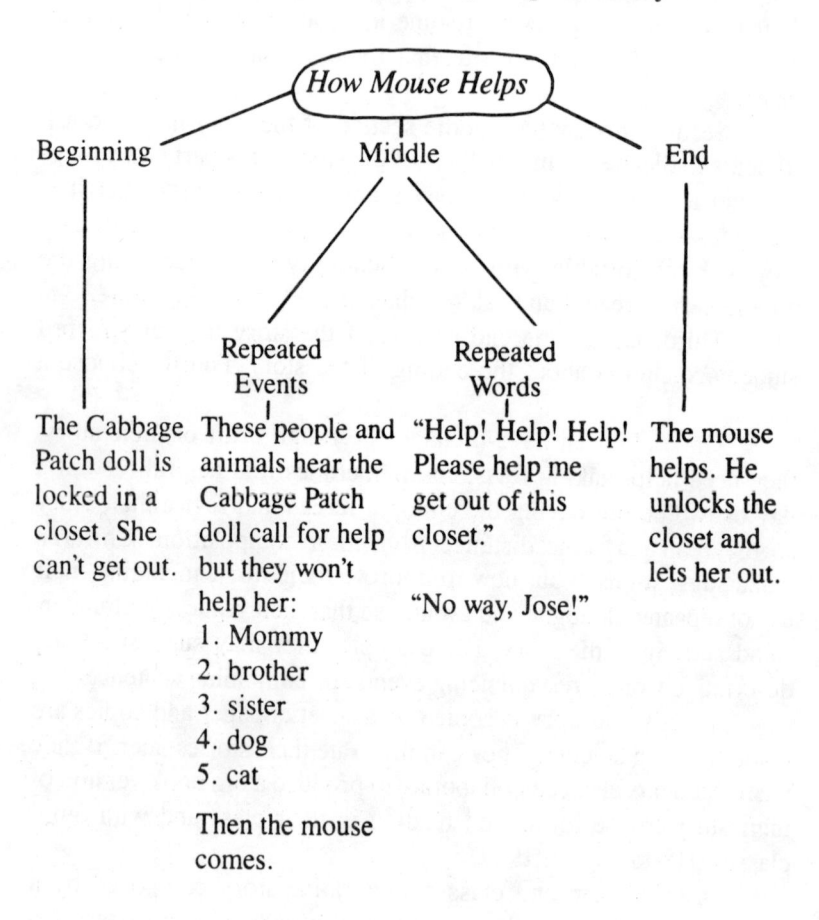

How Mouse Helps

Beginning — Middle — End

Middle: Repeated Events / Repeated Words

Beginning: The Cabbage Patch doll is locked in a closet. She can't get out.

Repeated Events: These people and animals hear the Cabbage Patch doll call for help but they won't help her:
1. Mommy
2. brother
3. sister
4. dog
5. cat

Then the mouse comes.

Repeated Words: "Help! Help! Help! Please help me get out of this closet."

"No way, Jose!"

End: The mouse helps. He unlocks the closet and lets her out.

How Mouse Helps

Once upon a time a Cabbage Patch doll was locked in a closet. She couldn't get out. Her mommy came. Cabbage Patch doll said, "Help! Help! Help! Please help me get out of the closet." But mommy said, "No way, Jose! There's no one at home to play with you."

Then brother came. Cabbage Patch doll said, "Help! Help! Help! Please help me get out of the closet." But brother said, "No way, Jose! I don't like dolls."

Then sister came. Cabbage Patch doll said, "Help! Help! Help! Please help me get out of the closet." But sister said, "No way, Jose! I can't play with you right now."

Then dog came. Cabbage Patch doll said, "Help! Help! Help! Please help me get out of the closet." But dog said, "No way, Jose! I want a bone."

The cat came. Cabbage Patch doll said, "Help! Help! Help! Please help me get out of the closet." But cat said, "No way, Jose! Meow."

Finally mouse came. Cabbage Patch doll said, "Help! Help! Help! Please help me get out of the closet." Mouse said, "OK." He unlocked the closet and let her out.

The End

Step 5: Compose Individual Stories Using Repetition

Kindergartners and first graders may dictate individual stories using repetition or draft their own stories using invented spelling. Older children may write individual stories using the process approach to writing, in which they develop a story map to plan their stories and then write a rough draft. Or, they might use informal drama or storytelling to plan their stories.

Later they meet in writing groups (often using reading groups) to share their stories and get feedback from classmates on how to revise their stories. The writing group's suggestions focus on ways to improve the story, including using repetitive events and dialogue consistently and creatively. After making revisions, children proofread their stories and work with their teacher to correct mechanical errors. Finally, students recopy their stories and share them with an appreciative audience of classmates, younger students, parents, grandparents, or pen pals.

Sample Lesson

The purpose of this sample lesson is to expand second graders' awareness of repetition as a literary device to make the plot of a story more complex and more interesting. Through this lesson, students will identify repeated events and repeated words in stories they listen to or read silently. They will also compose their own collaborative and individual stories that incorporate repetition. The sample lesson is designed for a two week period, with activities presented in a day by day format.

Day 1

Read, discuss, and complete the suggested activities presented in Step 1 of the instructional strategy using *The Gingerbread Boy* (Galdone, 1975). Talk about how the gingerbread boy's journey creates the opportunity for the author to use repeated events and dialogue. Make a copy of the chart illustrated in Figure 1, listing the two characteristics of repetitive stories. Invite students to draw pictures of the repeated events and add them to the chart. Then ask students to add the gingerbread boy's refrain.

Next, retell the story with students using a clothesline storyline. Pass out pictures depicting story events and have students clip the pictures on a clothesline as they retell the gingerbread boy's journey.

Day 2

Have students read *The Little Red Hen*. Talk about how little red hen's dilemma (she needs help growing the wheat and making the bread) provides the author with the opportunity to use the repetitive pattern in the story. Invite children to recall the events and words that are repeated. Refer students to the repetition chart developed on Day 1 and compare the two stories and how the author used repetition in each. Next, have students retell the story by developing a story map, as shown in Figure 3. Students may develop the story map as a group or individually, depending on their prior experience with story maps.

Day 3

Have students read two or three additional repetitive stories from the list of tradebooks or the list of basal reader stories presented earlier. Next, talk about the stories and why authors used repeated events and/or dialogue, and ask students to describe the repetition of events and/or words in the stories.

Days 4-5

Brainstorm a list of the repetitive stories students have read and ask them to choose their favorite one to retell. Students write and illustrate their own version of the story and then compile the pages to make a booklet. Next, have students share their stories with their classmates. Finally, review the characteristics of repetitive stories using the chart developed on Day 1 and ask students to point out how they used repetition in their stories.

Day 6

Write a collaborative story that incorporates repetition of events and words. As a group, have students select an idea and develop a story map. Have the students dictate the story and record it on the chalkboard. After writing the rough draft, ask students to reread the story, checking to be sure they have communicated clearly and that events and words are repeated consistently. Then ask students to suggest ways to revise the story. After making revisions and correcting mechanical errors, make a copy for each student.

Days 7-10

Have students write original stories that incorporate repeated events and/or words. Students may want to develop a story map to organize their ideas before writing. Have students use the process approach for drafting and revising their stories. After writing their rough drafts, children share their drafts with a writing group. Classmates check to see that events and/or dialogue have been repeated consistently and make general revision suggestions. Children revise their stories on the basis of feedback received from their classmates. Next, children proofread their stories to locate and correct mechanical errors. Finally, they recopy their stories in booklet form and share them with classmates or with younger children in the school. Finished booklets also may be placed in the class library.

Summary

Repetition is one literary device writers use to make stories more complex and interesting for their readers. For centuries, storytellers have valued this structure, and young children find it equally useful for both comprehending and producing stories because of its predictability. The instructional strategy presented in this chapter is a field tested approach for helping primary grade students become more aware of this structure.

References

Applebee, A.N. *Child's concept of story: Ages 2-17.* Chicago, IL: University of Chicago Press, 1978.

Botvin, G.J., and Sutton-Smith, B. The development of structural complexity in children's fantasy narratives. *Developmental Psychology,* 1977, *13,* 377-388.

Bridge, C.A. Predictable books for beginning readers and writers. In M.R. Sampson (Ed.), *The pursuit of literacy: Early reading and writing.* Dubuque, IA: Kendall/Hunt, 1986.

De Beaugrande, R., and Colby, B.N. Narrative models of action and interaction. *Cognitive Science,* 1979, *3,* 43-66.

Golden, J.M. Children's concept of story in reading and writing. *The Reading Teacher,* 1984, *37,* 578-584.

Heald-Taylor, G. How to use predictable books for K-2 language arts instruction. *The Reading Teacher,* 1987, *40,* 656-661.

Hoskisson, K., and Tompkins, G.E. *Language arts: Content and teaching strategies.* Columbus, OH: Merrill, 1987.

Johnson, N., and Mandler, J. A tale of two structures: Underlying and surface forms in stories. *Poetics,* 1980, *9,* 51-86.

Leondar, B. Hatching plots: Genesis of storymaking. In D. Perkins and B. Leondar (Eds.), *The arts and cognition.* Baltimore, MD: Johns Hopkins Press, 1977, 172-191.

McClure, A. Predictable books: Another way to teach reading to learning disabled children. *Teaching Exceptional Children,* 1985, *17,* 267-273.

Rhodes, L. I can read: Predictable books as resources for reading and writing instruction. *The Reading Teacher,* 1981, *34,* 511-518.

Sadow, M.W. The use of story grammar in the design of questions. *The Reading Teacher,* 1982, *35,* 518-522.

Spiegel, D.L., and Fitzgerald, J. Improving reading comprehension through instruction about story parts. *The Reading Teacher,* 1986, *39,* 676-682.

Stein, N.L., and Glenn, C.G. An analysis of story comprehension in elementary school children. In R.O. Freedle (Ed.), *New directions in discourse processing.* Norwood, NJ: Ablex, 1979.

Tompkins, G.E., and Webeler, M. What will happen next? Using predictable books with young children. *The Reading Teacher,* 1983, *36,* 498-502.

Wason-Ellam, L. Using literary patterns: Who's in control of the authorship? *Language Arts,* 1988, *65,* 291-301.

Whaley, J.F. Story grammars and reading instruction. *The Reading Teacher,* 1981, *34,* 762-771.

Christine J. Gordon

Teaching Narrative Text Structure: A Process Approach to Reading and Writing

> This chapter describes a process approach to teaching narrative text structure in reading and writing. The author presents an instructional strategy which combines a direct teacher explanation approach and a process approach for teaching narrative text structure. In the sample lesson provided, reading and writing are viewed as composing processes with teacher and students switching continually from one to the other. The strategy is most appropriate for students in grades four through nine, although it can be adapted for use at lower levels.

Enhancing sense of story through instruction in narrative text structure is one method that has been used successfully to improve children's reading and writing abilities (see Fitzgerald, this volume). This instruction is designed to complement actual story reading and story writing, not serve as a substitute for them. In addition, instruction in narrative text structure is an intermediary step, not an end in itself. It is a step toward automatic, unconscious, and independent use of text structure as a framework for comprehension and writing. It is a step toward making students strategic readers and writers.

In this chapter, a strategy will be presented for teaching narrative text structure within a process approach to reading and writing. In a process approach, students develop a concept of reading and writing as active involvement with text—the thinking and behaviour during reading and writing are made explicit. The process approach combines teacher centered instruction (the teacher has primary responsibility) with learner centered instruction (students gradually assume responsibility for their own learning). Supporting evidence for the critical components of the strategy is provided, the purposes of the strategy are outlined, the steps are described, a sample lesson using the strategy is presented, and the chapter concludes with suggestions for using this strategy in the primary grades.

Instruction in Narrative Text Structure

Instruction in narrative text structure is helpful if the instruction occurs over an extended period (Gordon, 1980) and includes a component for transferring knowledge and use of text structures to new or more difficult tasks, such as reading unfamiliar selections or writing one's own stories (Gordon, 1983; Gordon & Braun, 1982, 1983, 1985, 1986). An even more successful method involves combining a process approach to reading and writing (Collins, Brown, & Larkin, 1980; Flower & Hayes, 1981; Graves, 1983) with direct teacher explanation (Duffy & Roehler, 1987) of narrative text structure (Gordon, 1988). In such an integration, reading and writing are viewed as composing processes (Tierney & Pearson, 1983) so closely related (Rubin & Hansen, 1984) that teacher and students continually move from one process to the other rather than beginning with an emphasis on teaching narrative text structure as an aid to reading comprehension and then moving into writing. Indeed, the composing of stories often comes first. Students are involved in reading and writing as corequisite processes with narrative text structure serving as the transfer link between the two.

When teaching narrative text structure, the teacher makes explicit the structure underlying the organization of stories (Gordon, 1983). Through think alouds (Davey, 1983), the teacher models the reasoning processes during reading and writing, showing how the knowledge of structure helps in the process of understanding the story being read or in framing the story being written. In addition, teacher/student interactions include informal assessment of students' reasoning and further explanation (Duffy & Roehler, 1987) if students' answers to questions reveal misunderstandings.

Although the strategy outlined in this chapter focuses on using text structure in the thinking/reasoning process during reading and writing, other aspects of the thinking process (inferencing, accessing prior knowledge, affective states) are not neglected. Obviously, meaning is not constructed only on the basis of narrative text structure. So that use of narrative text structure becomes internalized, guided practice is provided following teacher modeling. Responsibility is gradually released to students during the course of instruction (Gordon, 1985; Pearson, 1985). Collaborative learning (Trimbur, 1985), particularly in the form of discussion, conferencing, collaborative writing (in triads), and peer editing, is a key step toward independent application. Revisions based on feedback from the teacher and/or peers and multiple drafts also characterize the process approach. Student/student interactions and the joint writing of compositions provide the necessary social context for input on the basis of unique abilities, for greater risk taking (since the end products are initially co-authored), and for active involvement in one's own learning through sharing and feedback.

Purposes of the Instructional Strategy

The primary purposes of the instructional strategy include: (1) predicting story content prior to or during reading; (2) guiding comprehension by serving as a framework for organizing what is read/learned; (3) framing oral and written story recall; (4) planning a story before, as well as during writing; (5) revising a story at the local level (one aspect of the structure) or the global level (the whole organizational framework); and (6) using questions based on text structure to monitor meaning during reading and writing.

Components of the Instructional Strategy

In general, the instructional strategy contains a variety of elements—process writing, think alouds, collaborative learning, questioning, clarification—within an instructional model that has four basic components in each lesson. These basic components are introduction, direct explanation, guided practice, and independent application (Baumann, 1983, 1984, 1986a, 1986b; Blanton, Moorman, & Wood, 1986; Gordon, 1985; Pearson, 1984, 1985). Depending on the particular focus of a lesson, one element may be emphasized more than other elements in any of the four components. For example, in the *sample lesson* that follows, teacher explanation (using questioning and clarification) is the focus in *direct explanation*.

Nevertheless, explaining narrative text structure within a process approach is the overarching framework.

Introduction. The introduction informs students of the goals/objectives of the lesson (what they are studying) in language they can understand, makes explicit why they are studying narrative text structure, when and how this knowledge can be used in a variety of learning situations (Baumann & Ballard, 1987; Baumann & Schmitt, 1986), and relates the lesson to students' past experiences or previous teaching.

Direct explanation. This component is the heart of the lesson. Questions, examples, teacher modeling of thought processes, and demonstration are all aspects to attain the stated purposes. The teacher leads the lesson and actively involves the students in question answering, providing further explanation for any required clarification. Students' own compositions or the stories of published authors are used to make explicit the role of text structure in the reasoning process. Initially, the teacher provides an overview of the narrative text structure by beginning with fairy tales, myths, or legends, as these have a fairly tight and consistent organization. This type of instruction makes narrative text structure explicit and teaches students how to use story elements as metatextual aids in dealing with the content of their reading and writing.

The teacher can deal with specific elements of story structure (Fitzgerald, this volume) while reading or writing complete stories. In any one lesson or series of lessons, the teaching/learning might focus on any specific element of story structure, just as the sample lesson in this chapter focuses on plot. Setting, goals, resolutions, or characters are elements that a teacher might highlight in the study of a story.

Instruction could begin using either the reading or writing mode but move back and forth in the direct teacher explanation. The focus is on both text structure instruction and the way we process during reading and writing. Through think alouds, the teacher models how to use text structure and how to think while reading. Process/content/structure discussions tie in any prior knowledge. In the direct teacher explanation, story diagrams (Tompkins & McGee, this volume) may be used to improve comprehension during reading, to aid story recall, and to plan and compose narratives.

Suitable stories from basal readers, trade books, or from children's own writing can be used in the teacher directed instruction. Gradually introduce stories that are not well structured so students learn that not all stories can be understood or appreciated in terms of such an organization. (However, not every story should be studied with an emphasis on text structure.)

Guided practice. In this component, students assume more responsibility for learning. While the teacher continues to provide guidance and direction, more of the lesson is student directed. Students are expected to apply what they have learned to new contexts under teacher supervision. The responsibility for teaching/learning becomes a shared one in reciprocal reading/writing situations. In reciprocal teaching, the teacher continues to model some reasoning related to text structure, story content, and the reading/writing process, but gradually relinquishes responsibility to students for this kind of modeling, predicting, or question asking. For example, in a reciprocal teaching approach students learn to ask and answer questions keyed to structure, content, and process. These questions serve as a basis for self-questioning during reading and writing and during conferencing with others. The goal is to develop awareness and control over processing so that students then can apply these processing strategies independently to monitor their reading/writing/learning.

In guided practice, there should be continual transfer of the knowledge of narrative text structure from reading to writing and from writing to reading. In other words, reading and writing need to be viewed as composing processes with more similarities than differences, processes wherein readers/writers are encouraged to construct meaning in multiple drafts.

Independent application. In the final step of each lesson, students assume total responsibility, moving from a shared student/student responsibility to totally independent application. In pairs or triads, students choose stories for reading and discussing or choose topics/ideas for compositions. They collaborate in "coming up" with the story comprehension or in composing the narrative. While the focus is on narrative text structure as a heuristic (vehicle) for reading and writing, content and process concerns should not be neglected. Conferences are held with peers (or the teacher) on aspects ranging from topic choice/idea generation to revisions the groups wish to consider. As students become more confident in group comprehension and/or composition, they are encouraged to begin to work independently.

Sample Lesson

The lesson that follows is designed for intermediate grade or junior high school students. It uses the process approach to teaching narrative text structure and is designed to blur the distinction between reading and writing.

The following conventions have been used in the sample lesson: (1) statements which can be made by the teacher are in lower case type (these are not intended to be verbatim utterances); (2) comments or annotations are in upper case type; (3) information in figures is intended for transparencies, charts, or handouts; and (4) examples of story parts are in lowercase boldface italics.

This lesson includes an introduction where the purpose is set, students' prior knowledge is assessed, the skill is named, and students are told when, why, and how they can use the knowledge they are acquiring. Direct explanation is provided where the teacher models thinking processes, demonstrates, and provides examples. The next component of the lesson is guided practice. In this step, the shared or reciprocal teaching approach is adopted. Finally, students assume much of the responsibility for reading and writing. Here students discuss, conference, read, write, and revise.

This lesson is based on several assumptions. It assumes that students have some knowledge of the elements of story structure and have diagramed some stories into their component parts (for an explanation of story diagraming, see Tompkins & McGee, this volume). Students have had an opportunity to ask questions, provide responses, and be involved in reciprocal teaching situations. They also have conferenced stories and their own compositions. They either know the conference form (see Figure 1) to use as a guide for their discussion or have access to it in chart form. The lesson should be a model, but not a script, for teachers to use.

Introduction. Today we will continue learning about the organization of stories. First, let's review briefly what we know about the ways stories are organized. Remember there is an order to the way things happen in most stories, at least stories that are well organized—they more closely follow a structure or organization than do stories that start straying from the structure.

Stories are somewhat like events that might occur in your everyday life. Things happen in a kind of order. The place where you are, the setting, could be your home; it is early in the morning. You get up, dress, have breakfast, and get ready for school. Your doorbell rings and someone wants you to call an ambulance, and so the events in your life or in a story unfold. If we think about how the author planned the story you are reading or how you can plan a story you want to write, there is a structure or a framework, which is like a skeleton on which we can hang all the ideas in that story.

In the past few days, we learned about the main parts in a story. For example, when I start reading a story, I know I can expect to find the *Setting* first. I predict that in a setting I'll be introduced to the time, place, and some of the characters. Then I expect the problem to unfold, and I watch for it. That is generally part of the *Theme* in the story. Once I detect the problem or goal, I expect various events, which are part of the *Plot*. These events lead me to predict a *Resolution* or story ending.

We also read and wrote different settings, themes, characterizations, and resolutions. We used our sheet to hold a conference (see Figure 1) for the stories we read and wrote. In some conference sessions we talked more about one story part than another, because that was the part we were focusing on those particular days. We also learned that we keep these headings in our head; we don't write them into our story.

The story plot has more than one part. Today we are going to learn about the various parts of plot: the happenings or events in a story. Why is it important to study the structure of the plot? STUDENT RESPONSES. Yes, you're right, we can use this knowledge to ask questions as we're reading, to remember the story to tell someone, to write it out from memory, or to plan what might go into a story when we are writing.

Direct explanation. Look at this chart (see Figure 2) on the overhead projector. At the top are the five main story parts. Look under the box that says *Plot*. There are two episodes or happenings

Figure 1
Process/Structure Conference Sheet*

1. One member of the group reads the whole story (or episode) to the audience (the other group).
2. Members of the group then ask members of the other triad to respond to the following questions.
   - What was the story (or the episode) about?
   - Something happens that starts our first episode and moves the story forward. What is it?
   - What is the character's goal or intent?
   - What action does the character take that brings him or her closer to the goal?
   - Let's talk about the outcome. How does this episode end? Does this ending fit in with the whole story?
   - Are there any feelings, thoughts, or actions in our story that are reactions to any part of the plot?
   - What did you like about our story (or episode)?
   - Were there any parts of the episode where you wondered what we were trying to say? Which part(s)?
   - Were there any parts in the episode you wanted to hear more about? Which part(s)?

*Adapted from Bissex, 1982; Gordon and Sveen, 1985, 1986.

in this story that are diagramed on this chart. Short stories usually only have one or two episodes. Longer stories may have as many as 20. Who will read the parts of each episode in the plot? STUDENT RESPONSES. Excellent. Not all episodes have the same parts. Sometimes the goals, thoughts, feelings, or plans are not given. Sometimes reactions are not given, but you might know what they are anyway. For example, if a boy came home with a very bad report card and the mother's reaction to this event was not given, what could you think or infer her reaction might be? STUDENT RESPONSES.

Yes, disappointment, anger. However, usually each episode has a *Starter Event*, an *Action*, and *What Happens* or an *Outcome* in that order. But the parts of an episode are not always in the same order. Sometimes an *Inner Response* comes before a *Starter Event*. The *Reaction* jumps around. Sometimes it is last, sometimes between the others.

Now let me explain each part. After my explanations, we will go back and read a story about events that occurred in an everyday life. EXPOSE THE FIRST EPISODE OF THE STORY (See Figure 3) ON THE OVERHEAD TO THE END OF "BAGGY PINK SWEAT SUIT." ALSO PROVIDE STUDENTS WITH A HANDOUT OF THE EPISODE. One important element of the plot is the *Starter Event*. This is the action or occurrence that gets the story rolling. Otherwise, if I stopped the story after the *Setting*, after "my school books," I would say to myself, "Ho, hum, so what? Nothing is really happening."

Let's take a look at Episode 1 in the story. What occurrence changes the course of events in this story? STUDENT RESPONSES. You said knocking, Susan. But knocking is very much like ringing. However, it might make sense that the person rang, and then knocked as well if there was some anxiety, if the person wanted someone to answer the door quickly. But does that move the story forward? Look back in the episode, Susan, to see what happens that takes the story a step further. STUDENT RESPONDS. Yes, that's correct, Susan, the plea to call an ambulance is important because the story cannot move ahead if no one answers the door. Now this story moves further.

Another important element in the plot is *Inner Response*. It's the plan, feeling, goal, or thought of the character about what he/she has to do. If there is a main goal in the story, the *Inner Response* is related to the main goal or theme. Words like *wanted, thought, felt, decided, said to himself,* and *realized* are cues to *Inner Responses*. Let's read the episode to find if there is a goal or plan of the character in our story. Who can tell me what the *Inner Response* is? STUDENT RESPONSES. Jason said, " 'At this time in the morning?' I asked myself as I yawned. 'Why...who would...?' " But his answer is not correct. I did say that *Inner Responses* are internal, but *Reactions* can be also. (We're studying *Reactions* a little later in this

Figure 2*
"Morning Blues"

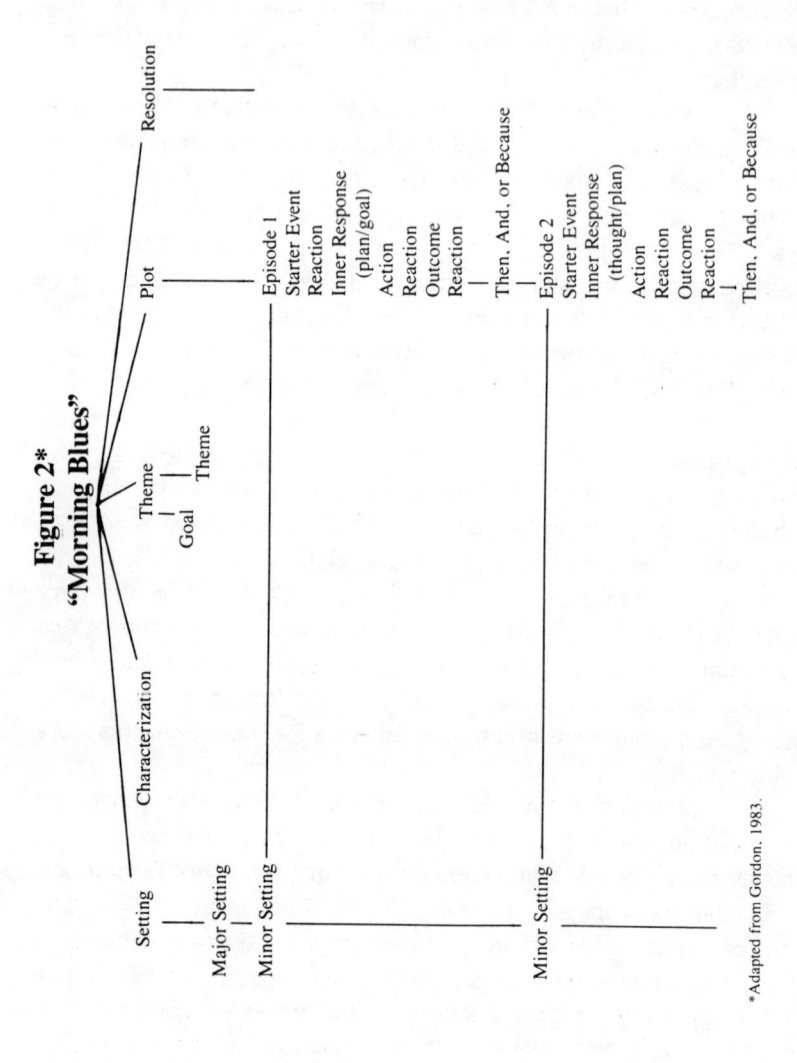

- Setting
  - Major Setting
  - Minor Setting
  - Minor Setting
- Characterization
- Theme
  - Goal
  - Theme
- Plot
  - Episode 1
    - Starter Event
    - Reaction
    - Inner Response (plan/goal)
    - Action
    - Reaction
    - Outcome
    - Reaction
  - Then, And, or Because
  - Episode 2
    - Starter Event
    - Inner Response (thought/plan)
    - Action
    - Reaction
    - Outcome
    - Reaction
  - Then, And, or Because
- Resolution

*Adapted from Gordon, 1983.

Figure 3
Story: Setting and Episode 1

It was 7:00 in the morning. The house was still dark. My eyes wouldn't stay open long enough for me to wake up. First one foot, then the other, I finally made it out of my warm bed. Dressing was painful. Even brushing my teeth didn't wake me up. I barely knew what I had eaten for breakfast as I started gathering my school books.

In a sudden noise and clatter, the doorbell rang with some urgency. "At this time in the morning?" I asked myself as I yawned, "Why...who would...?"

"Please call an ambulance!" blurted an ashen, breathless face. Instantly, I was awake.

As my mother dialed 911, I thought, "Maybe, I can help. I know CPR. I'm young; I'm strong, I can pull the victims out of their vehicles."

I dashed past the doorbell ringer onto the street but there were no cars. Nothing.

In that instant, the ringer slumped to the ground. I noticed the tennis shoes and the baggy pink sweat suit.

---

lesson.) The clue here is that there must be a goal related intent. What do we do now? STUDENT RESPONSES. Yes, read further to see if we can find a thought, a feeling, a plan that is internal and expresses an intent. ALLOW READING TIME. STUDENT RESPONSES. Yes, correct. It's "Maybe I can help. I know CPR; I'm young; I'm strong...." As I read, I think to myself, ah yes, the words "I thought" are here. This statement is clearly the goal. The statement "At this time in the morning...why, who would...?" is not the goal because it does not tell us what he intends to do to help the person at the door. Let's remember to come back to this discussion after we study the ***Reaction*** element in this episode. We'll doublecheck to see if we are correct. By the way, what is CPR? STUDENT RESPONSES.

A third important element of the plot is **Action**. It's what the character does to carry out goals or thoughts or feelings. Is there an **Action** in this episode? STUDENT RESPONSES. Yes, the person ran out into the street to help the "victims in the car accident." The action is related to the intent or the goal. Do you see this relationship? STUDENT RESPONSES. Yes, correct, the character did what he thought should be done.

A fourth important element of the plot is the **Outcome**. This is what happens because the character did what he or she did. This is how the action ends. Reread the episode. Who can tell me the **Outcome?** STUDENT RESPONSES. You are only partially right, Marsha, when you say there was no accident. What else did the main character (our hero) learn? STUDENT RESPONSES. Right, Marsha, that the jogger slumped to the ground on the doorstep.

There is one more element we need to learn about—**Reaction**. The reactions are feelings or actions that result because of starter events, actions, outcomes, or other reactions. Let's reread the episode to identify the reactions. Write them on the paper you have on your desk. What have you jotted down? STUDENT RESPONSES. Yes, you have identified these:

> "At this time in the morning?" I asked myself as I yawned, "Why...who would...?"—a reaction to the doorbell ringing.
>
> Instantly, I was awake—a reaction to the cry for an ambulance.
>
> I noticed the tennis shoes and the sweat suit—a reaction to the jogger passing out.

Can you see the difference between an **Inner Response** and a **Reaction?** DISCUSSION FOLLOWS with further instruction or elaboration as required.

Now let's talk about what else was happening in our heads as we read this story. BE SURE EPISODE 1 (SETTING AND EPISODE 1) ARE EXPOSED OVERHEAD. As I read the first paragraph, I thought of other people I know who are just like this character—people who just can't seem to wake up in the morning. Did you think of them, too? STUDENT RESPONSES. What in the story reminds you of such characters? STUDENT RESPONSES. Examples of responses include: eyes won't stay open; can't put one foot in front of the other; brushing teeth doesn't help wake him or her up; and unaware of the food eaten for breakfast.

STUDENTS MAY RELATE CHARACTERISTICS OF PEOPLE THEY KNOW WHO ARE SIMILAR TO THIS CHARACTER. Yes, we often relate what we know to what we read. We bring in our own experiences so the picture of the character each of us gets in our heads can be different from the picture someone else gets. Let me tell you about a picture that comes to my mind as I read this paragraph. I recall a teacher who was on the same staff as I was some years ago. He would come to school, eyelids at half mast, grab a cup of coffee, circle his hands around the cup, and sit there hunched over, going "Ummm, mmm, mmm" still in a "doze." Then the 8:50 A.M. school bell would ring, and in an instant, he was awake, alert, and fired up!

Clues in the story indicate that there might have been a car accident. In the *Starter Event*, there is noise, clatter, and the need to call an ambulance; there is the character's *Internal Response* that he could pull the victims out of their vehicles. I think as I read that, in such a situation, it would not be unusual for a passerby to be shaken, pale, and out of breath while ringing the doorbell for help. Even the *Action* in this episode confirms in my mind (at least in the beginning) that there probably was a car accident. Yes, of course, because one of our characters tears out onto the street. But then what happens? STUDENT RESPONSES. Yes, that's right. I have to change the whole picture I had formed in my mind because there are other clues that make me start building a different picture. There were no cars; and the doorbell ringer slumped to the ground. The main character notices that the runner was wearing tennis shoes and a baggy sweat suit. Now I make the inference that the doorbell ringer is a jogger who is probably having a heart attack. The clues I used to figure that out were in the story. The story tells me that the jogger, ashen faced, breathless, slumps to the ground, in tennis shoes and a pink sweat suit. I also have some clues from my own experience because I have heard on TV and read in newspapers and magazines that there is a possible risk of heart attack during strenuous exercise. I also think the jogger is female because the jogging suit is pink. Right? STUDENT RESPONSES.

Guided practice. It's your turn now (See Figure 4). What are some questions about the plot we should be asking ourselves as we read on the handout the next episode of the story we started earlier? STUDENT RESPONSES. TEACHER WRITES THEM ON THE BOARD AS THEY ARE ELICITED. TO ASSIST STUDENTS IN PHRASING QUESTIONS, THE TEACHER ALSO INSTRUCTS STUDENTS TO LOOK AT THE TRANSPARENCY, WHERE A DIAGRAM OF THE STORY (See Figure 2) IS DISPLAYED.

IS THERE A DIFFERENT MINOR SETTING FOR THIS EPISODE?
ARE PLACE, TIME, CHARACTERS THE SAME?
WHAT HAPPENS TO MOVE THE STORY FORWARD? THAT IS, WHAT IS THE STARTER EVENT?
WHAT IS THE MAIN ACTION?
WHAT IS THE OUTCOME?
IS THERE A GOAL? IF SO, WHAT IS IT AND IS IT RELATED TO THE ACTION AND THE OUTCOME?
WHAT ARE THE REACTIONS? ARE NONE GIVEN SO THE READER HAS TO MAKE INFERENCES ABOUT THEM?

(WHEN STUDENTS BECOME PROFICIENT IN ASKING QUESTIONS, ENCOURAGE THEM TO MAKE THEIR QUESTIONS MORE STORY SPECIFIC.) Now let's read this episode, thinking of these questions as we read silently. Then you will take turns asking and answering some of these questions following the reading. THE QUESTIONS ARE ASKED AND ANSWERED FOLLOWING THE READING, WITH THE TEACHER PROVIDING FEEDBACK AND ELABORATION IF DIFFICULTY IS EXPERIENCED OR MISUNDERSTANDING OCCURS.

Again, let's talk about how we changed our thinking from Episode 1 to Episode 2, how we did that to build an understanding of the story thus far. First let's talk about what we've learned about our character. STUDENT RESPONSES. Yes, he is awake but not very observant. How do you know he is not observant? STUDENT RESPONSES. Yes, he had not noticed that the lady runner was pregnant. His **Reaction** to the **Outcome** (a baby was about to be born) is surprise when he notices that the doorbell ringer is going to have a baby.

We made an inference in Episode 1 that is supported in Episode 2. We decided that the runner is a lady on the basis of the pink

Figure 4
Story: Episode 2

Calmly and carefully my mother bent down, picked up the frail, childlike figure and placed her on the floor of our entrance hall. She started taking the runner's pulse rate while I ran for a cold compress.
"My grief," I worried, "we must save her life."
We worked feverishly. The runner stirred, opened her eyes and whispered.
"The labour pains have begun. My baby is coming early." My jaw dropped to my chest. I had not even noticed, but I was certain my mother had.

---

sweat suit. How is this fact confirmed in Episode 2? What were the clues? STUDENT RESPONSES. Ah, yes, in the *Outcome* of this episode we learn this person is going to have a baby. What about the other clues? NO STUDENT RESPONSES. Look in the first paragraph of Episode 2. STUDENT RESPONSES. Yes, the author says "placed *her* on the floor...," "save *her* life," and "opened *her* eyes...."

At what point could we still have thought the mother and her child had to deal with a heart attack victim? STUDENT RESPONSES. Yes, halfway into the second episode. The measures being taken to help the runner—taking her pulse and the words "We must save her life" might continue to lead us to believe that is the case. At what point in the second episode do you begin getting a different picture? STUDENT RESPONSES. Correct, at the *Outcome*. Do you see that as you read, you make revisions or changes on the basis of what you read and what you know? How do you make revisions when you are writing, that is, composing a story? STUDENT RESPONSES AND DISCUSSION OF HOW REVISIONS IN READING AND WRITING ARE SIMILAR.

What is going to happen in Episode 3 of the story? That's what you're going to write about.

Independent application. I'd like you to work in groups of three, as we usually do. Since there are six of you in each row,

Teaching Narrative Text Structure

please split up into triads. In your group, talk about what you want to say and think about the main parts in an episode of the plot. These parts are on the chart at the front of the room: *Starter Event, Inner Response, Action, Outcome,* and *Various Reactions.* Then plan and write the next episode of this story. I'm available for conferencing with each group if you need me. When you have finished writing, find another group that has finished, read your episode to them, and hold a conference on your episode, or on the whole story thus far. Use your conference sheets if you have to (see Figure 1).

WHEN STUDENTS HAVE FINISHED CONFERENCING, REMIND THEM THEY CAN MARK ON THEIR SHEETS WHATEVER REVISIONS THEY AGREE ON AS A GROUP AFTER THE CONFERENCE. FURTHER, INDICATE THAT THOSE STUDENTS WHO HAVE NOT BROUGHT THEIR STORY TO A RESOLUTION CAN WRITE THE THIRD AND FINAL EPISODE THE NEXT DAY. INDICATE THAT THE NEXT DAY STUDENTS WILL THINK ABOUT ALL OF THE PARTS IN AN EPISODE OF THE PLOT AS THEY BEGIN WRITING A NEW STORY.

Adaptations to Primary Grades

Although the strategy described here may work best with upper elementary and junior high school students, it also can be adapted for primary children. First, a more simple diagram, designed to capture the underlying organization of less complex narratives, should be used with primary grade children. It will not overwhelm them with terminology. Figure 5 illustrates such a diagram.

Second, the process/structure conference questions in Figure 1 (which are to be used as a guide to questioning until internalization occurs and/or students can produce their own questions) require modification for younger students. Figure 6 provides an example of conference questions that could be used at the primary level when reading "The Three Billy Goats Gruff."

Third, each young author, sitting in the "author's chair," might conference with the whole class, using the conference questions as a guide. Two or three students could provide responses to each question, under the guidance of the teacher. All of these adaptations, as

Figure 5
Schematic Representation of Story Structure*
(primary school)

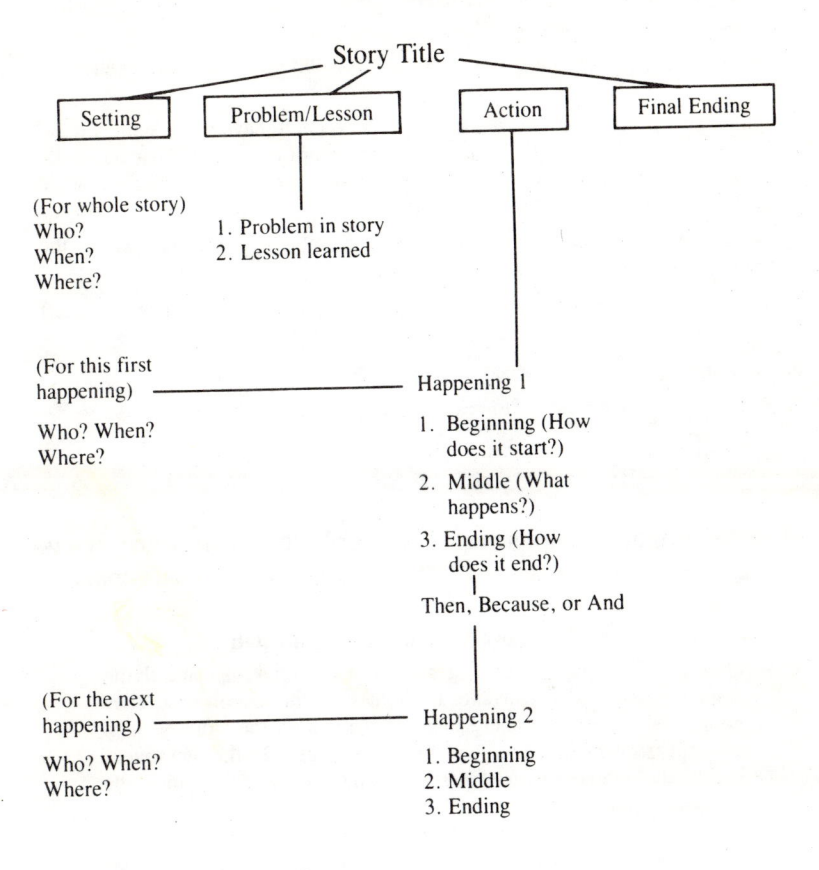

```
                        Story Title
         ┌─────────────┬──────────┬──────────────┐
      Setting    Problem/Lesson   Action      Final Ending
```

(For whole story)
Who?
When?
Where?

1. Problem in story
2. Lesson learned

(For this first
happening) ──────────────── Happening 1

Who? When?
Where?

1. Beginning (How does it start?)
2. Middle (What happens?)
3. Ending (How does it end?)

Then, Because, or And

(For the next
happening) ──────────────── Happening 2

Who? When?
Where?

1. Beginning
2. Middle
3. Ending

* Adapted from Gordon, 1983.

well as the one given here, have been used successfully at the second grade level.

Consideration also must be given to the developmental stage of primary grade children in choosing materials and determining the depth and length of the explanation in the think alouds during each

Figure 6
Conference Questions Specific to *The Three Billy Goats Gruff*

1. What problem do the three goats have? In other words, what are they trying to do throughout this whole story?
2. How many times did the goats try to get past the troll? Tell me about those times.
3. Although the author doesn't tell us, the goats seem to have made some kind of plan to deal with the troll. What is the beginning of this plan? What action did each goat take? That is, what does each goat do to carry out the plan? How did each action turn out?
4. Does the writer tell us about the feelings or thoughts of any of the goats or the troll?
5. Let's talk about the ending. How does the story ending (getting rid of the troll) fit with the problem the goats had at the beginning?
6. What did you like about the story?
7. Which parts would you like to hear more about?

of the four main components. The simple lesson provided below uses a story written by a third grade student, my son Christopher.

"The Monkeys That Invaded Manhattan"

One spring morning everything was fine until monkeys came flying from everywhere. They invaded the homes and the schoolyards. They even invaded the newspaper stands. In the homes, the monkeys kept on tipping over everything and throwing dishes. In the newspaper stands, the monkeys were throwing around newspapers, comics, the *TV Guide*, and *The Sun*.

When the news was on, the monkeys jumped on the announcer and the camera person in the newsroom. Then at the gas station the monkeys started spraying gas and oil all over, rolling tires, throwing tools, and kissing the customers.

One monkey thought that every day was Christmas! Another monkey kept on cracking eggs over its head and eating the shells. Nobody seemed to be able to stop the monkeys.

The monkeys were in Manhattan for a month until one Saturday morning the whole community got together (except the monkeys) to make a plan to get rid of them.

One person said, "Let's take them to the zoo." Everybody yelled, "'No, the whole month we've been trying to catch the monkeys."

Then another person said, "Let's ignore the monkeys instead of yelling and screaming and running after them. They will have no fun and probably leave." Everyone agreed to what that person said.

So on Monday they ignored the monkeys. It took until Thursday afternoon for the monkeys to leave the city. After the monkeys left, the people started to clean up every place.

Here is how the story might be used for instruction at the primary level.

Introduction. Today we are going to learn more about how authors put stories together. We have already learned that many stories have a **Setting** (who is in the story, when and where the story takes place), a **Problem** or **Lesson, Action,** and a **Final Ending,** usually in that order. These are the skeleton of the story. In real life, we also do things in a certain order. When we wake up, we get out of bed, wash our face, brush our teeth, dress, eat, and then go to school. We don't go to school, eat, get out of bed, wash, and wake up. That would make no sense.

Today we will study one important part of the story skeleton—*Action*. We will look at each part of the *Action* in each of the happenings.

Direct explanation. Look at Figure 5. Look at the box that says **Action.** How many parts are there to Happening 1? STUDENT RESPONSES. Yes, there are three. Name them, Paul. PAUL'S RESPONSE. Now let me give you examples of the parts in a happening. I find a tiny stray kitten (that's the *beginning*), then I look for its owners (this is the *middle*). When I find the kitten's home, that's the *ending*. Let's talk about our thinking as we understood this happening. I haven't told you the color of the kitten, but could you think of the colors it might have been? STUDENT RESPONSES. Yes, white, grey, black, brown, orange, or mixtures of any of those colors. How do you know kittens are those colors? STUDENT RESPONSES. Yes, because you have seen real live kittens in those colors. You figured out the answer from what you knew in real life. Is this kitten a baby or more grown up? STUDENT RESPONSES. That's right, it's probably a baby. How did you know that? STUDENT RESPONSES. Yes, the word *tiny* gave you the clue. When we read, we also think about what we know and about what is in the story; we put those ideas together to come up with "new" ideas.

I have a copy of a story written by a boy in third grade, the same story we talked about yesterday. You will enjoy rereading this story. Let me pass the story out to you. Read it and then I'll talk about what goes on in my head as I read Happening 1 in the story. I'll think out loud in "slow motion" for you.

ALLOW TIME FOR READING

First of all, as a review, what is the problem in this story? STUDENT RESPONSES. Right, the monkeys have invaded Manhattan and are causing trouble.

Now, let me think out loud to show you what happens in my mind as I read Happening 1.

As I read, it seemed to me that the *beginning* of Happening 1 was when the monkeys came flying from everywhere. They started tipping things, throwing dishes, and then throwing newspapers and all kinds of reading materials that we can buy at a newsstand. I thought about the names of some of the newspapers they would be throwing around, especially our other newspaper, *The Herald*. I even wondered why Christopher, the author, especially mentioned that the monkeys were throwing around *The Sun*; I think probably because some people don't like reading *The Sun*. I laughed out loud when I got a picture in my head of what happened in the *middle* of this happening. I could "see" the monkeys spraying gas, kissing customers, and cracking eggs. But nobody could stop them. The *ending* of this happening comes when no one can stop them. If the writer had stopped writing the story at this point, you can imagine what might have happened to Manhattan. Had the author chosen, the rest of the story could have been different from the one we have. We would have had a different picture in our heads of what would go on in the story and how people would have had to learn to live with the monkeys.

Guided practice. Now, you can share your thinking with me. I will ask you some questions as we read *Happening 2*. How does the next happening begin? What is the *beginning?* What do people do to get this story moving? STUDENT RESPONSE. John said the people got together. There is more, John. Why did they get together? That information is important because again this happening does not really begin until we know why people got together. What is the reason? JOHN RESPONDS THAT THEY WANTED TO MAKE A PLAN TO GET RID OF THE MONKEYS. Excellent, John, that's correct. Now what happens in the *middle* of this happening? STUDENT RESPONSES LIST SUGGESTIONS GIVEN BY MEMBERS OF THE COMMUNITY. Let's talk about the first suggestion. Who can tell me why taking the monkeys to the zoo was not a good suggestion? STUDENT RESPONSES. Correct, if you can't catch the monkeys you can't take them to the zoo. How did you figure out that answer? STUDENT RESPONSES. Yes, it was in the story, but as you told me, you had to think about what people need to do first before they can bring animals to the zoo. They need to catch them. Then you need to connect this idea to the suggestion about the zoo. How does this happening *end?* STUDENT RESPONSES. Yes, all the people agree to ignore the monkeys.

Now I'll have you work in small groups. You'll deal with the rest of the story in groups.

INDEPENDENT APPLICATION WOULD FOLLOW BEFORE THE LESSON WAS OVER. IN THIS CASE, THE STUDENTS WOULD BE ASKED TO WRITE IN GROUPS A DIFFERENT FINAL HAPPENING TO THIS STORY. SOME DISCUSSION AND DIRECTIONS WOULD BE NECESSARY AT THIS POINT.

Alternate Concepts of Story Mapping Instruction

Other concepts for direct teaching of narrative text structure that may be as effective and more easily adapted for younger children include those described by Alberta Education (1986) and Baumann and Ballard (1987). While these involve some aspects of direct instruction, there is less direct explanation of processing when reading and writing. Nevertheless, a teacher may wish to begin with any of the simpler approaches before progressing to the approach described in this chapter.

The simplest level is a teaching strategy outlined by Alberta Education (1986). In this procedure, students arrange into a sequence cut apart story sections. Younger or less proficient readers deal with only the three main concepts in a story: beginning, middle, and ending. Each small group is given a copy of one story section. As the students in each group silently read the section, they try to determine which group has the beginnning of the story. Discussion (based on teacher posed questions) follows on why they think it is the beginning and what clues tell that it is the beginning. Responses are elicited so that "in the beginning we find out who the characters in the story are, where the story takes place, and what might happen" (p. 78). Similar questions are asked and discussions held to help the students identify the next two story sections. The critical learning that takes place is that "in the middle of the story the characters have adventures" (p. 79) and "at the end of the story we find out how the characters solved their problems or how the adventure ends" (p. 80). As students become more proficient, stories can be cut into more sections.

Baumann and Ballard's (1987) technique (which is more readily accessible than the Alberta Education technique) uses the notion of a story map to aid students in understanding the main elements of plot and in composing their own stories. The map includes only the setting, the problem, the goal with attempts to solve the problem, and an ending.

Following a discussion of the *what* and *why* of the lesson, the teacher presents the *how* and the *why*. Direct instruction is provided wherein the teacher assumes full responsibility. That is, after explaining each story element, the teacher completes the story map using a think aloud procedure. In guided practice using another story, students complete the map or portions of it under teacher direction (shared responsibility), with the teacher monitoring students' work and providing feedback and further instruction. Independent practice in the use of story maps is eventually assigned, and students assume full responsibility. Baumann and Ballard's approach is less complex and yet it can be used effectively at upper elementary and secondary school levels.

Summary

The main purposes for teaching narrative text structure as a strategy are to enable students to predict story content, to use text structure as a plan for story writing, to guide their story comprehension and composition, to frame their story recall, and to revise story drafts. Teaching the strategy outlined in this chapter involves the following steps which combine direct explanation with a process approach: (1) an introduction which makes explicit what will be learned and brings to awareness when, why, and how the strategy will be useful; (2) direct explanation which involves demonstration and modeling by the teacher; (3) guided practice which involves shared responsibility in a reciprocal teaching situation; and (4) independent application which places responsibility for learning completely on the students.

The sample lesson, which can be used with students in grades four to nine, deemphasizes distinctions between reading and writing, since both are viewed as composing processes. Suggestions also are provided for simplified strategy use at primary levels.

References

Alberta Education. *Diagnostic reading program: Instructional strategies.* Edmonton, AB: Student Evaluation Branch, 1986.
Baumann, J.F. The direct instruction of main idea comprehension ability. In J.F. Baumann (Ed.), *Teaching main idea comprehension,* Newark, DE: International Reading Association, 1986a, 133-178.
Baumann, J.F. The effectiveness of a direct instruction paradigm for teaching main idea comprehension. *Reading Research Quarterly,* 1984, *20,* 93-115.
Baumann, J.F. A generic comprehension instructional strategy. *Reading World,* 1983, *22,* 284-294.
Baumann, J.F. Teaching third grade students to comprehend anaphoric relationships: The application of a direct instruction model. *Reading Research Quarterly,* 1986b, *21,* 70-90.
Baumann, J.F., and Ballard, P.Q. A two step model for promoting independence in comprehension. *Journal of Reading,* 1987, *30,* 608-612.
Baumann, J.F., and Schmitt, M.C. The what why, how, and when of comprehension instruction. *The Reading Teacher,* 1986, *39,* 640-646.
Bissex, G.L. Alternatives to the red pencil. *Learning,* November 1982, 74-77.
Blanton, W.E., Moorman, G.B., and Wood, K.D. A model of direct instruction applied to the basal skills lesson. *The Reading Teacher,* 1986, *40,* 299-304.
Collins, A., Brown, J.S., and Larkin, K.M. Inference in text understanding. In R.J. Spiro, B.C. Bruce, and W.F. Brewer (Eds.), *Theoretical issues in reading comprehension.* Hillsdale, NJ: Erlbaum, 1980, 385-407.
Davey, B. Think aloud—Modeling the cognitive processes of reading comprehension. *Journal of Reading,* 1983, *27,* 44-46.
Duffy, G.G., and Roehler, L.R. Improving reading instruction through the use of responsive elaboration. *The Reading Teacher,* 1987, *40,* 514-520.
Flower, L., and Hayes, J. A cognitive process theory of writing. *College Composition and Communication,* 1981, *23,* 365-387.
Gordon, C.J. Contexts for narrative text structure use: What do the kids say? *English Quarterly,* December 1988, *21.*
Gordon, C.J. *The effects of instruction in metacomprehension and inferencing on children's comprehension abilities.* Unpublished doctoral dissertation, University of Minnesota, 1980.
Gordon, C.J. *Improving reading comprehension and writing: The story grammar approach.* Calgary, AB: Braun & Braun, 1983.
Gordon, C.J. Modeling inference awareness across the curriculum. *Journal of Reading,* 1985, *28,* 444-447.

Gordon, C.J., and Braun, C. Mental processes in reading and writing: A critical look at self-reports as supportive data. *Journal of Educational Research*, 1986, *79*, 292-301.

Gordon, C.J., and Braun, C. Metacognitive processes: Reading and writing narrative discourse. In D.L. Forrest-Pressley, G.E. MacKinnon, and T.G. Waller (Eds.), *Metacognition, cognition, and human performance*, Volume 2. New York: Academic Press, 1985, 1-75.

Gordon, C.J., and Braun, C. Story schemata: Metatextual aid to reading and writing. In J.A. Niles and L.A. Harris (Eds.), *New inquiries in reading: Research and instruction*. Rochester, NY: National Reading Conferences, 1982, 261-268.

Gordon, C.J., and Braun, C. Using story schema as an aid to reading comprehension and writing. *The Reading Teacher*, 1983, *37*, 116-121.

Gordon, C.J., and Sveen, R. *Evaluation/revision of narrative text in the writing conference: Theory into practice*. Paper presented at the International Reading Association Annual Convention, New Orleans, Louisiana, May 1985.

Gordon, C.J., and Sveen, R. *Evaluation/revision of stories in the writing conference*. Paper presented at the International Reading Association's Seventh Transmountain Conference, Vancouver, British Columbia, May 1986.

Graves, D.H. *Writing: Teachers and children at work*. Portsmouth, NH: Heinemann, 1983.

Pearson, P.D. Changing the face of reading comprehension instruction. *The Reading Teacher*, 1985, *38*, 724-738.

Pearson, P.D. Direct explicit teaching of reading comprehension. In G.G. Duffy, L.R. Roehler, and J. Mason (Eds.), *Comprehension instruction: Perspectives and suggestions*. New York: Longman, 1984, 222-233.

Rubin, A., and Hansen, J. *Reading and writing: How are the first two "R's" related?* Reading Education Report No. 51. Champaign, IL: Center for the Study of Reading, University of Illinois, 1984.

Tierney, R., and Pearson, P.D. Toward a composing model of reading. *Language Arts*, 1983, *60*, 568-580.

Trimbur, J. Collaborative learning and teaching writing. In B.W. McClelland and T.R. Donovan (Eds.), *Perspectives on research and scholarship in composition*. New York: Modern Language Association of America, 1985, 87-109.

Charles W. Peters
Marilyn Carlsen

Using a Literary Framework to Teach Mysteries

> This chapter provides a systematic approach to teaching mysteries that is consistent with an interactive view of the reading process. The activities are presented in the context of a literary framework that emphasizes four phases to Informed Teaching: Strategic Planning, Before Reading, During Reading, and After Reading.

One major concern with instructional activities designed to enhance comprehension is that in many situations they minimize the overall importance that domain or content knowledge assumes in the learning process (Peters, 1987; Peters & Hayes, 1989; Voss, 1986). Rather than use the conceptual foundations of the various disciplines as the primary basis for developing activities, reading educators have imposed their views and attendant strategies with minimal regard for how content experts view their own fields.

In effect, this perspective to some extent has neutralized the acquisition and integration of content knowledge by focusing on reading skills and strategies. For example, reading teachers frequently use graphic organizers or story maps without establishing a purpose that is guided by content considerations. While these strategies are useful and should be used to enhance instruction, we must remember that content goals determine process goals.

The purpose of this chapter is to present a balanced approach between content and process, one that does not minimize or ignore how those who teach and write about literature conceptualize the reading process. This balanced approach shifts the perspective from a predominant focus on skills to a focus on the types of knowledge (e.g., concepts, principles, strategies) students need to know in order to interpret literature, because when content is ignored, important literary considerations are often sublimated to a skills oriented approach to reading.

To understand why it is important to have a balanced approach between content and process, we begin by describing the need to integrate current views of the reading process with current views of the literary process. A literary framework emerges that integrates the views that underlie both the interactive view of reading and literary theory into a theoretical structure that serves as a guide for informed teaching. The steps for developing the activities described in this chapter emerge through informed teaching.

The application of the literary framework will be presented in the context of a mystery unit. We have selected mysteries because they appear frequently in students' reading materials, and they illustrate why it is essential to understand how content considerations influence such factors as text structure and strategy usage.

Balancing Content and Process

In this section, we will examine what is meant by an interactive perspective and how it fits within the context of literary theory. We then will explain how the literary framework, a merging of the two perspectives, becomes the conceptual and theoretical structure from which instructional activities for the mystery unit are derived.

As previous chapters in this book have suggested, our concept of the comprehension process has changed dramatically in the past fifteen years. We have moved away from a static view of reading that does not account for such important factors as prior knowledge, text structure, or metacognitive knowledge toward one that explains how the interaction among these factors influences comprehension.

A synthesis of current research suggests that reading is a process of constructing meaning through the dynamic interaction among the reader, the text, and the context of the reading situation (Anderson et al., 1985; Wixson & Peters, 1984). At the core of this interactive perspective is the constructivist assumption that comprehension consists of representing or organizing information in terms of one's previously acquired knowledge. In other words, reading comprehension depends on *how* readers use the various types of knowledge they possess to construct meaning from the printed page (e.g., how a text is structured, how the structure is influenced by domain or content knowledge, and how domain knowledge is used to construct meaning).

This implies that comprehension involves constructing a holistic representation of a text, and to do this readers must be sensitive to the relationship among the various elements of information within a text so they can integrate the new knowledge with existing knowledge. Finally, the interactive perspective suggests that readers cannot strategically select the appropriate skills or strategies to use until they are aware of the *purposes* for learning, the *structure* of the material, and the assigned *task,* because all of these factors significantly influence reading performance.

Because the interactive perspective uses purpose as the focal point of strategic planning, it places a greater emphasis on the importance of domain knowledge. This means that the initial phase of instructional planning must begin with the establishment of content goals rather than process goals because process can flow only from content. Readers must know why they are reading (*purpose*) and what type of material they are reading (*text*) before they can determine how to read it (*strategies*).

Therefore, to incorporate a content perspective into instructional planning, reading teachers can no longer afford to minimize how those who teach and write about literature conceptualize the reading process. In the past, reading teachers have been more concerned about the skills or particular strategies being taught and less about what students need to know about interpreting literature.

Unfortunately, when skills are the focus, the emphasis is not on what literary theorists' would argue students need to know about literature and how it works. To better understand how to identify important literary goals, reading teachers must understand what literary theorists have to say about literature in general and mysteries in particular.

Literary Theory

Literary theories (formalism, structuralism, deconstructionism, poststructuralism, modernism) provide useful insights into how those in literature conceptualize the reading process. For example, structuralists look at the relation between structure and interpretation and emphasize the literary know how or competencies readers must bring to works of literature for comprehension. According to Scholes (1985), we need to provide the reader with textual power. This involves systematically providing students with the textual knowledge and skills that allow them to read, interpret, and criticize literary materials, requiring the reader to unlock the narrative codes embedded within literature. These codes take the form of cultural and generic codes, and together they influence strategy selection (see Figure 1, page 127).

Cultural codes. Cultural codes refer to the type of information that allows readers to construct a fictional world, to orient themselves in it, and to understand the characters and their actions. The more culturally at home in a text students become, the less dependent they will be on guidance from teachers, suggesting that reading teachers need to examine literature from more than a linguistic perspective. In other words, the author's philosophy or perspective guides the conscious selection of characters, setting, plot, and theme. An important part of literary interpretation is understanding how cultural codes influence the underlying meaning of a selection.

For example, Sir Arthur Conan Doyle, whose stories are the focus of our mystery unit, created Sherlock Holmes and Dr. Watson during a period in which people believed that if they thought like scientists in a rational and logical manner (scientific rationalism), all problems could be solved. Doyle adopts this perspective with his detective, Sherlock Holmes, and one's ability to figure out how Sherlock Holmes solves mysteries is linked in part with understanding his investigative techniques. Doyle embeds these beliefs or cultural codes in his mysteries, and readers need to be aware of how these codes influence their comprehension. (For a more detailed description of cultural codes in mysteries, see column 1 in Figure 2, page 128.)

Generic codes. Generic codes are the second component of narrative codes. According to Porter (1981), generic coding serves as a structural guide that provides form to the content of a literary work. Generic codes allow the reader to understand how the structure of a narrative text is influenced by the cultural codes an author uses. The term *generic* should not be confused with the generic notion of story grammars used in psychological and educational research. To literary theorists, generic codes denote the unique structural features that comprise the various types of literature found in the field.

If literary theorists are correct, then generic codes become extremely important in assisting teachers to differentiate between the various types of literature. Figure 2 (column 2) presents an overview of these features in the context of a mystery. In a mystery, they take the form of inverted temporal order where the crime is committed before the reader knows why, and deliberately constructed impediments or hidden clues that often divert the readers from their goal of solving the mystery. Such generic coding plays an important role in distinguishing mysteries from other types of literature. Both the cultural and generic codes influence the strategies that readers must use to understand mysteries, as shown in column 3 of Figure 2.

The Literary Framework

As students unlock the cultural and generic codes found in literature, they begin to understand the interrelationship between the two. In essence, they begin to formulate a literary schema or literary framework (Figure 1). Not only is the notion of a literary framework consistent with an interactive view of reading, but it also allows readers to transcend the generic notion of narrative text that is so pervasive in reading and permits them to think in ways more consistent with a literary perspective. The literary framework suggests that focusing on cultural and generic codes helps students understand the differences that exist within and across various types of narrative materials. Readers need to understand how a writer's use of generic and cultural codes is highly interactive.

Without a literary perspective, important theoretical principles that form the precepts upon which the literary framework is based will continue to be overlooked or taught in isolation. When this occurs, process becomes the primary focus—not literary concepts. Thus it is the literary framework that provides the content focus. This perspective requires teachers to help readers break the hermetic seal around the literary text so they can understand how narrative codes operate within the context of the literary framework. When this occurs, readers can engage in what Todorov (1975) calls "metareading," a process by which the reader notes the methods of the narrative instead of falling under its spell, allowing the reader to match wits with the author, not the characters in the story.

This approach in turn leads to what Iser (1974) refers to as the process of continual modification, which closely parallels the way readers gather experiences in life. As he points out, we "look forward, we look back, we decide, we change our decisions, we form expectations, we are shocked by their nonfulfillment, we question, we muse, we accept, we reject" (page 288).

The literary framework provides a way to integrate each perspective (literary, reading, and research) in a manner that will highlight salient information that must become the basis for instructional planning.

Applying the Literary Framework to Mysteries

In mysteries, as Billman (1984) and Porter (1981) point out, authors implicitly require the reader to participate in the guessing game of detection. The reader plays at sleuthing to discover "whodunit," to resolve the plot, and to find out how this specific literary narrative operates.

According to Cawelti (1976), a fundamental literary principle that governs the process of narrative coding in a mystery is the progressive/digressive dichotomy of time. This refers to the writer's attempt to synchronize time by closing the logical temporal gap created by the mystery. In other words, unlike many other types of narrative materials, in a mystery time is jumbled. The writer presents results (the mystery) before there are reasons (suspects and motives).

To solve the mystery, the reader must put time in chronological order. To help the reader close the time gap, the author often employs the "great detective" who generally uses some quasiscientific approach to solving mysteries. To maintain interest and create suspense, the author employs tricks or impediments to confuse the reader. These impediments are used by the author to disrupt the temporal sequence and postpone the ultimate solution. It becomes the function of the detective to guide the reader through this circuitous journey toward a successful conclusion.

Therefore, to be successful at solving mysteries requires the reader to recognize and understand how these cultural codes affect the structural features of a mystery. Students must understand more than "whodunit"; they must understand how this type of literature works. To do this students need to acquire a literary framework. Consider how time assumes such an important role in a mystery. Time influences the technique the detective uses to figure out important clues (cultural codes); this in turn influences how the author presents the information in the mystery (generic codes). By helping students understand the relation between cultural and generic codes, teachers can select the most appropriate strategies (see Figure 2).

This approach contrasts sharply with how time typically is handled in many reading activities that accompany mysteries. Generally, students are asked to do such activities as sequence events without regard for how time dramatically influences the structure of a mystery. When one adheres to a literary framework, activities take on a different perspective. The goal shifts from merely ordering events to understanding *why* it is important to attend to time or *how* the treatment of time differs from the more traditional logical/temporal order found in other types of literature. For readers to move beyond surface level information, such as who, what, when, where, and why, teachers must focus on literary concepts that provide the appropriate knowledge base and necessary conceptual linkage so students can develop a literary framework essential for comprehending, interpreting, and criticizing literature.

This need suggests that the goals of the discipline must assume a greater role in the instructional decision making process. Information no longer can be decontextualized. If literature is the focus, students must not merely focus on generic skills that do not account for differences within various types of narrative materials.

Sample Development of Instructional Activities

This section focuses on (1) the systematic planning and development of instructional activities and (2) a recommended sequence for instruction. Both are derived from the theoretical assumptions that underlie the literary framework. As mentioned previously, mysteries will be used because they provide a good example of how a teacher can move from a more traditional and decontextualized view of reading to one based on an interactive view of learning that is consistent with the literary framework. In addition, because of their popularity and unique structure, mysteries provide a rich source for teaching students how to read and interpret literature.

The activities described in this section are based on an instructional planning process called Informed Teaching. Informed Teaching requires the teacher to follow a systematic plan for developing and implementing activities consistent with the views that underlie the literary framework. Informed Teaching begins with the Strategic Planning Phase. During this phase, instructional decisions are guided by the identification of content goals. With a clear content focus, teachers select materials and identify activities that will lead to the attainment of the goals. To be consistent with the literary framework, the activities must have a holistic focus and must help students acquire the type of knowledge that will lead to the development of a literary framework or schema. Once the activities are developed, they are implemented in the next three phases of Informed Teaching—Prereading, During Reading, and After Reading.

The Strategic Planning Phase

The Strategic Planning Phase is the beginning point of Informed Teaching. During this phase, all important decisions regarding instructional planning are made. The four components for this phase are goal selection, text selection, strategy selection, and the development of literary processing guides.

Goal selection. Before materials and strategies can be selected, instructional goals are identified. These goals should be the direct outgrowth of a broader set of curricular goals that are in part derived from the literary framework. Curricular goals are important, because they become the basis for establishing the more specific text goals. Text goals operationalize the curricular goals by focusing on specific features of a literary text and the processes required to interpret them.

For example, one broad curricular goal might be to help students understand the relationship between an author's purpose/philosophy, the structure of the material, and the strategies required to interpret it. In order to teach to this goal, the teacher must select materials and identify strategies that demonstrate a direct connection between the broader curricular goals and the more specific text goals. Therefore, during this phase teachers do not merely select the next story in the basal or anthology but must decide what type of literature best fits conceptually with their overall curriculum. With Informed Teaching, the text does not become the curriculum; instead, the literary goals direct the learning process.

Since mysteries are the literary text used in this chapter, we must establish a specific set of text goals that focus on the unique literary features of mysteries (content goals) and the strategies needed to interpret them (process goals). As Figure 2 illustrates, authors like Sir Arthur Conan Doyle use cultural and generic codes that influence the way a mystery is written. To develop the text level content goals, teachers must decide what important literary concepts are embedded within the cultural and generic codes students must know to understand this type of literary text.

With a mystery, these concepts might include how Sherlock Holmes's investigative techniques influence the structure of the mystery; how the major structural elements of a mystery influence the strategies used to solve it; how important literary concepts such as progressive/digressive use of time, the distinction between important and unimportant clues, and characterization influence its plot structure; and how the important logical linking of suspect, motive, and clues lead to understanding the holistic focus of a mystery.

Next, the teacher must develop a set of text level process goals designed to help students understand how they might go about reading a mystery. Some examples are understanding *when, why,* and *how* to use strategies such as reorganizing time chronologically, making observations and predictions and formulating hypotheses; understanding *why* linking clues to a suspect and motive is a good strategy; understanding *why* it is important to distinguish between making predictions and formulating hypotheses in a mystery; and understanding *why* some strategies are different in a mystery than in other literary materials.

Text selection. The second step is to match text level goals with a suitable set of mysteries. In making this decision, several criteria are used. First, teachers should use several mysteries by the same author (Scholes, 1985) because if students are to understand fully how literature works, they must be given the opportunity to read several selections by one author. It is through such extended exposure that students begin to understand the relation between cultural and generic codes and the impact they have on comprehension. This is an important distinction and one that differentiates the literary framework from conventional approaches to teaching reading where students are likely to read only one selection by an author.

Second, when multiple selections are used, teachers must make sure that each mystery contains structural features consistent with the established curricular and text goals. For example, if understanding the relationship between how time is used in a mystery and the type of strategies needed to arrange it in its proper chronological order, then the mystery must be organized so that when readers use the appropriate strategies, they can figure out the ending. A mystery that keeps important clues from the reader until they are explained at the end would be inappropriate. Students must see that appropriate strategies work.

Third, mysteries should be available in a variety of forms (print, audio, visual). This is important because many students may not have the reading skills to comprehend mysteries adequately. Using a video or audiotape allows the teacher to introduce students to the complexities of solving a mystery before they read one. We have found that by beginning with videos and moving to audiotapes, we are able to develop the necessary literary framework for mysteries. This does not mean circumventing print; instead it suggests that if knowledge about the reading process, in this case mysteries, is an important factor that influences comprehension, then one can use alternatives to print to help facilitate the transition to print. With knowledge of the literary framework in place, the transition to print is expedited.

These criteria worked well with the Sherlock Holmes mysteries because there were numerous works from which to select; they were available in a variety of forms; they were available at varying reading levels; and they were formulistic in nature. All of these criteria must be considered carefully.

It is not always easy to identify mysteries that contain all the necessary narrative codes. Mapping procedures were developed to allow teachers to attend to textual information in a systematic manner. The notion of narrative mapping is not new, but conventional story maps are inappropriate because they do not contain some of the key structural elements (generic codes) of a mystery. For this reason, a map was developed that was more consistent with the unique features of a mystery (see Figure 3, page 129). As is the case with all of the activities that follow, the map in Figure 3 is based on Doyle's mystery, "The Adventure of the Dancing Men." The mapping procedures described were in part based on the story maps developed by Wixson and Peters (1987). However, they are modified to reflect the generic codes of a mystery.

As Figure 3 shows, there are three major components to the mystery map. The first component provides the holistic focus by addressing the important question, "What is the mystery?" The second component identifies the important elements in the plot structure that help the reader solve the mystery, such as suspects, motives, and clues. For example, one cannot solve a smotive, and themystery without understanding the relationship among such key elements as investigative techniques used by the detective. In "The Adventure of the Dancing Men," only one character is a legitimate suspect with a reasonable motive. The identification of the suspect can be determined by following the investigative techniques used by Sherlock Holmes. The clues elicited by his investigative techniques must be noted. The map is used to help identify those clues. If they are not readily apparent, this is a good sign that the mystery is not appropriate for the goals previously identified. When all the clues have been identified, the reader should know the suspect, the motive, and how these together help answer the question, "What is the mystery?"

Information from the first two components of the map are used to identify the third component—important literary techniques, such as unfinished sequences and clever impediments that sidetrack the reader. Literary techniques are important because they are part of the narrative codes writers often use to confuse readers. For example, in "The Adventure of the Dancing Men," one of the leading characters, Mr. Walker, becomes a primary suspect because of his abrasive personality. However, he has no motive. If readers fall for this red herring, teachers must be able to identify the source of the difficulty and plan an activity that redirects the reader toward a more plausible suspect. The map is important because it highlights these features.

Strategy selection. The information included on the map serves as the basis for planning instructional activities. Once the map has been completed and the mystery judged appropriate, the teacher focuses on the third part of the Strategic Planning Phase—the identification of essential strategies needed to solve a mystery. While Figure 2 shows the relation between cultural and generic codes and strategy usage, it does not explicitly delineate the steps a reader might go through in solving a mystery. A more detailed listing is provided in Figure 4 (page 130). It is important to identify these steps for several reasons: (1) they form the basis for explaining to students the procedures for solving a mystery, (2) Sherlock Holmes used steps similar to these in his quasiscientific approach to solving mysteries, and (3) they provide the processing focus for activities.

In the next section, these steps will be translated into a series of activities designed to provide a more explicit guide for modeling how a good reader solves mysteries. When the mental steps that underlie the problem solving process of a mystery are made explicit, their teaching becomes more direct.

Guided instruction. Once the essential strategies for solving a mystery have been identified (Figure 4), Literary Processing Guides (LPGs) are developed. The LPGs are charts and diagrams designed to help students understand how to read, interpret, and criticize literature. They are not generic guides that have as their primary focus reading skills or strategies presented in a decontextualized manner. Instead, the LPGs juxtapose both content and process in a manner consistent with the assumptions that underlie the literary framework. More specifically, their purposes are to model explicitly some of the implicit cognitive operations that underlie the assignments in the unit. In most classrooms, students are either assumed to possess these skills or the skills are taught indirectly through questioning guides or classroom discussion.

The LPGs focus students' attention on the various cognitive operations they employ when trying to solve a Sherlock Holmes mystery. Thus, the guides provide both conceptual and procedural focuses that allow students to better understand the strategies they used to generate their responses and how these strategies vary as the purpose, text, and task change. There are essentially three types of LPGs: before reading, during reading, and after reading. Each type corresponds to the remaining phases of Informed Teaching and will be discussed in the context of that phase.

Before Reading Phase

The purpose of the Before Reading Phase is to evaluate, motivate, and stimulate students' prior knowledge. Figures 5 (page 131) and 6 (page 132) provide examples of two activities based on an instructional technique called ACCESS (Peters & Hayes, 1989), which involves accessing and evaluating students' prior knowledge about a specific topic. Three categories are used to evaluate students' knowledge: (1) Can students generate words that describe key concepts? (2) Can they generate examples of these concepts? and (3) Can students interrelate them?

Unlike some prior knowledge assessment techniques, which are limited to the explicit information contained in a new reading selection, the concepts selected for use with ACCESS are derived from the collective knowledge required to attain the two levels of goals identified in the Strategic Planning Phase—curricular and text. In most cases, these tend to be superordinate concepts not mentioned directly in the text. A good source for identifying these concepts is the mystery map, because it generally contains concepts that are important to understanding the holistic focus of a specific mystery.

Figure 5 presents an activity that evaluates the reader's knowledge of several major concepts important to constructing a holistic understanding of both the content of a mystery and the process used in solving a mystery. Students are asked to list words that describe these concepts, provide examples, and then relate two or more important concepts. The difference between the descriptive words and the example category is that the descriptive words focus on critical attributes of a concept, and the examples focus on concrete instances of the concept. The relational category is designed to determine how students see important concepts going together in a superordinate, coordinate, or subordinate manner. In order to construct a holistic interpretation, it is important for students to see how concepts are related.

The advantage of an activity like this is that it allows the teacher to evaluate the breadth and depth of an individual's knowledge. The teacher looks at the number of appropriate words generated as well as the qualitative difference between the types of words used. For *suspect* you would expect a student with a good deal of knowledge about mysteries to generate synonyms related to the context of a mystery. A person with some knowledge of *suspect* might generate words that come from a context other than a mystery. Those who do not know the meaning of the word would provide little or no information. In the example category, students with knowledge of mysteries should be able to provide an example of a suspect from a previous mystery they have read or watched. If students have little knowledge of mysteries, an example may be difficult to provide. This activity allows teachers to see where students need additional background information. If students do not understand the concepts "suspect," "motive," and "clue," teachers must provide appropriate experiences to build that knowledge before students read the first mystery. Without an appropriate level of knowledge, students will not understand mysteries at a level commensurate with the process and content goals that have been established. Prior knowledge assessment does not involve merely having students complete the activities before moving on to the next phase. If student knowledge is lacking, appropriate steps must be taken.

In a second version of ACCESS (Figure 6), the depth of students' knowledge of one concept, scientific process, is probed. It was selected because Holmes bases his investigative technique on a quasi-scientific approach to problem solving. In addition, one of the processing goals for this unit is to improve logical reasoning in the context of solving mysteries. Students must understand how this process works in order to make accurate predictions about suspects, motives, and clues. Without some knowledge of the scientific process, it will be difficult for them to attain the level of independence they need to be strategic readers.

The categories used in the activity come from concept attainment research. The categories are characteristics, example, nonexample, definition, and relationships with other key concepts. Figure 6 provides a specific example for each category. Students place known information into each of these categories. To evaluate student responses, teachers should examine both the quantity and quality of the information, much as they did for the first activity. The "Reason it qualifies as an example" category is particularly useful in making such determinations. Here students must justify their responses. Often, their explanations allow the teacher to determine their levels of understanding.

In the activities based on ACCESS, the concepts fall into both the cultural and generic coding areas. Typically, most prior knowledge assessment procedures limit their assessment to concepts that come directly from the text. In addition, there is no distinction made between the levels of importance these concepts assume in constructing a holistic interpretation of the material. All the concepts selected for inclusion in ACCESS are central to understanding the mystery.

Based on the results of these activities, the teacher must decide whether students can comprehend the material they will be asked to use or whether some type of additional teaching is required. Since prior knowledge assumes such an important role in the constructive process, it does not make sense to proceed unless students understand the major concepts.

While ACCESS' primary function is evaluation, it also activates student thinking about the nature of mysteries and can be used for more direct methods of stimulating and motivating student background knowledge. One useful technique that could follow the ACCESS activities is to have students write a short mystery. This provides an additional check on prior knowledge and stimulates student thinking about various aspects of a mystery. This same activity can be used at the end of the unit to measure how much students learned. Have them write a second mystery and compare it with the first one. It is interesting to see how many of the components presented in the unit end up in the second version.

Another useful Before Reading activity is reading the mini-mystery published by Scholastic Press and found in either *Track Down* or *Scope Magazine*. These activities require students to detect a flaw in the statement of a person who is suspected of committing a crime. Because of their form, they are useful in introducing students to the detailed reading required to identify essential clues and logically connect them with a suspect and a motive. Finally, there is an excellent video entitled *Young Sherlock Holmes*. It is a fictional account of how Holmes and Watson met in boarding school. The video provides students with a wealth of knowledge about the two characters and their relationship at the beginning of Holmes's investigative career and introduces them to Holmes's first attempt at solving a complex mystery. These activities help prepare students for the next phase.

During Reading Phase

The primary purpose of the During Reading Phase is to develop activities that will guide students through some of the complex cognitive operations that underlie the successful attainment of goals identified in the Strategic Planning Phase of Informed Teaching. Since solving mysteries is one of the primary goals, the purpose of the first activity is to provide students with a Literary Processing Guide that focuses their attention on the essential clues of a mystery. Since observing is one of the first things detectives do when attempting to solve a mystery, it is the first step that is explicitly modeled in the During Reading Phase.

The Observation LPG (Figure 7, page 133) is designed to focus students' attention on three important questions: What is the mystery? Who is the suspect? and What is the motive? These questions direct students toward the key features of the mystery and ultimately provide them with a means for synthesizing their observations in a way that guides them toward potential solutions. These questions also provide criteria for sorting important from unimportant information, because observations that do not directly answer one of the three questions are considered unimportant to the mystery. Therefore, from the beginning, students are encouraged to think in terms of how the observations they make help them identify the suspect and motive.

A second purpose of the Observation LPG is to link a clue to one or more characters. In mysteries, unlike other types of literature, readers must attend to all characters, no matter how trivial their roles, because they may be potential suspects. The problem is that readers often do not associate certain actions, thoughts, or feelings with a name. As a result, important clues are overlooked or ignored. The Observation LPG addresses the issue by placing the names at the top so readers will have a continuous reference. Every observation must be linked with a name. Once an observation is made, students must determine whether it helps them answer one of the three important questions at the top of the sheet.

By attending to this detail, students learn that when Sherlock Holmes asks a question or makes an observation, they must note the person's answer and try to determine why Holmes asked the question, because his actions are often indicative of his thinking. Since there are numerous observations, students quickly learn they must be written down. As students become more efficient, this step should be eliminated. A third purpose of the Observation LPG is to model the steps Sherlock Holmes or other detectives use when trying to solve a mystery. As readers come to understand these investigative techniques, they can apply them to their own reading.

The next step in solving a mystery is to organize the clues by systematically formulating impressions of characters. The Observation LPG allows students to note important details but does not provide any structure for helping them organize their clues into meaningful categories. The Character Summary LPG (Figure 8, page 134) helps readers formulate impressions about characters by focusing on two important dimensions: character traits (which must be supported by observations they have made), and conclusions that can be drawn about the character based on these traits and observations.

The goal of the Character Summary LPG is to have students describe each character. Much of the information placed in the Character Traits category comes from the Observation LPG. Next, students must provide observations or clues that support their character traits. Finally, students must decide what these traits reveal about the character. The Character Summary LPG is an important first step in making focused predictions; many readers tend to ignore important clues that are part of the character's personality or actions. Important insights emerge only when this information is synthesized. If the viewing, listening, or reading of a mystery takes place over several days, this activity is repeated each day. These written observations provide students with a record of their speculations and how these change as they acquire additional information.

Once students have formed their general impressions of characters, they make predictions about the suspect and motive, based on the Character Summary LPG. The Predictions about the Mystery LPG (Figure 9, page 135) takes the mystery solving process one step further. It provides a framework for moving from observations about characters to formulating predictions about the suspect and motive.

While some students already may have tentative feelings about "whodunit," it is important for them to provide support that comes from their observations and analysis of characters. For those who have difficulty making a prediction, it is equally important to show them how to make a *focused* first guess. By looking at the conclusions from the Character Summary LPG (Figure 8), it is often possible to identify one or more suspects. Next students should try to figure out a motive. This link is essential, since legitimate suspects must have a plausible motive.

Notice that the Predictions LPG (Figure 9) provides space for students to list as many suspects as they feel are appropriate. This is done so they realize that a good mystery has more than one suspect and that part of being good at solving mysteries is narrowing the list as you go. The multiple listing of suspects and motives also helps communicate that it is perfectly acceptable to make some incorrect predictions. Students should know that very few readers can solve a good mystery in the first page or two.

The Predictions LPG becomes increasingly important as students progress through the mystery, because they tend to be unfocused when they begin making predictions. Initially, this is not too disruptive since many of their impressions come from experiences with other mysteries. However, these unfocused predictions can become detrimental to problem solving, because future clues often are ignored in favor of the "off the wall" prediction. The Character Summary LPG helps students see that characters with no suspect traits usually are not prime candidates.

This activity provides a means for verifying impressions with actual clues. Students should not have suspects without evidence. Finally, when students make predictions, they become psychologically and emotionally involved in actively solving the mystery. Carefully focused thought is required to solve mysteries, and this is what LPGs are designed to model.

Once students become more adept in their predictions about potential suspects and motives, they are shown how to formulate hypotheses about suspects and motives. This is where the Hypothesis Formulation LPG is introduced (Figure 10, page 136). The distinction between predictions and hypotheses is somewhat arbitrary but is a useful step in the mystery solving process. Readers are accustomed to making predictions while they read. They are not accustomed to being concerned with accuracy, which is essential for solving mysteries.

Predictions are generally a mixture between what the readers' prior experiences have revealed to them about human behavior and the content of the mystery. This means that predictions are based as much on feelings readers have about suspects and motives as on actual clues that come directly from the mystery. In many cases, predictions deal more with guessing than with making informed decisions. While the Predictions LPG is designed to focus the process, some readers require an additional step, the formulation of hypotheses.

A hypothesis is based on information that comes predominately from the mystery. The intent is to move students from making tentative predictions to the more informed step of formulating a hypothesis. When readers feel confident that they have a suspect and a motive supported by the clues they have gathered, they formulate a hypothesis. The crucial factor is the evidence they use to support the hypothesis. The hypothesis represents a clear, concise logical argument. For this reason, its formulation comes later in the mystery.

As mysteries become more complex, solving them becomes more difficult. Some readers will make mistakes even when using all of these LPGS. This is natural, because writers employ many clever impediments. When students discover their mistakes, they are encouraged to make changes, and they must explain why they have changed their minds. Figure 10 provides an example.

Although the hypothesis formulation stage may seem unnecessary, it is particularly useful for those students who have difficulty sticking to the clues presented in the mystery. By forming a hypothesis solely on the information from the mystery, students' focus their attention on the clues they have gathered, the character analyses they have developed, and the predictions they have made. This is one of the final steps in the process. Once again the emphasis is on knowing *why* as opposed to merely making right or wrong responses.

In mysteries, one of the major impediments is how authors use time. They typically begin with a mysterious event that has occurred in the past and then proceed to take readers on a circuitous journey. To be successful at solving the mystery, readers must synchronize time. However, many readers are unaware when the time shifts take place and do not use a strategy for synchronizing these events.

The Timeline LPG (Figure 11, page 137) was developed to provide a means for organizing time chronologically and for interpreting the clues in the context of the mystery. When this is done, it generally directs students' thinking in ways that will give them new insights into the suspect and motive.

Many times, readers can make new discoveries by arranging information in chronological order. These insights come only after an examination of crucial information. As the questions at the bottom of the activity suggest, readers are encouraged to draw new conclusions about suspects and motives. Two additional questions are asked that focus on the activity's usefulness and additional changes that might be made to improve it. These questions are designed to get students to think about a strategy's usefulness and how they might modify it if it does not meet their needs. These questions provide a link to the final phase of Informed Teaching, After Reading.

After Reading Phase

The After Reading Phase has three primary purposes: to evaluate the effectiveness of the LPGs, to discuss how the LPGs can be improved or modified, and to develop plans for transferring the appropriate strategies to future assignments. Therefore, the main emphasis during this phase is on the relationship between narrative codes and strategy selection, two integral components of the interactive process. This approach suggests to the student that more than just the content of the mystery is important and that to be a strategic reader of literature requires the use of varying types of knowledge.

After the During Reading discussions have been completed, students are asked a series of questions that examine the relationship between the structural features of mysteries (generic codes) and strategy usage. They analyze the purpose and function of important structural features found in the mystery. For example:

How did Holmes use the scientific process in this mystery?

How did the author jumble the logical/temporal sequence of events?

What is an example of an important unfinished sequence?

What is an example of an important impediment used by the author?

It is important to take this questioning one step further and ask for judgments about the impact these structural devices have on the comprehension process. In other words, do students make a connection between an author's use of a particular literary device and its impact on meaning? To do this, students must relate the strategies modeled in the LPGs to specific situations in which they were used. To help make this connection, questions are asked that examine different types of cultural and generic code relationships. For example, "What strategies did you use when Sherlock Holmes employed his scientific process?" Students are expected to connect the strategy with a specific generic code. In this example, the strategy would be sequencing clues in order to make a prediction or formulate a hypothesis.

Students also must understand that as the relationship between cultural and generic codes changes, so should the strategy. For example, if the question changed to "How did the author jumble time, and what strategy did you use to place it in proper chronological order?" they should suggest a different strategy such as the use of a timeline.

Another method for evaluating strategy usage is to ask a series of questions aimed at the overall appropriateness of the LPGs. Appropriateness is determined by the context in which the LPGs are used. For example, asking "Which LPG worked best for you when you were attempting to identify the suspect and motive?" and "Why do you think it worked best?" would help to determine the appropriateness of the strategy in relation to its purpose.

The second purpose of the After Reading Phase is to focus on the modification of the LPGs. Since the primary goal is to solve a mystery, students must determine the strategy's effectiveness in helping them attain that goal. A sequence of questions is used. The first question is aimed at determining the LPG's overall utility, "How useful was the Character Summary LPG?" If students found it useful, they must identify the elements that made it useful. The goal is not merely to elicit a positive response, but to have students tell why it worked. Conversely, if their response was no, they are asked to state why it did not work.

In addition, students must provide examples of the types of revisions they would make to improve the Character Summary LPG. These questions are repeated for each of the LPGs. By consciously focusing on why they used a particular LPG and whether it was useful in attaining their goal, students can monitor, regulate, and modify their strategy selection in a manner consistent with the interactive perspective.

The third purpose of the After Reading Phase is to determine the extent to which students can transfer these strategies to varying situations (i.e., other Sherlock Holmes mysteries, other mysteries in general, other types of literature, and materials other than literature).

In the first type of transfer activity, the task is designed to determine whether students, when asked to solve another Sherlock Holmes mystery, can devise a plan that addresses these questions: What is the mystery? Who is the suspect? What is the motive? Once they have devised a plan, they must provide a rationale for its selection and determine a way for evaluating its overall effectiveness. To complete this activity, students must move beyond a type of evaluation that merely examines some of the various strategies used in reading a mystery to the development of a fully integrated plan. It is one thing to know when and why you might use individual strategies, yet another to provide an integrated plan for solving mysteries. Activities like this encourage students to become independent, flexible readers by learning how to devise a plan, to evaluate its effectiveness, and to make the necessary revisions.

The second type of transfer activity examines students' ability to transfer some of the strategies modeled in the LPGs to a different type of mystery. Students begin by examining what they believe are important features of the Sherlock Holmes mystery they have been reading. Next, they are asked to predict how these features might be similar or different in other mysteries. Finally, they are asked, "What would you tell a person who was about to read a Sherlock Holmes mystery for the first time?" These questions attempt to evaluate what the student believes is important to know when preparing to read another mystery.

The third type of transfer activity examines whether any of the strategies modeled in the LPGs are appropriate for other types of literature. The questions include:

How are mysteries different from other literature you have read?

Give me an example of the difference.

What accounts for the difference?

How does the difference influence your reading?

What are some important components of a mystery?

How are mysteries similar to other literature you have read?

Give me an example of the similarity.

The fourth type of transfer activity involves evaluating a student's ability to transfer information to other types of content materials. These questions are used after students have had an opportunity to read several different mysteries. A sampling of these questions would include the following:

How could you apply these strategies to other reading materials? Provide a specific example.

Which strategies would be the most effective and which ones the least, in reading a chapter on the problems leading to the Civil War?

Which strategies would be the most effective and which ones the least, in reading a chapter on the theories of animal intelligence?

Under what circumstances might you use strategies for solving a mystery outside school?

This full range of questions is designed to ascertain whether students see any utility in the strategies beyond the context of literature. The questions examine the impact that varying purposes and texts have on strategy selection. For example, in answering questions on animal intelligence based on a general science text, there would seem to be some similarity between examining the evidence scientists use to prove a theory about animal intelligence and supporting a hypothesis about a suspect and motive. While the text and content are different, some modification can be made in the strategies for making observations and formulating a hypothesis. In this case, they would have to fit the structure of a scientific experiment.

With a history chapter on the problems leading to the Civil War, there would be less overlap. The strategy modifications would be substantial. In this context, strategies for problem solving would have to take into account regional differences (social, political, economic) embedded within a series of historical events causally linked.

As the topic and text change, so must the strategies. This is an important difference that exists within and across the various content areas. Students must learn to make modifications consistent with content and its structure. Merely changing some minor aspects is not appropriate.

Summary

The purpose of this chapter has been to provide a systematic approach to planning and teaching mysteries that is consistent with an interactive constructive view of the reading process. The activities developed from this perspective were presented in the context of a literary framework that emphasizes four phases of Informed Teaching: Strategic Planning, Before Reading, During Reading, and After Reading. These activities were designed to provide the appropriate knowledge base and necessary conceptual linkage so students could develop a literary framework essential for comprehending, interpreting, and criticizing literature.

It should be clear that the emphasis is not on a process that yields right or wrong answers but rather on a process that emphasizes thinking about how you can move students through higher levels of reasoning. It is important to understand that these are not merely worksheets that students passively complete but are Literary Processing Guides designed to follow the assumptions that underlie the literary framework.

This approach suggests that the goals of the discipline must assume a greater role in the instructional decision making process. Information no longer can be decontextualized. If literature is the focus, students must learn how to read it and not merely focus on generic skills that do not account for differences existing within various types of narrative materials.

**Figure 1
The Literary Framework**

Building a Literary Framework
↓
(requires knowledge of)
↓
Narrative Codes
↓
(have)
↙   ↘
Cultural Codes   Generic Codes
↓   ↓
(e.g.)   (e.g.)
↓   ↓
Knowledge of the writer, the context in which the writing occurs, and literary language used by the writer   Structure of literary works, mysteries, adventure stories, fables, myths

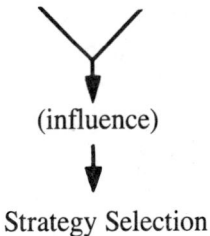

↘   ↙
(influence)
↓
Strategy Selection

Figure 2
Narrative Codes and Their Relationship to the Strategic Selection of Reading Skills

Cultural Codes	Generic Codes	Reading Strategies
1. Author's goal is to create suspense, motivate reader (aesthetic). 2. Author often uses formulistic elements of the mystery in writing. • Establishes sequence of causality that has an inverted time order • Uses deliberate impediments • Creates circuitous journey through which the reader must travel 3. The art of literary detection depends largely on the author's ability to divert readers on their way to the solution. • Creates detective or investigator, e.g., Sherlock Holmes, who uses a systematic method based on problem solving techniques	1. The mystery's unique structure has • Inverted temporal order, i.e., crime committed without knowing reason • Unfinished sequence of events • Clues, motives, suspects, and super sleuth • Deliberately constructed impediments (hidden clues) • Progressive/digressive elements • Jumbled chronological order 2. The mystery has rhetorical structure that governs its form. • The investigation is sequenced, i.e., fixed point of departure to fixed point of destination • It goes from mystery to solution	1. The mystery requires the reader to use a variety of strategies. • Detailed reading • Seek closure of logical temporal gap • Establish causal link among the clues in the mystery • Order information in a logical manner • Distinguish between important and unimportant observations • Make predictions • Formulate and test hypotheses 2. The reader must know: • When, how, and why certain strategies must be used

Figure 3
"The Adventure of the Dancing Men" Mystery Map

1. What is the Mystery?
2. Plot Structure
   A. Characters

Suspects	*Character Traits*	*Motives*
1. Mr. Walker	Abrasive	None
2. Abe Slaney	Violent	Former lover

Other Characters	*Character Traits*	*Function*
1. Elsie Cubbit	Secretive	Defender
2. Hilton Cubbit	Kind, Devoted	Victim

Detectives	*Character Traits*	*Investigative Techniques*
1. Holmes	Intelligent	Logical reasoning
2. Watson	Helpful	Guessing

   B. Clues
   1. Elsie sees dancing men.
   2. Hilton explains why Elsie is upset.
   3. Hilton explains how he met his wife.
   4. Elsie receives a letter from Chicago.
   5. Holmes asks Hilton if there are any strangers in the area.
   6. Holmes begins working on the "code."
   7. Someone appears at the window.
   8. More drawings appear on the door.
   9. Message says "come/never."
   10. Holmes decodes first message, "I am here Abe Slaney."
   11. Hilton awakes and Elsie is not in bed.
   12. Hilton gets his gun and goes downstairs.
   13. Gunshots fired.

3. Important Literary Techniques
   Progressive/Digressive Use of Time
   Unfinished Sequences
   Clever Impediments

Figure 4
Essential Strategies for Solving a Mystery

1. Defining the Mystery
   Becoming aware of the mystery
   Formulating a statement of the mystery
   Making initial predictions

2. Formulating a Hypothesis
   Making observations
   Identifying clues
   Seeking relationships
   Drawing logical inferences
   Identifying a suspect
   Identifying a motive

3. Testing the Tentative Hypothesis
   Assembling the clues
     Identifying relevant clues
     Evaluating relevant clues
   Arranging evidence
     Interpreting clues
     Classifying clues
   Analyzing the clues
     Seeking relationships
     Noting similarities and differences
     Identifying trend, sequences, and regularities

4. Reaching a Conclusion about the Mystery
   Making meaningful patterns or relationships
   Stating the conclusion

Figure 5
"The Adventure of the Dancing Men"
Prior Knowledge Assessment

Concepts	Words That Describe These Concepts	Examples of Each Concept	Relating Concepts
Sherlock Holmes	Intelligent Inquisitive Logical Detective	A detective developed by Sir Arthur Conan Doyle	How are Sherlock Holmes and Dr. Watson related? Dr. Watson helps Sherlock Holmes with his cases. He is also the person who chronicles them.
Dr. Watson	Medical doctor Sherlock Holmes's assistant Diligent Sensitive	A character developed by Sir Arthur Conan Doyle	How is Sherlock Holmes related to the investigative process? Sherlock Holmes was one of the first detectives to use the scientific process to solve mysteries.
Clues	Hint Answer Suspicion Tip	A knife left at the scene of the crime A fingerprint	How are clues, suspect, and motives related? Clues, suspects, and motives are the key elements of a mystery.
Motives	Reason for a crime Purpose Basis	Jealousy Revenge	
Suspects	Presume Suppose Predict	A relative who might become rich because of a wealthy uncle's death	
London in 1900	Developing city Crowded Industrial	There is no example of this concept	

Figure 6
Prior Knowledge Assessment
Target Concept: Scientific Process

1. Characteristics

   Systematic
   Used to solve problems
   Contains hypotheses, observations, and conclusions
   Method used to test ideas

2. Example

   A doctor tests a new drug intended to cure the common cold.

   Reason it qualifies as an example

   In order for a doctor to make sure his new drug works, he has to identify what he wanted to investigate, i.e., cure for common cold; develop a hypothesis; test the hypothesis; and form some conclusions.

3. Nonexample

   Identify the capital of Michigan.

   Reason it qualifies as a nonexample

   This is not a scientific statement that requires the use of the scientific process.

4. Definition

   It is a systematic method used to develop and test ideas.

5. Relationships with Other Key Concepts

   Here are two ways logical reasoning and the scientific process are related.

   They are both used to solve problems.
   Logical reasoning is part of the scientific process.

Figure 7
"The Adventure of the Dancing Men"
Observation LPG

Name: _____ Date: _____

Characters
Sherlock Holmes
Dr. Watson
Mr. Walker
Hilton Cubbit
Elsie Cubbit

What is the mystery?
Who is the suspect?
What is the motive?

1. Hilton goes to see Holmes.
2. Hilton explains why Elsie is upset.
3. Hilton believes someone is threatening Elsie.
4. Hilton explains how he met his wife.
5. Elsie Patrick was from America.
6. Hilton marries Elsie Patrick.
7. Elsie doesn't want Hilton to know about her past.
8. Elsie gives Hilton a chance to back out of the marriage.
9. Elsie receives letter from Chicago.
10. Elsie burns letter before opening it (Holmes and Watson made sure this was correct).
11. Hilton says drawings appeared after letter.

Using a Literary Framework to Teach Mysteries

Figure 8
"The Adventure of the Dancing Men"
Character Summary LPG

First Day

Characters	Character Traits	Observations	Conclusions Drawn about the Character
1. Elsie Cubbit	Secretive Caring Sensitive Frightened	Elsie does not tell Hilton about her past. She does not want to see Hilton get hurt. She is afraid of the dancing men figures.	She seems to love Hilton but is unwilling to share her past with him. She appears to have something important to hide. She could be a suspect, but there are no real clues to support it.
2. Hilton Cubbit	Caring Concerned Devoted Responsible	Hilton goes to Sherlock Holmes to enlist his help in finding out why Elsie is frightened by the dancing men. His family has lived in the same house for 500 years.	He is a devoted husband who would do anything to protect Elsie.
3. Sherlock Holmes	Intelligent Thoughtful Inquisitive Questioning Observant	Holmes is a detective who has solved many mysteries. He asks Hilton many questions about his past. He is able to tell Watson why he is not investing in South African gold securities.	He is an intelligent detective who continually probes people for more information. He believes that the dancing men are a code.
4. Dr. Watson	Reserved Observant Helpful Insightful	Watson takes notes for Sherlock Holmes. He asks Hilton to explain why Elsie burned a letter from Chicago without opening it.	He is an assistant to Sherlock Holmes. While not as smart as Holmes, he helps the reader understand Holmes's methods.
5. Unnamed Character	Secretive	Left drawings on a garden bench. Tried to communicate with Elsie.	Not enough information has been presented to form a conclusion.

Figure 9
"The Adventure of the Dancing Men"
Predictions LPG

First Day

Suspect	Motive	Evidence to Support Your Predictions
1. Someone from Elsie's past	To get Elsie to steal Hilton's money	1. Elsie will not tell Hilton about her past. 2. She received a letter from Chicago. 3. She knows who this person is.
2. Elsie	Wants Hilton dead so she can have his money	No real clues thus far. It is only a feeling I have about her. She does not want to tell Hilton about the man who is leaving the messages.
3.		
4.		

Using a Literary Framework to Teach Mysteries

Figure 10
"The Adventure of the Dancing Men"
Hypothesis Formulation LPG

Second Day

Suspect	Motive	Evidence to Support Your Predictions
1. Someone from Elsie's past	Not sure	He shows up at the house and Elsie tries to protect him. Elsie writes him a message. Holmes sends a letter to the Chicago Chief of Police.
2. Mr. Walker	Wants Hilton's money. Dislikes Hilton	He is rude to Hilton. He looks like the man in the window whom Elsie was trying to protect.
3.		

Change of Opinion

	Reason
I believe Elsie is no longer a suspect.	There is no real evidence to support my hypothesis. While Elsie will not reveal her past, she seems to be devoted to Hilton and wants no harm to come to him. In fact, she tries to encourage him to leave so he won't get hurt.

Figure 11
"The Adventure of the Dancing Men"
Timeline LPG
Chronological Order of Important Events

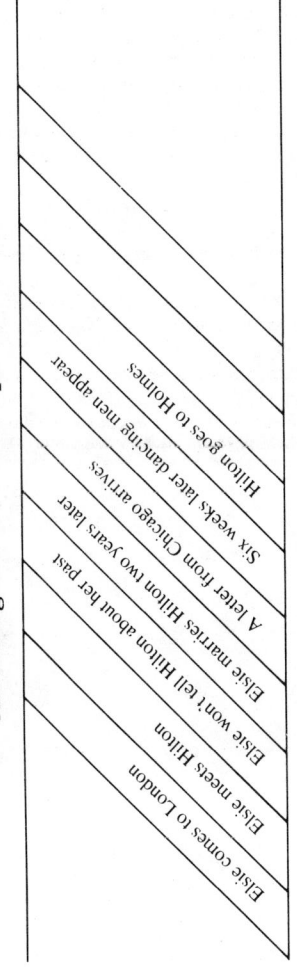

- Elsie comes to London
- Elsie meets Hilton
- Elsie won't tell Hilton about her past
- Elsie marries Hilton two years later
- A letter from Chicago arrives
- Six weeks later dancing men appear
- Hilton goes to Holmes

Summary of Mystery

1. What new clues does the timeline reveal?
   Someone from Elsie's past has traced her to London.
2. What new conclusions about the suspect were revealed?
   He is in the area and is writing secret messages to Elsie.
3. What new conclusions about the motive were revealed?
   He wants something from Elsie.
4. How did the timeline help you?
   It helped me sort out important clues.
5. How would you change it?
   I would not change it, because it helped me understand important clues.

References

Anderson, R.C., Hiebert, E.H., Scott, J.A., and Wilkinson, I.A.G. *Becoming a nation of readers: The report of the commission on reading.* Washington, DC: National Institute of Education, 1985.

Billman, C. The child reader as sleuth. *Children's Literature in Education,* 1984, *15,* 1.

Cawelti, J. *Adventure, mystery, and romance.* Chicago: University of Chicago Press, 1976.

Doyle, A.C. *The complete Sherlock Holmes.* Garden City, NY: Doubleday, 1905.

Iser, W. *The implied reader.* Baltimore, MD: Johns Hopkins University Press, 1974.

Peters, C.W. Using a literary model of thinking as a guide for selecting software in literature. In C. Canning and K. Bunting (Eds.), *Developing thinking skills across the curriculum and how they can help.* Westland, MI: MACUL, 1987, 45-51.

Peters, C.W., and Hayes, B. The role of reading instruction in social studies. In J. Flood and D. Lapp (Eds.), *Instructional theory and practice for content area reading and learning.* Englewood Cliffs, NJ: Prentice Hall, 1989.

Porter, D. *The pursuit of crime: Art and ideology in detective fiction.* New Haven, CT: Yale University Press, 1981.

Scholes, R. *Textual power: Literary theory and the teaching of English.* New Haven, CT: Yale University Press, 1985.

Todorov, T. *The fantastic Richard Howard.* Ithaca, NY: Cornell University Press, 1975.

Voss, J.F. Social studies. In R.F. Dillon and R.J. Sternberg (Eds.), *Cognition and instruction.* Academic Press, 1986, 205-239.

Wixson, K.K., and Peters, C.W. Comprehension assessment: Implementing an interactive view of reading. *Educational Psychologist,* 1987, *22,* 333-356.

Wixson, K.K., and Peters, C.W. Reading redefined: A Michigan Reading Association position paper. *Michigan Reading Journal,* 1984, *17,* 4-7.

Part Two
Expository Text

Wayne H. Slater
Michael F. Graves

Research on Expository Text: Implications for Teachers

This chapter provides a comprehensive definition of good expository text. The authors synthesize current findings from research studies conducted with elementary school, middle school, high school, and college students focused on readers' comprehension of exposition. The chapter also includes a classification system for types of expository text to assist teachers in conceptualizing attributes of exposition for teaching purposes. Finally, the authors provide a model for instruction and specific teaching strategies that are designed to enhance students' comprehension of exposition.

During the past fifteen years, researchers have focused increasing attention on questions involving the comprehension of expository text. Their investigations have concentrated on such issues as structure, cohesion, and coherence (Britton & Black, 1985; Garner, 1987; Just & Carpenter, 1987; Kinneavy, 1971; Mandl, Stein & Trabasso, 1984; Meyer, 1975; Murphy, 1982; Otto & White, 1982; van Dijk & Kintsch, 1983). Recently, many researchers have begun to investigate instructional procedures for improving students' comprehension of expository text that can complement the existing methods for the teaching of narratives (Aulls, 1982; Harris & Sipay, 1985; Spache & Spache, 1986; Taylor, Harris, & Pearson, 1988). Our purpose is to review current research findings on exposition and to draw implications for instructional practice.

A Definition of Good Expository Text

Providing a comprehensive definition of expository text is not simple. One approach is to give a dictionary definition of exposition: "setting forth of meaning or intent; explication; elucidation" (Morris, 1979). Unfortunately, like most dictionary definitions, this one fails to fully characterize the concept. The following discussion attempts a fuller characterization by discussing four attributes that are characteristic of most, although not all, good exposition.

1. *Good expository text as informational text.* The primary function of expository text is to present to the reader information about theories, predictions, persons, facts, dates, specifications, generalizations, limitations, and conclusions. The following excerpt exemplifies its informational nature.

> In Philadelphia, in May of 1775, the Second Continental Congress met. Some of those at the meeting were Benjamin Franklin of Pennsylvania, John Adams of Massachusetts, and Thomas Jefferson of Virginia. The Congress chose a Virginian named George Washington to lead the American army (Schreiber et al., 1986, p. 157).

At the same time, good expository text must be more than informational. Students need more than a string of leaden facts — something all too typical of many school texts — if they are to understand new information (Anderson & Armbruster, 1984; Graves & Slater, 1986). Often, authors of informational text simply present facts and dates without taking into account the background knowledge and interests of readers at those particular grade levels. That is, the reader is somehow expected to provide the analyses and syntheses across the barren facts presented without much assistance from the authors. Information is the focus of this type of text, but unless it has been made comprehensible and compelling by the author, it is simply a listing of facts. Texts that present new facts or concepts are incomprehensible for most students unless they incorporate explanatory features.

2. *Good expository text as explanatory text.* Good expository text incorporates meaningful explanations and elaborations that are included to explain the theories, predictions, persons, facts, dates, specifications, generalizations, limitations, and conclusions included at the informational level. The following expository text clearly explains the significance of the concepts being presented.

> Independence would mean that the new nation would have to protect itself. The English army would no longer protect

it from Indians or other nations. It would have to elect its own citizens to make laws and decisions. It would also have to learn how to trade with other nations.

Many Americans felt that this was too much responsibility. America had always been a part of England, and they liked it that way. They felt America should fight, but only until the English agreed to treat them fairly. Then they would again be loyal to England (Schreiber et al., 1986, p. 157).

Good exposition is information made meaningful and compelling by authors who consider readers' prior knowledge (see Ogle, this volume). By taking into account readers' prior knowledge, authors can provide explanations and elaborations at strategic points to explain to readers why and how certain facts, persons, dates, and the like are important and should be remembered.

3. *Good expository text as directive text.* Good expository text frequently has a directive quality. This means that the author provides explicit cues—introductions, headings, subheadings, and summaries to help readers identify main ideas and supporting information. Additionally, throughout the text, the author may provide statements about significant and important information so that readers can identify crucial concepts, definitions, and explanations. The following excerpt demonstrates the authors' involvement in directing readers' attention to important information by using headings, highlighting, and explicit definitions.

Chapter 17 Lesson 1 New Freedoms and New Problems
Lesson 2 Southern Whites after the Civil War
Lesson 3 Blacks Lose Their Rights

The New South
The Civil War tore the United States apart. After the war, Americans had to **reconstruct,** or put the nation back together again. Great changes took place during the four years of war. It took many years for people to learn to live with the changes.

Lesson 1 New Freedoms and New Problems
In December of 1865, the Thirteenth Amendment was

added to the Constitution. An **amendment** to the Constitution means a change. In this case, the change meant that slavery was abolished in the United States (Schreiber, et al., 1986, p. 270).

By being directive, the author is actively present in the text and establishes a dialogue with the reader. This dialogue presents the author as a significant presence who is showing, telling and guiding the reading and comprehension of the reader. Thus, for a piece of expository text to be directive, it must manifest the active involvement of an author who gives readers specific cues as to what is important and what needs to be understood. Without this directive attribute, the information provided by the author may not be fully understood. Unfortunately, in many textbooks, directive information is incomplete or missing.

4. *Good expository text and narrativity.* Good expository text has narrative attributes that have been incorporated into the exposition. Authors of good exposition include brief anecdotes, myths, tales, or stories to illustrate their points and to make the information more comprehensible, interesting, and compelling to readers (Graves & Slater, 1986; Graves et al., in press). A good narrative anecdote can provide the elaboration needed to make information meaningful. For example, in a discussion of the battles of Lexington and Concord, Schreiber et al. (1986) include the following anecdote by British Lieutenant John Barker:

> We waited at Lexington a long time, and then went on our way to Concord....[At Concord we destroyed] three pieces of cannon, several gun carriages, and about one hundred barrels of flour....Three companies of soldiers were sent across the river to search some of the houses there.
> During this time the people were gathering together in great numbers....Across the river, the rebels were about one thousand strong, on the hill above, covered by a wall....
> The rebels marched into the road and were coming down upon us. The rebels when they got near the bridge halted and faced us. The fire soon began from a shot on our side....

> After taking care of our wounded as well as we could, we set upon our return....We were fired on from houses and behind trees, and before we had gone half a mile we were fired on from all sides, but mostly from the rear, where people had hid themselves in houses till we had passed (pp. 155-156).

This brief narrative gives readers a richer understanding of the events and the people in these battles than would a mere listing of names and dates.

To summarize, good expository text is prose in which an author presents information to a reader. Good expository text is explanatory in that the author provides the necessary explanations to enable readers to understand the information being presented. Good expository text is also directive in that the author actively engages readers in a dialogue that highlights information and tells readers what is and is not important. Finally, much good expository text incorporates narrative elements to give life to the prose and to portray people in a more compelling and comprehensible manner.

What Research Tells Us about Readers and Expository Text

The task of translating the results from research studies focused on readers and their recall and comprehension of expository text is difficult for two major reasons. First, the expository passages used in research studies are not always typical of the passages found in classroom textbooks. They are often chosen or created for research studies to test the specific research hypotheses of the study involved, such as structure, headings, or signal words. Second, the content of the passages may be contrived or dull because researchers are asking structural questions while neglecting the impact of interesting content.

Given these qualifying conditions, the following research findings based on studies that use passages and implement instruction similar to that found in classrooms offer important insights for teachers.

Developmental findings. Students from fourth grade through college increasingly develop their ability to use expository text structure and/or main ideas to facilitate comprehension and recall. The results from studies conducted with students in elementary schools (Berkowitz, 1986; Taylor, 1982; Taylor & Samuels, 1983; Williams, Taylor, & Ganger, 1981), middle schools (Garner et al., 1986; Taylor & Beach, 1984), high schools (Meyer, Brandt, & Bluth, 1980; Slater, Graves, & Piché, 1985), and college (Slater et al., 1988) have generally shown that students' ability to use text structure and/or main ideas for comprehension purposes increases with age. The general conclusion for this developmental trend is that the ability to capitalize fully on text structure is probably a late developing skill (Baker & Brown, 1984).

Recall findings. Students who can identify and use text structure and/or main ideas remember more of what they read than do students who cannot or do not. Study after study (Meyer, Brandt & Bluth, 1980; Slater et al., 1988; Taylor, 1982; Taylor & Beach, 1984) generally confirm the notion that those students who can identify and use text structure and main ideas remember more of the content of passages than those students who cannot or do not. In examining the data, text structure appears to provide a framework for remembering important ideas and concepts in the passages for readers who are able to identify and use it.

Main idea and supporting idea findings. Main ideas generally are retained better than lower-level ideas. Studies where students are asked to recall information from passages they have read usually demonstrate that main ideas are more memorable than supporting ideas (Meyer, 1975, 1984; Meyer & Rice, 1984; Piché & Slater, 1983; Voss, Tyler, & Bisanz, 1982). The main thrust of a passage appears to be the easiest aspect of the text to remember and is a good measure of students' comprehension. However, it is important to remember that some research suggests that interesting and/or concrete supporting ideas can distract students and inhibit their retention of main ideas (Anderson et al., in press; Baumann, 1982; Hidi & Baird, 1986).

Identifying text structure findings. Students can be taught to identify expository text structure and main ideas. Studies at elementary school level (Berkowitz, 1986; Taylor, 1982), middle school level (Taylor & Beach, 1984), high school level (Bartlett, 1978; Slater, Graves, & Piché, 1985), and college level (Slater et al., 1988) provide evidence that students who are given instruction focused on identifying expository text structure and main ideas can identify those elements more reliably than students who have not received such instruction. Richgels, McGee, and Slaton (this volume) describe a strategy they designed to teach expository text structure to elementary school students.

Using text structure findings. Training in the use of text structure and main ideas improves reading comprehension. When students have been taught procedures they can use in identifying text structure, those students who use the procedures comprehend and recall more of the information from texts than those students who do not (Armbruster, Anderson, & Ostertag, 1987; Baumann, 1984).

Prior knowledge and text structure findings. Failure to use expository text structure has a more negative impact when the topic of the material is unfamiliar. This result is found in studies that checked for students' prior knowledge of the content of the experimental passages (Meyer, Brandt, & Bluth, 1980; Taylor, 1982; Taylor & Beach, 1984). An analysis of the data indicated that comprehension and recall decreased significantly when reading unfamiliar text if text structure and main ideas were not identified and used by readers.

Taken together, these findings suggest that students' knowledge and understanding of expository text structure in prose is crucial for the comprehension of the information in texts. Based on these findings, teachers at all levels need to give serious consideration to providing explicit instruction in identifying text structure and main ideas to improve students' comprehension.

Comprehensive Classification System for Expository Text

Given what research tells us about the importance of students' understanding and use of expository text structure in reading, it is important for classroom teachers to have as thorough an understanding of the types or categories into which expository text may be classified as they do of the structural components of narrative text. By acquiring this knowledge, teachers will be able to better understand the nature of exposition and to make judicious instructional decisions for their students. Also, knowledge of expository structure when combined with appropriate examples from students' texts provides a powerful means of teaching the reading of exposition at various grade levels.

The classification scheme presented here is not a simple one. Instead, it represents the complexities and realities of expository text as it exists in textbooks, newspapers, and magazines. The scheme was formulated by Calfee and Curley (1984), and it is based on the examination of exposition Aristotle discusses in *The Rhetoric* (c. 335 B.C./1984), which continues to serve as one of the most comprehensive discussions of exposition available. In the Calfee and Curley synthesis of Aristotle's ideas (Table 1), there are five major categories for expository text style: Description, Illustration, Sequence, Argument and Persuasion, and Functional.

Description. Three categories are included under the first major classification, description: definition, division of classification, and comparison and contrast. Thus, authors have three major options to provide descriptive content for their readers. Simple definitions can be used to define terms, to describe major features, or to delineate relationships with other objects. The following definition both describes and specifies relationships:

> ...dirty, dark *tenements*. These were cheap apartment buildings with small rooms, few windows, and few bathrooms. Trash could often be found everywhere (Schreiber et al., 1986, p. 317).

Division of classification allows authors to describe and characterize parts of members of an object or class and then relate members according to similar traits. The following excerpt classifies the roles of women in the Civil War.

> A few women dressed as men and fought in the front lines. Others, like Pauline Cushman for the North and Belle Boyd for the South, served as spies. Several thousand women on both sides worked in hospitals as nurses. Clara Barton

Table 1
Categories of Rhetorical Styles

Description

    Definition — Definition elaborates on the meaning of a term. It may identify features, uses, or relationships with other known objects, events, or ideas.

    Division and Classification — Division distinguishes the parts or members of an object or class. Classification relates groups of objects, events, or ideas according to a principle of similarity.

    Comparison and Contrast — Comparison generally highlights similarities among two or more entities, while contrast emphasizes differences.

Illustration

    Analogy — Illustrative analogy is a comparison between two different things or activities for the purpose of explanation.

    Example — Illustration through a sample of typical or outstanding instances.

Sequence

    Process — Process is a series of connected instances, each developing from the preceding one, that results in something—a decision, a product, an effort of some kind.

    Cause and Effect — A sequence of events which is related in a causal chain.

Argument and Persuasion

Deductive Reasoning	An argument from generalities to particulars, where the conclusion necessarily follows from the premises.
Inductive Reasoning	An argument from particulars to generalities. A given outcome may be characterized as more or less probable depending on the strength of the evidence in relation to the conclusion.
Persuasion	A line of argument laid out so as to present the ideas in the most convincing manner. The correctness of the argument is not necessarily a criterion.

Functional

Introduction	An opening statement in which the author indicates a point of view and perhaps also the ways the subject is to be developed.
Transition	Establishes a framework for integrating prior information with forthcoming information. Emphasizes the relationships among ideas or explains changes in theme.
Conclusion	Generally includes review of thematic material. Ties together any lines of thought left uncompleted.

From R. Calfee and R. Curley. Structure of prose in the content areas. In J. Flood (Ed.), *Understanding reading comprehension.* Newark, DE: International Reading Association, 1984, pp. 161-180.

served as a nurse on the Union side. Sally Tompkins worked in hospitals for the Confederacy. Most women stayed at home during the Civil War. They ran farms and worked in factories and in offices (Schreiber et al., 1986, p. 255).

Finally, comparison and contrast provides the options of describing similarities or differences among entities. In the following excerpt, the authors describe similarities and differences between slaves and free people.

> Southern slaves did many of the same jobs as whites in both the North and South. Yet there was a difference. Slaves rarely got paid for their work. They received whatever food, clothing, and housing their owners decided to give them.
> Sometimes slaves lived in the same houses as their owners. But usually, they lived in cabins away from the homes of the slaveholders.
> The lives of slaves and free people differed in other ways, too. Slaves could not marry without their owner's approval. Even with that approval, slaves could not be sure their families would be kept together. Husbands, wives, and children could be sold separately to new owners (Schreiber et al., 1986, p. 239).

Each of these stylistic elements allows authors to provide elaborated descriptions to enhance readers' understanding of concepts being presented.

Illustration. The second major classification is illustration, which is related to description. The first category under illustration is analogy. Through this stylistic device, authors can establish a comparison among different ideas, objects, or activities in order to illustrate relationships. Glynn and White (this volume) demonstrate that an analogy has great potential for explanatory power. The following excerpt presents an analogy between the Canadian and the United States governments.

> Today, Canada is a strong and independent nation. Its government is much like that of the United States. Each prov-

ince has control over its own taxes, health, and education. They send representatives to the Canadian Parliament. The Parliament is made up...(Schreiber et al., 1986, p. 406).

Example is a second stylistic device that can be used to provide illustrations for readers. By selecting typical or outstanding instances of particular events and situations, authors can give illustrations that increase readers' understanding of abstract or difficult ideas. The following examples from Benjamin Franklin's *Poor Richard's Almanack* provide readers with specifics on the content included in a typical almanac of that period.

> Franklin's almanac also gave wise and witty sayings. Here are a few examples.
> Well done is better than well said.
> Wish not so much to live long, as to live well.
> A true friend is the best possession.
> Haste makes waste (Schreiber et al., 1986, p. 141).

Sequence. Sequence is the third major classification in this discussion. As the first category under sequence, process allows authors to delineate a number of connected examples or events in order to demonstrate that the previous examples or events were necessary for some kind of result. A process may focus on how a decision is made, on how a product is created, or on any other topic. The following excerpt specifies the process involved in making decisions at a New England town meeting.

> City Council meets on Tuesday night at 8:00 PM. All are welcome to attend. The following ideas will be discussed....
> This is a common notice that appears in the newspapers of small towns and cities all across America today. The notice is saying that all citizens of a community can help govern themselves. And notices like it have been appearing for more than two hundred years. The practice began in small New England towns like Plymouth.

At early town meetings, the people elected officers to do a certain job. The job might be to serve as sheriff, tax collector, or even collector of stray hogs.

Decisions at town meetings were made by majority rule of those present. People who had not voted with the majority had to obey the decision, but were allowed to openly disagree. All citizens had the right to speak and write freely. They also had the responsibility to vote carefully (Schreiber et al., 1986, p. 124).

Cause and effect give the additional option of specifying a series of events in a causal chain. The following explanation discusses some of the causes and effects of the Great Depression.

For the next ten years, the country was in a depression. The Great Depression, it has been called. The country had seen other depressions. None lasted so long or were so hard as this one, though.

Was it all caused by people "playing" in the stock market? No, the Great Depression had other causes, too.

Industry produced too much. Throughout the 1920s, American industry produced new and wonderful products. Americans had many products that helped them in the home and made their life more enjoyable. But Americans could only buy so many radios, vacuum cleaners, washers, and cars. By the end of the 1920s, many warehouses were filled with a surplus of these and other goods.

Laying off workers. When businesses did not sell their products, they began to lay off their workers. By 1930, over four million people were out of work. These unemployed people bought little more than the necessities of life (Schreiber et al., 1986, p. 347).

Argument and persuasion. As the fourth major classification in expository style, argument and persuasion allows authors to present information while expressing opinions and views about that information. Deductive reasoning involves working from generalities about the content to specifics that further explain the content. The following paragraph is written using deductive reasoning.

> People were changing their environment without even knowing it. Farmers used dangerous chemicals on their land to make crops grow faster and more abundantly. Drivers ran their cars on gasoline that fouled the air. Private companies and government leaders in cities and towns allowed waste to be dumped into lakes and rivers. Factory owners ran machines that poured unhealthy smoke into the air. Miners dug giant holes in the earth (Schreiber et al., 1986, p. 390).

In contrast, inductive reasoning involves working from specific details that explain the content to generalities that result from the cumulative effects of these details. In the following inductive paragraph, the authors present the series of events which led to growth in New France.

> France sent Samuel de Champlain to Canada in 1603 to set up a trading post. With the help of Indians, he explored much of the St. Lawrence Valley and the area around the Great Lakes. In 1608, he started the trading settlement of Quebec. Soon, other traders and missionaries explored Canada. Small farming villages developed in the next fifty years. New France was now growing in the New World (Schreiber et al., 1986, p. 403).

Finally, persuasion involves presenting a series of arguments in the most convincing manner in order to support a particular idea or opinion. In the following excerpt, the authors provide a strong argument for establishing national parks.

> Was the decision to set aside land a wise one? In 1898, the famous explorer, John Muir, thought that it was. "Thousands of nerve-shaken, overcivilized people are beginning to find out that going to the mountains is going home; that wildness is a necessity." In other words, the parks give people a chance to breathe the open air and understand nature (Schreiber et al., 1986, p. 395).

Functional. The fifth and final classification for expository text is functional. This classification may be the most obvious, because its three components are used extensively by authors of exposition. Introduction is the first category; authors use it to orient readers to their purpose and focus. The following general introduction concentrates on changing ways of life in the eastern United States in the first half of the nineteenth century.

> Between 1800 and 1860, the United States changed in many ways. You have already read about some important changes in the West. Large areas of land there were added to the United States. People moved from settled areas in the East to these western lands.
> During these sixty years, there were also important changes in the East. Factories opened in New England. In the factories, people started to use machines to produce goods. Cities grew up around the factories because people wanted to be closer to their place of work (Schreiber et al., 1986, p. 215).

In a somewhat similar way, transition emphasizes the relationships between old information and new information within and between paragraphs. In the following paragraphs, the authors establish transitions by merely repeating the words "Industrial Revolution" and "change." Notice that the word "too" at the end of the first sentence indicates that "change" has been discussed in previous paragraphs.

> The Industrial Revolution changed life on farms, too. Americans made new machines that helped farmers do their work quickly and easily. In 1834, Cyrus McCormick made a machine that cut wheat. Three years later, John Deere made a steel plow. These all helped farmers produce twice as much wheat and corn in 1859 as they did in 1839.
> The Industrial Revolution changed the United States. At first, most of the changes took place in the northern states. Most of the factories and cities developed there. Farming remained the main way southerners made their living. These differences between the North and South caused two ways of living to develop in the country (Schreiber et al., 1986, p. 218).

As the last category under function, conclusion allows authors to review the information covered and to sum up important ideas and opinions. The following concluding paragraph deals with Brazilian plantations.

> Brazilian plantation workers and owners alike look forward and backward daily. Modern machines help plant and transport crops east to thriving ports and markets. To the west, plantations are backed by untamed jungles and deserts. Many areas of Brazil, especially along the Amazon, are still as mysterious to Brazilians as they were to Portuguese explorers four hundred years ago. The future of Brazil may lie in learning how the wilderness can help the nation prosper (Schreiber et al., 1986, p. 448).

By understanding the categories for describing and classifying expository text, teachers can select appropriate examples from textbooks and other student reading materials to illustrate the categories and to explain to students why and how authors use these devices to communicate information. With continued practice focused on making students independent in identifying and understanding these expository text features, reading expository text should become a more efficient task.

Teaching Students to Read Expository Text

Having provided a definition of good expository text, the research findings on reading exposition, and a classification of expository text types, we turn to the issue of effectively teaching readers to more efficiently comprehend expository text. Such text constitutes increasing amounts of students' reading, beginning about fourth grade. In discussing ways of enhancing students' comprehension of exposition, we will first present a general model of instruction and then describe four procedures that research has shown to be effective.

A model of instruction. The model of instruction proposed here is not a new one. At the same time, it is worth briefly reviewing the tenets in this model, which recently has been called the Gradual

Release of Responsibility Model of Instruction (Campione, 1981; Pearson & Gallagher, 1983). The model (Figure 1) specifies the proportion of responsibility for the completion of a learning task by teachers and students. The breakdown of the responsibilities of the teacher and student is presented graphically from left to right.

At the beginning of instruction, teachers model the learning task to be mastered. In doing so, they assume full responsibility for selecting materials for instruction, for explicitly demonstrating and modeling the task in such a way that students can observe the important aspects of task performance, and for completing the task so that students can see a finished product. As teachers continue to model and receive students' feedback that indicates a beginning mastery of the task being presented, they gradually move from the central position of providing all the instruction and work toward guided prac-

Figure 1
The Gradual Release of Responsibility Model of Instruction

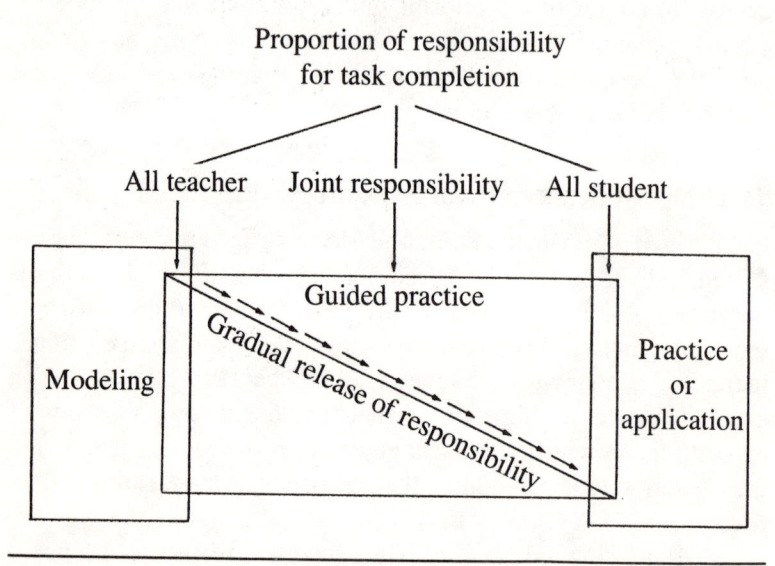

From P.D. Pearson and M.C. Gallagher. The instruction of reading comprehension, *Contemporary Educational Psychology,* 1983, *8,* 317-344.

tice, in which students assume more of the responsibility for performing the task. During the guided practice phase, teachers and students have joint responsibility for learning the material. As the students become more independent through guided practice, teachers bring them to the stage where they are completely responsible for task completion, and they achieve independence in task performance. Of course, the objective in this model is to make students independent learners with careful teacher centered instruction based on explicit modeling, guided practice with teacher-student joint responsibility, and independent practice and/or application by students.

Four suggestions for teaching students how to read expository text more effectively are structural organizers, outlining, summarization procedures, and questioning routines. Each of these can be taught using the Gradual Release of Responsibility Model of Instruction in Figure 1.

Structural organizers. The structural organizer is a process for identifying expository text structure and generating blank outline grids with labeled slots for main and supporting ideas (Slater, 1985). Its purpose is to highlight these ideas for students. The following structural organizer was created for a paragraph in which there was one main idea with five supporting ideas:

Main Idea _____
Supporting Idea 1 _____
Supporting Idea 2 _____
Supporting Idea 3 _____
Supporting Idea 4 _____
Supporting Idea 5 _____

The paragraph employing this structure is shown here.

> In 1862, Congress passed a law to build the first transcontinental railroad. The Central Pacific and Union Pacific railroad companies were formed to do the work. From the start in 1867, the two companies were in a race across the country. Each railroad had been promised a bonus from the government. For every mile of track laid, the railroads received

land and money. The company that put down the most track would get the biggest bonus (Schreiber et al., 1986, p. 285).

Using an overhead transparency with a sample paragraph, teachers can demonstrate how to make a structural organizer by generating a grid similar to the one above for main and supporting idea sentences. With the blank structural organizer on one overhead transparency and the paragraph on another, teachers can show the class how the author has arranged main and supporting ideas. While filling in the grid, they read the paragraph aloud and explain why a particular idea is a main idea or a supporting idea. By completing a sample grid, teachers are constructing a visual display of the hierarchy of ideas in the paragraph.

After teachers have demonstrated this process with several examples, they can involve students in the procedure by asking them to help generate and complete structural organizers. Together, teachers and students can identify main and supporting ideas in the sample paragraphs and then fill in the outline grids. Again, it is appropriate to work with several examples at this joint responsibility stage.

When teachers determine students have a solid mastery of the concepts involved in generating and filling in structural organizers, it is time to move to the student responsibility phase. In this phase, students are to demonstrate independently that they are able to take paragraphs from their books, prepare structural organizers, identify main and supporting ideas, and fill in the organizers.

It is important to keep in mind that (1) the teacher should select from students' textbooks examples that adequately reflect the types of real texts students read; (2) those text samples initially should include paragraphs that explicitly contain main and supporting idea organization; and (3) if necessary, the structural organizer outline grid should be further broken down to include a more detailed hierarchy of main ideas and supporting details, such as main ideas, primary supports, and secondary supports.

As an instructional tool, the structural organizer allows teachers to highlight for students the standard expository passage organizations found in the Calfee and Curley classifications. At the same time, the structural organizer concept needs to be used with both well written and prototypic passages that clearly display a straightforward, hierarchical structure. Unfortunately, not all prose found in textbooks is either well written or prototypic in its organization, and students need to be aware of this.

Outlining. Our second suggestion for instruction, outlining, will work with well organized and prototypic passages and with less well written and less clearly organized passages (Baumann, 1984; Slater, Graves, & Piché, 1985). It seems reasonable to provide initial instruction on expository prose organization with clearly written examples and then to provide strategies to use with less clearly organized examples. Outlining provides the necessary flexibility. One standard format is shown here.

I. Main Idea
   A. Supporting Idea
   B. Supporting Idea
   C. Supporting Idea
   D. Supporting Idea
II. Main Idea
   A. Supporting Idea
   B. Supporting Idea

Building on knowledge that students have acquired from their work with structural organizers, teachers can demonstrate that outlines are somewhat less structured versions of structural organizers. Consider the following passage.

> Americans gazed longingly at store windows and advertisements. There they saw the many new products of American technology—electric refrigerators and vacuum cleaners, radios, washing machines, and cars. All of these products made life easier and more enjoyable (Schreiber et al., 1986, p. 334).

This passage does not conform to an explicit organization that would lend itself to a structural organizer. Instead, teachers in their modeling of outlining will need to show students that with such passages they still must identify main and supporting ideas and then sort those ideas into appropriate slots in an outline to make the information more comprehensible. Teachers might explain that the first sentence of a paragraph may not reveal the main topic and that further reading may be necessary. Once the main topic is identified and placed in an outline, teachers can model how the supporting details are organized under the main idea. In additional examples, teachers need to show students that sometimes they will be required to generate main idea sentences under which they will place supporting details.

After teachers determine that students understand the outlining principles, they can proceed in joint efforts with students by continuing with additional passages from which students will identify or generate main idea sentences and then fill in outlines together. The final stage of instruction comes when students can independently read expository text, identify or generate main idea sentences, and then fill in outlines with main and supporting ideas.

At this point, we offer a caution about teaching outlining. Sometimes the format of the outline can be emphasized at the expense of the purpose, which is to increase comprehension. In other words, the Roman numerals and capital letters become the object of the lesson rather than the purpose they serve. Initially, students should be allowed to place main ideas on the left and indent supporting ideas. A labeling system can be taught later.

Summarization. After students have mastered concepts provided by structural organizers and outlining, the third important strategy for them to master is summarization (Armbruster, Anderson, & Ostertag, 1987; Brown & Day, 1983). Students' practice with structural organizers and outlines provides much of the groundwork for teaching them how to prepare summaries of expository text content. Again, it is important to select representative passages from textbooks that students are reading. The following excerpt could serve as a stimulus in teaching students to write summaries.

> Germany's problems began as early as the end of World War I. At that time, Germany was officially blamed for starting

World War I. Because of this, Germany had to help pay the cost of the war for such nations as England and France. This was hard to do. The German government had little money of its own. And it could not borrow from Germany's businesses and industries. Most were ruined because of the war (Schreiber et al., 1986, p. 358).

First, teachers should read the passage aloud to determine the main idea of the paragraph—"Germany's problems began at the end of World War I." By continuing to think aloud, teachers could identify the important and the less important supporting details. Important supporting details include: (1) Germany was blamed for starting World War I, (2) England and France expected Germany to help pay the war costs, and (3) Germany had no money because of war damage to German businesses. Less important supporting details include: (1) The German government had little money of its own, and (2) it could not borrow money from German industries. Then the teacher could show students how to delete the less important details while including the important supporting details in the summary statement. A reasonable summary of the paragraph follows.

Germany was blamed for starting World War I. England and France expected Germany to help pay the war costs. Germany had no money to pay the costs because of war damage to German businesses.

After working through several examples, teachers could work with longer passages including multiple paragraphs. In working with longer units of text, teachers should continue to demonstrate how to identify important information and how to delete less important information. In the next stage, teachers can involve the students in the identification and summarization process. Finally, after full instruction, teachers can expect students to independently create their own summaries from expository passages.

Questions. The final suggestion for improving students' comprehension of expository text is to teach them question asking procedures for focusing their attention on text content (Anderson & Biddle, 1975; Reynolds & Anderson, 1980). In presenting structural organizers, outlining, and summarization procedures, teachers usually use questions to help students identify main and supporting ideas. These questions provide good models for students to use independently, but do not directly teach students how to ask questions.

The specific questioning routine suggested here involves converting headings and subheadings into questions that students need to answer as they read those sections of the text. The following excerpt could serve as a good model.

The 1920s: The Great Promise

"Every day in every way, things are getting better and better." This was an important idea in the 1920s. Many people then thought the future looked rosy. But like roses, futures can fade.

Lesson 1. Prosperity and the New Production

"This country believes in prosperity," said President Calvin Coolidge. He meant that Americans wanted to live well. Never before had so many Americans lived as well as they did during the 1920s.

Americans gazed longingly at store windows and advertisements. There they saw the many new products of American technology—electric refrigerators, vacuum cleaners, radios, washing machines, and cars. All of these products made life easier and more enjoyable.

During the 1920s, American workers produced more goods in a shorter time than ever before. There were at least two reasons for this. Americans were happy...(Schreiber et al., 1986, p. 334).

With this particular example, teachers can point out that the headings will serve as the basis for the questions to be generated. The teacher can convert the first major heading, "The 1920s: The Great Promise," into the question, "What was the great promise of the 1920s?" Then the teacher can move to the second heading, "Lesson 1. Prosperity and the New Production," and create two questions based on its content: What was the prosperity? and What was the new production? After the questions have been generated, the teacher can examine the text to find the answers.

After the initial modeling, teachers and students can work jointly to answer questions from headings and subheading and then search the text together for the answers. Finally, students can work independently with texts, create questions from appropriate headings, and then answer their questions. This fairly simple question generating procedure can assist students in focusing their reading of expository text and in improving their comprehension of that text.

Taken together, structural organizers, outlines, summarization, and questioning routines can provide students with a variety of tools to increase their efficiency in reading and comprehending expository text. Richgels, McGee, and Slaton (this volume) demonstrate how to use a variation of The Gradual Release of Responsibility Model of Instruction with another tool, the graphic organizer.

Conclusions

This discussion of expository text has had four major objectives: to provide a comprehensive definition of good expository text, to discuss research findings specific to how readers comprehend expository text, to present a comprehensive classification system for types of expository text to help teachers conceptualize the attributes of exposition for teaching purposes, and to describe specific teaching procedures which are designed to enhance students' comprehension of expository text.

The first section, which focused on defining good exposition, probably set the tone for the complex issues involved in teaching exposition. In the definition, its informational, explanatory, directive, and narrative attributes were discussed with the author of the text and the reader firmly in mind. No attempt was made to oversimplify issues. The complexities were included to capture the richness of good exposition and to point out the potential difficulties for readers in comprehending its content.

The second section focused on what research tells us about readers and expository text. The findings are generally straightforward and compelling: Structure is one of the most important variables in the comprehension of expository text. Students who are able to identify main and supporting ideas in expository texts generally recall significantly more information than those who do not. In other words, if we focus our efforts on helping students to identify and use structural cues when reading their texts, they will comprehend more of the information they encounter in these texts.

The third section classified types of expository text. The Calfee and Curley (1984) taxonomy was discussed because it is a comprehensive system capable of describing the diversity and complexity of exposition. The discussion focused on the categories within the taxonomy and on how teachers can use this scheme to become more knowledgeable about exposition so that more accurate instructional decisions can be made.

Finally, the fourth section described The Gradual Release of Responsibility Model of Instruction and examined methods for helping students become better readers of expository texts: structural organizers, outlining, summarization, and questions. The model of instruction emphasized the need for all-teacher modeling at the beginning of instruction, the move to joint teacher-student guided practice, and the final stage of all-student responsibility in practice and application. Each of the teaching methods was designed to enhance students' understanding of text structure by teaching them to use text structure to improve their mastery of the information in expository texts.

We hope this information will assist teachers in teaching students how to read expository text more effectively and efficiently. As more research is completed on the nature and purpose of exposition (Beck, McKeown, & Gromoll, 1986; Britton, 1986; Hidi & Baird, 1986; Slater, 1985), we hope that both teachers and researchers will gain additional insights in teaching students how to read expository texts.

References

Anderson, R.C., and Biddle, W.B. On asking people questions about what they are reading. In G.H. Bower (Ed.), *The psychology of learning and motivation,* volume 9. New York: Academic Press, 1975, 89-132.

Anderson, R.C., Shirey, L.L., Wilson, P.T., and Fielding, L.G. Interestingness of children's reading material. In R. Snow and M. Farr (Eds.), *Aptitude, learning, and instruction: Cognitive and affective process analyses.* Hillsdale, NJ: Erlbaum, in press.

Anderson, T.H., and Armbruster, B.B. Content area textbooks. In R.C. Anderson, J. Osborn, and R.J. Tierney (Eds.), *Learning to read in American schools: Basal readers and content texts.* Hillsdale, NJ: Erlbaum, 1984, 193-226.

Aristotle. *The rhetoric.* W.R. Roberts, translator. New York: Modern Library, c. 335 B.C./1984.

Armbruster, B.B., Anderson, T.H., and Ostertag, J. Does text structure/summarization instruction facilitate learning from expository text? *Reading Research Quarterly,* 1987, *21,* (3) 331-346.

Aulls, M.W. *Developing readers in today's elementary school.* Boston: Allyn and Bacon, 1982.

Baker, L., and Brown, A.L. Metacognitive skills and reading. In P.D. Pearson (Ed.), *Handbook of reading research.* New York: Longman, 1984, 353-394.

Bartlett, B.J. *Top level structure as an organizational strategy for recall of classroom text.* Unpublished doctoral dissertation, Arizona State University, 1978.

Baumann, J.F. The effectiveness of a direct instruction paradigm for teaching main idea comprehension. *Reading Research Quarterly,* 1984, *20*(1), 93-115.

Baumann, J.F. Research on children's main idea comprehension: A problem of ecological validity. *Reading Psychology,* April-June, 1982, *3*(2), 167-177.

Beck, I.L., McKeown, M.G., and Gromoll, E.W. *Issues concerning content and structure of expository text for young readers.* Unpublished paper, University of Pittsburgh, Learning Research and Development Center, June 1986.

Berkowitz, S.J. Effects of instruction in text organization on sixth grade students' memory for expository reading. *Reading Research Quarterly,* 1986, *21*(2) 161-178.

Britton, B.K. Capturing art to improve text quality. *Educational Psychologist,* 1986, *21,* 333-356.

Britton, B.K., and Black, J.B. (Eds.). *Understanding expository text: A theoretical and practical handbook for analyzing explanatory text.* Hillsdale, NJ: Erlbaum, 1985.

Brown, A.L., and Day, J.D. Macrorules for summarizing texts: The development of expertise. *Journal of Verbal Learning and Verbal Behavior,* 1983, *22*(1), 1-14.

Calfee, R., and Curley, R. Structure of prose in the content areas. In J. Flood (Ed.), *Understanding reading comprehension.* Newark, DE: International Reading Association, 1984, 161-180.

Campione, J. *Learning, academic achievement, and instruction.* Paper presented at the Second Annual Conference on Reading Research of the Study of Reading, New Orleans, April 1981.

Garner, R. *Metacognition and reading comprehension.* Norwood, NJ: Ablex, 1987.

Garner, R., Alexander, P., Slater, W., Hare, V.C., Smith, T., and Reis, R. Children's knowledge of structural properties of expository text. *Journal of Educational Psychology,* 1986, *78,* 411-416.

Graves, M.F., and Slater, W.H. Could textbooks be better written and would it make a difference? *The American Educator,* 1986, *10,* 36-42.

Graves, M.F., Slater, W.H., Roen, D.H., Redd-Boyd, T.M., Duin, A.H., Furniss, D.W., and Hazeltine, P. Some characteristics of memorable writing: Effects of revisions by writers with different backgrounds. *Research in the Teaching of English,* in press.

Harris, A.J., and Sipay, E.R. *How to increase reading ability: A guide to developmental and remedial methods,* eighth edition. New York: Longman, 1985.

Hidi, S., and Baird, W. Interestingness: A neglected variable in discourse processing. *Cognitive Science,* 1986, *10,* 179-194.

Just, M.A., and Carpenter, P.A. *The psychology of reading and language comprehension.* Boston: Allyn and Bacon, 1987.

Kinneavy, J.L. *A theory of discourse.* New York: W.W. Norton, 1971.

Mandl, H., Stein, N.L., and Trabasso, T. (Eds.). *Learning and comprehension of text.* Norwood, NJ: Ablex, 1984.

Meyer, B.J.F. Organizational aspects of text: Effects on reading comprehension and applications for the classroom. In J. Flood (Ed.), *Promoting reading comprehension*. Newark, DE: International Reading Association, 1984, 113-138.

Meyer, B.J.F. *The organization of prose and its effects on memory*. Amsterdam: North-Holland Publishing, 1975.

Meyer, B.J.F., Brandt, D.H., and Bluth, G.J. Use of author's textual schema: Key for ninth graders' comprehension. *Reading Research Quarterly*, 1980, *16*, 72-103.

Meyer, B.J.F., and Rice, G.E. The structure of text. In P.D. Pearson (Ed.), *Handbook of reading research*. New York: Longman, 1984, 319-351.

Morris, W. (Ed.). *The American heritage dictionary of the English language*. Boston: Houghton Mifflin, 1979.

Murphy, J.J. (Ed.). *The rhetorical tradition and modern writing*. New York: Modern Language Association, 1982.

Otto, W., and White, S. (Eds.). *Reading expository material*. New York: Academic Press, 1982.

Pearson, P.D., and Gallagher, M.C. The instruction of reading comprehension. *Contemporary Educational Psychology*, 1983, *8*, 317-344.

Piché, G.L., and Slater, W.H. Predicting learning from text: A comparison of two procedures. *Journal of Reading Behavior*, 1983, *15*, 43-57.

Reynolds, R.E., and Anderson, R.C. *The influence of questions during reading on the allocation of attention*. Technical Report 183. Urbana, IL: University of Illinois, Center for the Study of Reading, 1980.

Schreiber, J., Stepien, W., Patrick, J., Remy, R., Gay, G., and Hoffman, A.J. *America past and present*. Glenview, IL: Scott, Foresman, 1986.

Slater, W.H. Revising inconsiderate elementary school expository text: Effects on comprehension and recall. In J.A. Niles and R.V. Lalik (Eds.), *Issues in literacy: A research perspective*. Rochester, NY: National Reading Conference, 1985, 186-193.

Slater, W.H. Teaching expository text structure using structural organizers. *Journal of Reading*, 1985, *28*(8), 712-718.

Slater, W.H., Graves, M.F., and Piché, G.L. Effects of structural organizers on ninth grade students' comprehension and recall of four patterns of expository text. *Reading Research Quarterly*, 1985, *20*, 189-202.

Slater, W.H., Graves, M.F., Scott, S.B., and Redd-Boyd, T.M. Discourse structure and college freshmen's recall and production of expository text. *Research in the Teaching of English*, 1988, *22*(1), 45-61.

Spache, G.D., and Spache, E.B. *Reading in the elementary school*, fifth edition. Boston: Allyn and Bacon, 1986.

Taylor, B.M. Text structure and children's comprehension and memory for expository material. *Journal of Educational Psychology*, 1982, *74*, 323-340.

Taylor, B.M., and Beach, R.W. The effects of text structure instruction on middle grade students' comprehension and production of expository text. *Reading Research Quarterly*, 1984, *19*, 134-146.

Taylor, B.M., Harris, L.A., and Pearson, P.D. *Reading difficulties: Instruction and assessment*. New York: Random House, 1988.

Taylor, B.M., and Samuels, S.J. Children's use of text structure in the recall of expository material. *American Educational Research Journal*, 1983, *20*, 517-528.

Williams, J.P., Taylor, M.B., and Ganger, S. Text variations at the level of the individual sentence and the comprehension of simple expository paragraphs. *Journal of Educational Psychology*, 1981, *73*, 851-865.

van Dijk, T.A., and Kintsch, W. *Strategies of discourse comprehension*. New York: Academic Press, 1983.

Voss, J.F., Tyler, S.W., and Bisanz, G.L. Prose comprehension and memory. In C.R. Puff (Ed.), *Handbook of research in human memory and cognition*. New York: Academic Press, 1982, 349-393.

7

Donald J. Richgels
Lea M. McGee
Edith A. Slaton

Teaching Expository Text Structure in Reading and Writing

This chapter describes a method for teaching expository text structure. The method uses well-structured sample passages from textbooks and graphic organizers to show students what structure is, what clue words are, which ideas in a passage are most important, and how ideas are related to one another. Examples in this passage use *causation* structure, but the method can be used for any expository text structure.

In the elementary grades, students meet increasingly more text that is designed to inform or explain. They begin to read and write expository text. For example, elementary students may read health textbooks to learn about the heart and read trade books to find out how to keep their hearts healthy. Then they gather data on diet from family members and write reports about their "Heart Health."

As Slater and Graves explain (this volume), the purpose of reading and writing expository texts is to explain, describe, or inform. Because of this, elementary children must become masters at detecting main ideas and supporting details. They must be able to recognize relationships between ideas (e.g., too much cholesterol can cause heart trouble). Children must learn to write information in which the ideas are clearly supported and the reasoning is valid. Children must learn to recognize the organization of ideas in texts they read and to structure ideas in texts they write.

This chapter describes a method of helping students become more aware of how ideas are organized and related in what they read and write. This method will help students read their content material more effectively and help them write informative material more clearly.

This chapter begins with definitions of five expository text structures and a brief discussion of the role of text structure awareness in elementary students' textbook reading. These are followed by a seven step approach to teaching students about expository text structures. The approach is intended for use with one structure at a time. Our sample lessons illustrate its use with causation text structure.

Text Structures

While effective authors do not write to a formula, they do use some recognizable organizations or structures in their writing to help readers get the point. For example, writers use the order in which events happened over time to tell about a period of history. They compare and contrast the North and South to tell about causes of the Civil War. Although there are many ways to describe formats writers use to create expository texts (see Slater and Graves, this volume), we will describe five structures we have found useful in teaching elementary students. These descriptions are adapted from Meyer and Freedle (1984). Meyer and Freedle describe expository text structures in terms of their organizational components.

The *description* text structure is merely a grouping of ideas by association. With the *collection* text structure, other organizational components such as ordering or sequencing of elements are added. The *causation* text structure goes another step toward greater organization by including causal links between elements, in addition to grouping or sequence. The *problem/solution* text structure is related to the causation structure, but is still more organized. In this structure, a causal link is part of either the problem or the solution. That is, there may be a causal link that is disrupted by the problem and restored by the solution, or the solution may involve blocking the cause of a problem. Finally, a *comparison/contrast* text structure may have any number of organizational components, depending on how many differences and similarities the author includes.

These text structures are illustrated in five passages we have written about the United States Constitution. Slater and Graves (this volume) provide short illustrations for some of these structures. The somewhat longer examples included here illustrate the difference between content and structure. The five passages are very similar in content, but each is organized using a different expository text structure. Notice that all but the first passage have three basic strands: the conflict between the small states and the big states, the checks and balances principle, and the slavery issue. These are presented in different ways, with different text structures, depending on the kind of relations (among a strand's concepts) the author wanted to emphasize.

Description
The United States Constitution is the oldest written constitution in the world. It was written during the summer of 1787 and had received the required ratifications of nine states by June 1788. It still serves as the "ground rules" of the government of the United States.

Collection
The document that the delegates signed on September 17, 1787 contained several important compromises. **First,** under the proposed Constitution, big states would receive more votes than small states in the House of Representatives, whereas small states would receive the same number of votes as big states in the Senate. **Second,** the Constitution called for a stronger law making body (Congress) than the old Articles of Confederation had created and two new branches of the national government, the Presidency and the Federal Courts. But it also created a system of "checks and balances" among those branches. **Third,** the document allowed slave states to keep their slaves, but five slaves would be counted as the equivalent of only three free men when slave states figured their number of representatives in the House of Representatives.

Causation
With the ratification of nine states, the Constitution became the official "ground rules" for the new government of the United States. One **reason** many states agreed to the Constitution was that it created two houses of Congress. The big

states would receive more votes in the new House of Representatives than small states. The small states would receive the same number of votes (two) as the large states in the new Senate.

Many states were willing to ratify the Constitution **because** it contained a system of checks and balances among the three branches of government—the Presidency, the Congress, and the Courts. They were giving to the national government many powers that had formerly been theirs. But the national government was to operate under a clear definition of its powers and with a division of its powers among its three branches.

A strange system of counting slaves **resulted in** still other states' agreeing to the Constitution. Slave owning states would be allowed to keep their slaves. But nonslave holding states had at least been able to make an important point. If slave owners were not willing to free slaves and treat them as citizens, then the slave owners would not get full credit for slaves when figuring out how many representatives they could send to Congress. A slave was counted as three-fifths of a person when figuring representation!

Problem/Solution

The biggest **problem** facing the framers of the United States Constitution was that they represented so many different groups and interests. They wanted to create "a more perfect Union," but they themselves were far from unified on many issues. They disagreed about how to put together the Congress. Those from large states wanted to have more representatives than smaller states. Those from small states wanted all states to have the same number of representatives. They disagreed about the powers of the new central government. Those for a strong national government wanted no continuation of the disarray and rebellion that had occurred under the Articles of Confederation. Those for states' rights wanted to protect the powers of the state governments which had sent them to Philadelphia. They disagreed about slavery. Some opposed it. Others insisted that the new government protect their practice of owning slaves.

The **solution** to this problem was the same **solution** that has made our federal government work ever since

1787 – compromise. Unity could be achieved, differences could be overcome, if everyone agreed to give a little. For example, the big states gave the small states a Senate. The small states gave the big states a House of Representatives. Those against a strong national government went along with a stronger lawmaking body (Congress) than the old Articles of Confederation had created and two new branches of national government, the Presidency and the federal Courts. Those for a strong national government went along with a system of "checks and balances" among the President, the Congress, and the Courts. Those against slavery allowed slave owners to keep their slaves. The slave owners agreed to a system that counted slaves differently from free citizens for a state's representation in the House of Representatives.

Compare/Contrast
The framers of the United States Constitution were **alike** in many ways, but also **different** in many ways. They all believed in the United States. Most had been leaders during the War for Independence. They worried that individual states were becoming so selfish and shortsighted that the word "united" in their nation's name might no longer be accurate. But they all believed that self government was possible, that people could agree about matters that affected them all. In others words, the experiment that began on July 4, 1776 was worth continuing, even at the cost of their meeting and debating in the stuffy Assembly Room of the Pennsylvania State House through the long, hot summer of 1787. All admired and respected the man they had chosen as the President of the Convention, George Washington.

But there were many **differences** as well. Some delegates were farmers; some were city people. Some were from large states; some were from small states. Some were slave owners; some thought slavery was wrong. Some had come to the Constitutional Convention in order to create a strong national government; some were there to ensure that their state governments would not have to give up too much power.

As shown by the bold face words in the passages, writers often use signal or clue words to indicate which text structure organization they are using. Clue words provide information about the relationships between ideas in a passage. They do not provide additional content (Meyer, Brandt, & Bluth, 1980). In short, clue words are one way that authors can fulfill the "directive quality" of expository text that Slater and Graves discuss.

Clue words signaling collection structure include *first, second,* and *next.* Clue words signaling causation structure are *therefore, as a result, so that, in order to,* and *because.* Clue words signaling comparison/contrast structure are *similar to, different from, in contrast, however, but,* and *on the other hand.* Clue words signaling problem/solution structure are *problem, solution,* and *solve.*

The five text structures provide the means for talking about the organization of ideas in expositions. With those structures in mind, one can consider the characteristics of expository passages in elementary textbooks and the demands such passages place on students' reading abilities.

Text Structures in Elementary Textbooks

We know that readers who have structure awareness comprehend well structured texts better than poorly structured texts (Taylor & Samuels, 1983). We also know that many students, even in elementary school, are beginning to develop an awareness of text structure (McGee, 1982; Richgels et al., 1987) and, with good instruction, can improve their structure awareness and their use of structure guided reading comprehension strategies (Piccolo, 1987; Taylor & Beach, 1984).

Unfortunately, we also know that most content materials students read are not well organized (Schallert & Tierney, 1981). They do not have the four qualities Slater and Graves describe in their definition of good expository text. Because of this discrepancy, teachers must be especially vigilant. When they recognize well structured passages, they must take the opportunity to use them to teach their students about text structure.

As students come to know what an ideal, well structured passage for each of the five text structures looks like, they can be helped to rewrite drafts of their own expository writing, to rewrite less ideally organized texts found in their content materials, and to compensate for poorly structured texts as they read. The remainder of this chapter describes a teaching method that uses well structured passages from textbooks when they can be found. This method uses graphic organizers to show students text structure. It helps students compare well structured writing they have produced following a graphic organizer with their textbook passages.

Teaching Expository Structure: An Overview

We have developed a seven step approach to teaching students about expository text structure (McGee & Richgels, 1985) that is similar to Hennings' (1982) writing instructional sequence. This approach will help students use text structure for both writing and reading. The first two steps involve teacher preparation, and the last five steps involve instruction.

First, find a passage from the students' textbook that is well organized, represents one text structure, and has appropriate clue words. The passage can be from a basal reader or from content textbooks. The passage should be only a few paragraphs in length. Although it may be difficult to find a "perfect" passage, it is important to begin with a passage that does not deviate much from the text structure to be taught. Students cannot learn about exceptions until they learn about the ideal. Check to be sure that main ideas are stated clearly even if clue words are sometimes only implied. The passage should relate to content the students are learning or to part of their basal reading lessons.

Second, prepare a graphic organizer for the passage. (A sample graphic organizer is presented in the next section.) Graphic organizers are outlines of key ideas from a passage, arranged with more important ideas written higher on the page than less important ideas. Lines are drawn between related ideas to illustrate how they are related. To prepare an organizer, read the entire passage to determine the key ideas and how they relate. Then list the key ideas in order of importance and join related ideas with lines. The purposes of the graphic organizer are to teach the content of the passage and to demonstrate how the content is structured or organized.

Third, introduce students to the idea of text structure. One way to demonstrate text structure is to have students build several towers out of toy blocks. Each tower should have the same structural pattern but use differently colored blocks. Make the point that even though each tower was made of differently colored blocks, all the towers have the same structure. In the same way, tell the students that passages may be about different ideas, but each may be organized following the same structure.

Fourth, show the students the graphic organizer that has been constructed from their text. Explain that graphic organizers are special outlines that not only represent information from a passage but also illustrate how that information is related. Remember, the students will not have read the passage taken from their text. They will see only the graphic organizer created by the teacher.

Fifth, help the students use the graphic organizer to write a passage. Their passage must include the relationships shown in the graphic organizer and use appropriate clue words. Help students edit their passage so that it clearly states the information and relationships among ideas that are illustrated by the graphic organizer.

Sixth, have students read the passage from their text and compare it with the text they have written. Name the structure (collection, causation, problem/solution, or compare/contrast), list sample clue words, and make a poster illustrating the structure's organization for easy reference in future use of this text structure (see Piccolo, 1987).

This same sequence of six steps can be used to teach students additional text structures (with the exception that step 3 can be deleted). Our seventh step should be taken after students have learned about all the structures. In step seven, help students move beyond short, single structure passages to longer passages with more than one structure. This guides students in looking for the *overall* structure of such passages.

Sample Lessons

We will describe how this seven step method might be used with a fourth grade class. To simplify our description and to show

how to use the knowledge students already have about structure, we will describe lessons for a class that has already been through the first six steps in learning about one text structure, collection. This class is now learning about the causation structure. The students are studying the period of history following the Revolutionary War, and their teacher has found a passage from their American history textbook that quite faithfully follows a causation text structure.

The selected passage explains the causes of the War of 1812. The War of 1812 (the effect) is announced at the end of the passage. The passage describes four causes of the war with Great Britain: the British attacked American ships, the British kidnapped American sailors, American settlers feared the British in Canada, and peaceful solutions failed. Although there are no clue words (such as *cause, effect, because*) to signal the causation structure, the passage content is clearly about causes and effects. By deciding to use this passage to teach about causation structure, the teacher has completed step one of the seven step method.

Next, the teacher created the following graphic organizer to represent the ideas and content of this passage. The organizer emphasizes the importance of the effect (War of 1812) by placing it first, followed by the four causes.

The teacher's goals for the first day of instruction are that the students be able to (1) remember what a graphic organizer is, (2) recognize causation text structure in sample passages, and (3) explain how the graphic organizer for the selected passage illustrates causes and effects important to the War of 1812. The following activities and samples of teacher talk from a first day lesson plan lead students through step four of the seven step approach described earlier. (The students do not need to go through step 3 because they did so earlier when learning about the collection structure.)

1. Remind students of previous knowledge about the general idea of structure ("Remember when we used differently colored blocks to build towers that were different colors but had the same structure?") and about other text structures ("We already know some clue words and ways of arranging and relating ideas as a collection or listing structure."). Tell students that today they are going to learn about a new text structure.

Causes of the War of 1812

After the Revolutionary War, Great Britain and France were at war. At first, "the United States remained uninvolved or **neutral**. American ships continued trading with both countries. Great Britain, however, did not want France to get supplies from the United States. So Great Britain attacked American ships sailing to France. The French also tried to prevent other nations from trading with Great Britain. The French navy attacked American ships that were on their way to British ports.

"Between 1804 and 1807, the United States lost more than 700 trading, or merchant, ships because of British attacks. About 200 American ships were lost to the French. In addition, thousands of sailors were kidnapped from American ships by the British. Great Britain claimed that these sailors had run away from, or deserted, the British navy. These sailors were forced to serve in the British navy. Many of the sailors were American citizens. This practice angered Americans. Some called for war with Great Britain.

"American settlers in the Northwest Territory also wanted war with Great Britain. They feared the British and their American Indian allies to the north in Canada. The settlers hoped that a war with Great Britain would give them the chance to claim land in Canada for the United States.

"American leaders tried to find peaceful solutions. But none of them worked. In 1812, the President, James Madison, asked Congress to declare war against Great Britain. Congress supported him and the United States went to war."

Excerpt from "The War of 1812" from *Holt Social Studies: Our History*, edited by JoAnn Cangemi, copyright ©1983 by Holt, Rinehart and Winston, Inc., reprinted by permission of the publisher.

Figure 1
Graphic Organizer from the War of 1812 Passage

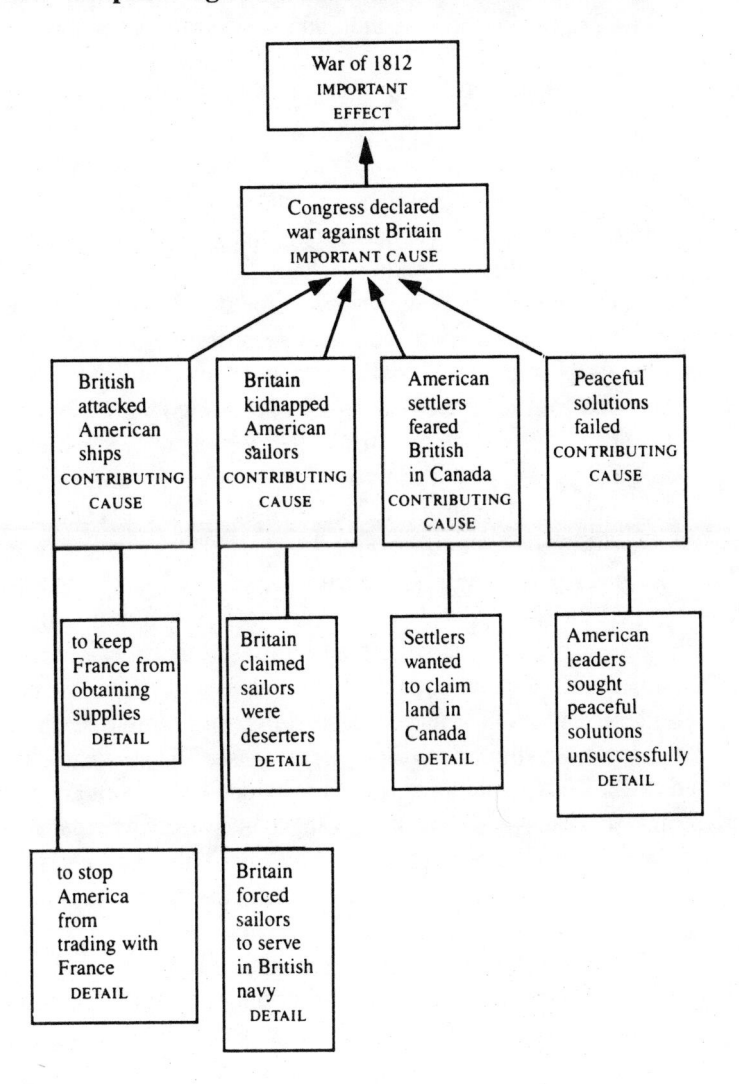

- **War of 1812** — IMPORTANT EFFECT
  - **Congress declared war against Britain** — IMPORTANT CAUSE
    - **British attacked American ships** — CONTRIBUTING CAUSE
      - to keep France from obtaining supplies — DETAIL
      - to stop America from trading with France — DETAIL
    - **Britain kidnapped American sailors** — CONTRIBUTING CAUSE
      - Britain claimed sailors were deserters — DETAIL
      - Britain forced sailors to serve in British navy — DETAIL
    - **American settlers feared British in Canada** — CONTRIBUTING CAUSE
      - Settlers wanted to claim land in Canada — DETAIL
    - **Peaceful solutions failed** — CONTRIBUTING CAUSE
      - American leaders sought peaceful solutions unsuccessfully — DETAIL

2. Compare a passage in the collection structure (known text structure) with a passage in the causation structure (new structure to be learned). For example, use the same collection and causation passages presented earlier. ("Both of these passages are about the United States Constitution. How are they different?") Students recognize that one is a collection passage, and the other is not. ("How is the second passage more than a listing of ideas? What key words tell what special kind of ideas they are and how they are related?") Students find the causal words, and the teacher writes causal sentences (or paraphrases of them) on the board.

3. Introduce the graphic organizer for the War of 1812 passage (Figure 1). ("Remember, we can show information and structure using a graphic organizer. This organizer looks different from the one we used for the collection passage we studied before.") Refer to the sample, empty organizer for collection structure, which is displayed on a poster you made with the class at the end of their learning about collection structure (see Piccolo, 1987). ("That is because it is a different structure from collection. The ideas are organized differently. But it will do the same kind of things: It will use ideas from the passage. It will arrange the ideas so that more important ideas are higher on the page than less important ideas. And it will use lines and labels to connect related ideas and show how they are related. The ideas are causes—just as the ones we wrote on the board for the Constitution passage were causes. That means that they led to an effect, something that they helped bring about. So on our organizer we have arrows that point from causes to what they caused. We also show some details that tell more about some of the important ideas and are connected to them in our organizer by lines.")

4. Talk through paths on the organizer, going from contributing causes to important causes to the important effect and emphasizing both supporting detail connections and causal connections. ("American settlers were afraid of the British in Canada. Remember that Canada still belonged to Britain, and the American settlers wanted to claim land there. This was one of the reasons Congress declared war against Britain. Under our Constitution, when Congress declares war, that causes the war to be official.")

5. Invite students to talk through other paths and eventually to talk through the whole organizer. In the process, they will be giving an oral expository report on the causes of the War of 1812.

The teacher planned a second day of instruction to complete step five of the seven step method. Depending on students' experience with text structure, with graphic organizers, and with writing, the teacher might plan to use the graphic organizer to compose a single class report (with the teacher as recorder). Or students may write reports independently. The teacher decided that this group of students could benefit from writing a passage from the organizer independently. They have already practiced writing passages as a group and know how to use a graphic organizer to guide their writing.

Figure 2 shows the first draft of a report written by one fourth grader, Ted, following the War of 1812 graphic organizer. Ted has followed the graphic organizer very well. All its elements are included except for the last detail, "American leaders sought peaceful solutions unsuccessfully." The relationship between important cause and important effect is implicit in Ted's title and his first and last sentences.

Ted has used a collection or listing structure within his causation structure ("There were several reasons....First.... Second....Third....Fourth...."). Still, he has included causation clue words ("reasons...to keep...because...caused..."), and his grouping of causes and their effects has made explicit most of the causes shown on the graphic organizer.

Based on Ted's use of the causation structure in his War of 1812 composition, the teacher planned a third day of instruction. A goal for this day is to consolidate students' knowledge of the causation structure and their growing ability to use it in their writing. The teacher will help Ted and other students make the relationship between important cause and important effect more explicit in their writing (see how it is more explicit in the teacher talk in activity four of the first day).

The teacher also planned to help the students include more information in the supporting details. Ted and the others might also be helped to think about the issue of using collection within

Figure 2
Ted's First Draft of "The War of 1812"
Written from the Graphic Organizer

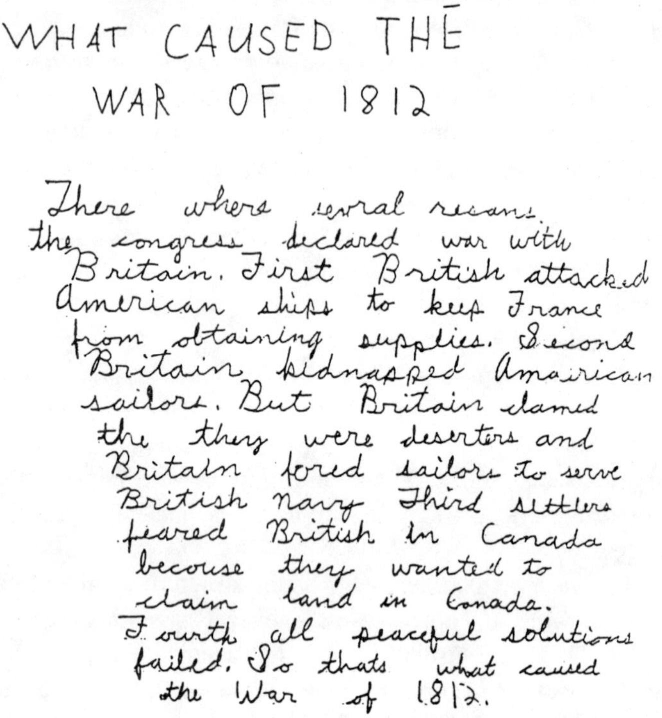

> WHAT CAUSED THE WAR OF 1812
>
> There where several reasons the congress declared war with Britain. First British attacked American ships to keep France from obtaining supplies. Second Britain kidnapped American sailors. But Britain clamed the they were deserters and Britain fored sailors to serve British navy Third settlers feared British in Canada becouse they wanted to claim land in Canada. Fourth all peaceful solutions failed. So thats what caused the War of 1812.

causation. Other students in a group sharing session might say, "Ted, it sounds to me too much like a collection with all that 'first,' 'second,' and 'third' stuff." Or the teacher might ask, "Are you giving the listing language too much prominence? Does it distract from the important causation relations? How could it be toned down so that the importance of the causal connections is obvious to a reader?"

On the fourth day of instruction, the teacher planned for the students to complete step six of the seven step method. They are to compare their various drafts of their War of 1812 passages and the passage from their textbook. This is a day for further consolidation of learning about the causation text structure. The teacher will be sure that

1. Students compare their drafts and talk about improvements from first drafts to edited, final drafts.
2. Students compare their final drafts with the textbook version and talk about strengths and weaknesses of each.
3. Students compare writing a passage (their own) in the causation text structure and reading a passage (each other's and the textbook's) in the causation text structure. ("How is meaning making the same/different when you are reading someone else's text and when you are writing a text with someone else in mind as a reader?")
4. Students and teacher create a poster that names the structure, lists often used clue words, and shows an empty sample graphic organizer (one with the labels IMPORTANT EFFECT, IMPORTANT CAUSE, CONTRIBUTING CAUSE, and DETAIL, with blank spaces and with arrows and lines as shown in Figure 3). This poster will be displayed in the classroom for future reference when reading and writing in the causation text structure.
5. The teacher warns students that not all texts are written with one, easily identified, "pure" text structure ("Remember how hard it was for *you* to write in the causation structure at first.") – that texts often follow several structures, especially if they are long. This paves the way for step seven, which the students will not complete until they have learned several other text structures.

Notice that many of these activities depend on student initiative. By now, the teacher's "gradual release of responsibility" (described by Slater and Graves, this volume) will be nearly complete for most students. If that is so, the teacher may help the students deal with the many poorly structured texts they will encounter in their daily reading.

On another day, the teacher and students may discuss poorly structured texts. The teacher can tell students that their poster may serve only as an approximation of what to look for when they need help comprehending real life causation texts. ("Often authors write about causes and effects but do not organize their ideas exactly as we have them in our graphic organizer. You can still try to find the

**Figure 3
Poster of Causation Structure**

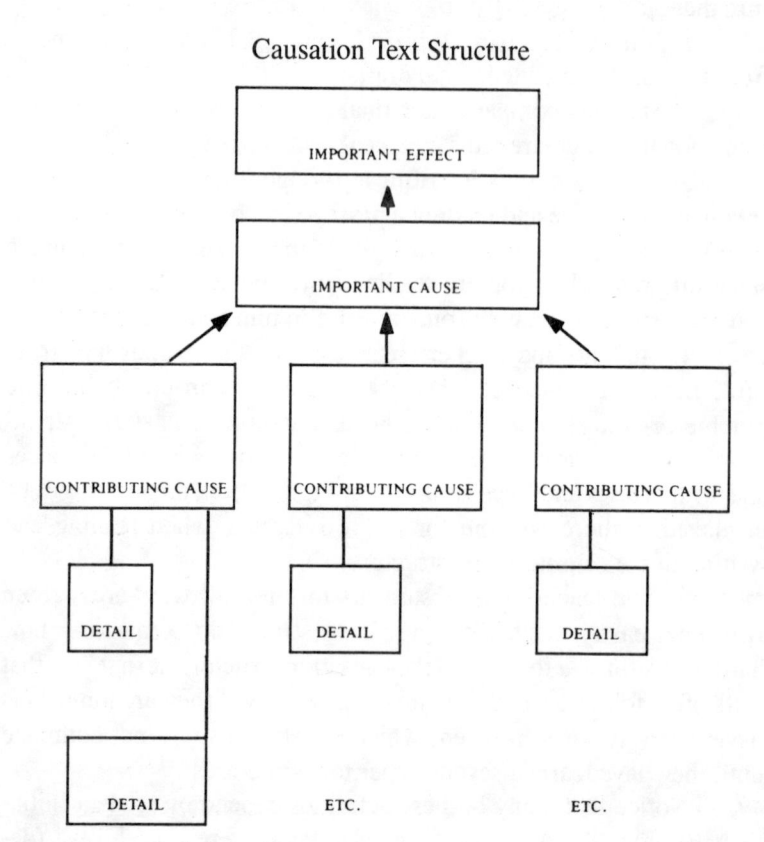

Causation Text Structure

kinds of ideas and connections our poster shows. You can look for causes and effects. Ask 'What is causing what? What are the causes and what are the effects? What is the most important cause-and-effect link? Which ideas are just details?' ")

The teacher and students may find and discuss a new causation passage from one of their textbooks. The students may be able to find such a passage by looking for clue words. When the passage does not exactly follow the organization shown on their poster, the teacher can help them use the empty graphic organizer to improve on the author's organization. ("Sometimes you can use our graphic organizer to organize what you read in your mind, even if it is not that way on the page. That will help you to understand and remember what you read.")

Summary

The teaching method we have described was designed with the realities of elementary classrooms in mind. Students need concrete examples and strong teacher involvement. Content area textbooks are often less than ideal. Learning can be a process of discovery if teachers themselves know what they want students to discover and have prepared carefully and with appropriate materials. Learning about reading and learning about writing go together. And learning about writing is a multiprocess, multistep, multiday endeavor (Calkins, 1986; Graves, 1983).

We end with a list of real life expository textbook passages that we feel come close to being "purely" organized in one of the text structures. We hope that this list will help you take the first step (and often the most difficult step) in the method we have described in this chapter, finding a well structured expository passage to use with elementary students.

Sample Passages

Collection text structure
Atkin, J., Asimov, I., and Galland, R. Vertebrae of the chest. *Ginn science series.* Lexington, MA: Ginn, 1973, 72.
Schneider, H., and Schneider, N. Clouds. *Science in our world.* Boston: Heath, 1968, 20.

Causation text structure
Cangemi, J. (Ed.). A community is people. *Communities.* New York: Holt, Rinehart & Winston, 1983, 32-34.
Richmond, J., and Pounds, E. (Eds.). Health around us. *You and your health.* Glenview, IL: Scott, Foresman, 1981, 115.

Problem/solution text structure
Kent, D. Subways on the move. In T. Clymer, R. Venezky, and R. Indrisano (Eds.), *Barefoot island.* Lexington, MA: Ginn, 1982, 254.
Schneider, H., and Schneider, N. Navigating by dead reckoning. *Science in our world.* Boston: Heath, 1968, 58.

Comparison/contrast text structure
Brewer, A., Garland, N., and Notkin, J. A model of a charge. *Learning by investigating.* Chicago: Rand McNally, 1972, 83.
Richmond, J., and Pounds, E. (Eds.). How do you and others grow in healthy ways? *You and your health.* Glenview, IL: Scott, Foresman, 1981, 116-117.

References

Calkins, L.M. *The art of teaching writing.* Portsmouth, NH: Heinemann, 1986.

Graves, D.H. *Writing: Teachers and children at work.* Portsmouth, NH: Heinemann, 1983.

Hennings, D.G. A writing approach to reading comprehension: Schema theory in action. *Language Arts,* 1982, *59,* 8-17.

McGee, L.M. Awareness of text structure: Effects on children's recall of expository text. *Reading Research Quarterly,* 1982, *17,* 581-590.

McGee, L.M., and Richgels, D.J. Teaching expository text structure to elementary students. *The Reading Teacher,* 1985, *38,* 739-748.

Meyer, B.J.F., Brandt, D.M., and Bluth, G.J. Use of top-level structure in text: Key for reading comprehension of ninth-grade students. *Reading Research Quarterly,* 1980, *16,* 72-103.

Meyer, B.J.F., and Freedle, R.O. Effects of discourse type on recall. *American Educational Research Journal,* 1984, *21,* 121-143.

Piccolo, J.A. Expository text structure: Teaching and learning strategies. *The Reading Teacher,* 1987, *40,* 838-847.

Richgels, D.J., McGee, L.M., Lomax, R.G., and Sheard, C. Awareness of four text structures: Effects on recall of expository text. *Reading Research Quarterly,* 1987, *22,* 177-196.

Schallert, D.L., and Tierney, R.J. *The nature of high school textbooks and learners: Overview and update.* Paper presented at the annual meeting of the National Reading Conference, Dallas, Texas, 1981.

Taylor, B.M., and Beach, R.W. The effects of text structure instruction on middle grade students' comprehension and production of expository text. *Reading Research Quarterly,* 1984, *19,* 134-146.

Taylor, B.M., and Samuels, S.J. Children's use of text structure in recall of expository material. *American Educational Research Journal,* 1983, *20,* 517-528.

8

Shawn M. Glynn

The Teaching with Analogies Model

> This chapter demonstrates how analogical reasoning can play an important role in elementary school children's comprehension of the concepts in their content area textbooks. The author argues that the process of relating concepts by means of analogy is a basic part of human thinking. Analogies can put new concepts into familiar terms for students, but analogies should be used cautiously because at some point every analogy breaks down. Analogies which are effective from the standpoint of instructional design contain certain key features which have been incorporated into a Teaching with Analogies (TWA) model.

This chapter will show how analogical reasoning can play an important role in elementary school children's comprehension of text in content areas. As an introduction, "listen in" on the following conversation between a seventh grade science teacher, Miss Davis, and one of her students, John.

John: I'm worried about the next science test, Miss Davis.
Miss Davis: Oh, what's giving you trouble, John?
John: The stuff on electricity and electric circuits in our text.
Miss Davis: Electricity can be a tough unit all right. Have you read your textbook carefully?
John: I sure have, lots of times. The reading is really hard. All the new terms get me confused.
Miss Davis: What were some of those confusing terms?
John: Well, I sort of know what a "circuit" is, but I'm not sure what "voltage" and "resistance" mean.
Miss Davis: What were some of the other electricity terms or ideas that you read about?
John: Uh, I read about "wires" and "batteries" and "switches."

Miss Davis: Yes, these are important parts of an electric circuit. You seem to remember all the important ideas from your reading. Can you put these ideas together and explain to me how an electric circuit works?

John: Ah, no. That's the problem. I can't get a picture in my head of how this electricity stuff works.

Miss Davis: Well, don't be discouraged, John. You learned a lot of important bits and pieces from the text. Let me see if I can help you put these bits and pieces together, so you will understand how an electric circuit works. Perhaps an analogy might help. Do you recall when you and your classmates set up the aquarium in the classroom?

John: Sure!

Miss Davis: And do you remember me explaining how the water circulated in the aquarium?

John: That was easy, not like this electricity stuff. When you explained how the water circulates, I could actually see the pump and filter.

Miss Davis: Right! Well, now I'm going to help you "see" how the electric circuit works by comparing it to water circulation in the aquarium. Look at the classroom aquarium while I describe again how the water flows through it in a circuit, or a connected path. A current of water is drawn through a pipe from the aquarium by a pump which controls pressure. The water then flows through a filter which slows the flow and catches impurities. Finally, the water returns to the aquarium through a pipe. Do you remember and understand that, John?

John: Sure, Miss Davis.

Miss Davis: Fine. Now think about this question. What might the water correspond to in an electric circuit? That is, what flows in the circuit?

John: Electricity?

Miss Davis: Exactly! Very good. Now, the water is carried from the aquarium into the filter and back into the aquar-

	ium by means of plastic pipes. What do these pipes correspond to in an electric circuit?
John:	The metal wires?
Miss Davis:	Right again. Now, in the aquarium, the pump provided the pressure to move the water through the tubes. In an electric circuit, what device provides the "pressure" to move the electricity through the circuit?
John:	How about a battery?
Miss Davis:	Yes, indeed, a battery, or a generator. Now, for a tougher question. Like a pump, the battery produces a sort of "electrical pressure." What's the correct name for this electrical pressure?
John:	I bet it's "voltage."
Miss Davis:	And I bet you're right! Now here's a really tough question. We stuffed cotton in the aquarium filter to clean the water. This also had the effect of reducing the amount of water that flowed through the pipes in a given period of time. Likewise, in an electric circuit, the use of some poorly conducting metals in wires can reduce the amount of electricity that flows in a given period of time. In an electric circuit, what do you call this reduction in flow?
John:	Resistance!
Miss Davis:	Correct, John, I think you've got it. To sum up, let's list here on the board the features of our aquarium water circuit which correspond to those in an electric circuit.

Water Circuit	**Electric Circuit**
water	electricity
flowing water	electric current
pipes	wires
pump	battery
pressure	voltage
filter	poor conductor
reduced flow	resistance

	Now, John, keeping these features in mind, explain to me how an electric circuit works.
John:	OK, I'll give it a try. An electric circuit is an unbroken wire path through which electricity can flow. In order for the electricity to flow, there must be a source of voltage, such as a battery. How much electricity will flow through a circuit in a given period of time depends on how much resistance there is in the material which makes up the wire. So how's that? I guess I've got this circuit business down pat.
Miss Davis:	Very impressive, but we're not done yet. I still have a few tricky questions.
John:	OK, Miss Davis, give me your best shot.
Miss Davis:	Look at this diagram of an electric circuit; it's similar to the one in your textbook. The circuit contains a charged battery and a lit light bulb. What would happen to the electricity flowing through the circuit if you cut the wire and pulled the ends apart? Would you get a different result if you cut the wire before or after the light bulb?
John:	Those are tricky questions, for sure. Hmm, let me use the aquarium water circuit analogy. If I cut the pipe returning water to the tank, the water would continue to flow, but probably spill out on the floor. On the other hand, if I cut the pipe taking water from the tank just above the water line, then the water would stop flowing. Now, I'll apply this analogy to your circuit. If I cut the wire before the bulb, then electricity would flow but spill out of the wire. If I cut behind the bulb, then electricity would stop flowing. Am I right?
Miss Davis:	No, you are not, although your reasoning is good. When you cut or break an electric circuit at any point in the circuit, the electricity stops flowing everywhere in the circuit. That's the function of an electrical switch, by the way; it interrupts the circuit, stopping the flow of electricity.
John:	But why wasn't I right, Miss Davis? I used the analogy.

Glynn

Figure 1
**Diagram of an Electric Circuit,
with a Charged Battery and a Lit Bulb**

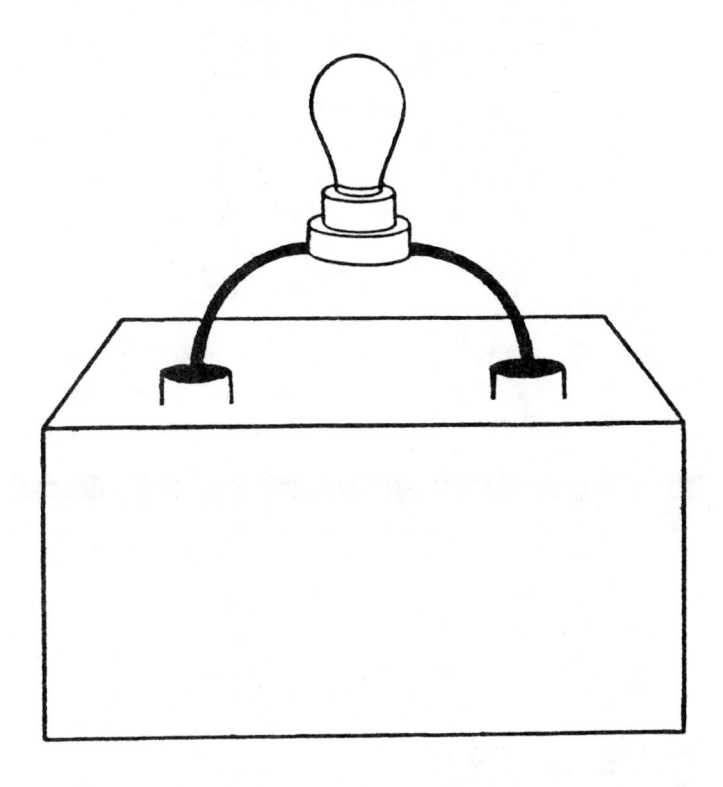

Miss Davis: Because, John, no analogy is perfect. Analogies help us to understand some aspects of a new concept, but at some point every analogy breaks down.

John: If analogies can lead us to wrong conclusions sometimes, then I think we shouldn't use them at all.

Miss Davis: That, John, would be like "throwing the baby out with the bath water" if you'll forgive me using another analogy. Analogies can be a big help to me when I explain new concepts and to you when you try to understand them. The trick is to use analogies carefully, keeping in mind their limitations and the wrong ideas

	which can arise when an analogy is carried too far. Used carefully, analogies can help you a lot, John, just as they've helped many of the famous scientists you've read about in your textbook.
John:	Which scientists?
Miss Davis:	Oh, astronomers such as Johannes Kepler, who drew an analogy between the movements of the planets and the workings of a clock. And physical scientists such as Joseph Priestly, who suggested the law of electrical force by drawing an analogy from the law of gravitational force.
John:	Oh, yes, I remember their names. They used analogies, huh?
Miss Davis:	Certainly. Analogies are important thinking tools. They can help us to make the jump between old ideas we already understand and new ideas we're trying to learn.
John:	Is science the only area where I can use analogies?
Miss Davis:	You can use analogies in all your subjects, John. They are powerful tools for understanding and problem solving. But do keep in mind their limitations.
John:	I will, Miss Davis. And thanks a lot. I'm not worried about the test anymore.

Teaching with Analogies

In the preceding fictitious conversation, the teacher effectively used an analogy to explain a complicated concept a student encountered in a textbook. The concept in question related to physical science, but it could just as easily have been a complicated concept in another discipline. For example, the science teacher could have been any of the following:

- A mathematics teacher explaining the concept of an equation by drawing an analogy to the balance used in science lab.
- A geography teacher explaining the concept of a glacier by drawing an analogy to a river of ice.

- A music teacher explaining the concept of harmony (i.e., musical background) by drawing an analogy of the concept of perspective in painting.
- An English teacher explaining the concept of a hierarchical outline by drawing an analogy to a tree and its branches.

Analogies are instructional tools which can be applied to concepts in all the disciplines.

By drawing an analogy spontaneously and using a guided discovery method with the student, the science teacher demonstrated how an analogy can be used in informal instructional situations. A formal, direct instructional method could have been used with similar success. Sometimes the analogies that text authors use to explain new concepts are clear and well developed, while other times they are vague and potentially confusing. What authors need is a model to guide their use of instructional analogies. Teachers who wish to extend or modify an author's analogy also need such a model. Teachers could use the model to develop their own analogies when none are offered in the text—analogies that are targeted to the specific background knowledge of the children they teach. For example, a Minnesota science teacher might help students to picture the earth rotating by comparing it to an ice skater spinning. A Georgia teacher, on the other hand, might draw a comparison to a roller skater, since southern children are more likely to have experience roller skating than ice skating.

Later in this chapter, a Teaching with Analogies (TWA) model will be presented and illustrated. Teachers and text authors can use this model to explain new concepts to students. To set the stage for this model, the processes of text comprehension and analogical reasoning will be discussed.

Meaningful Text Comprehension

An expository text is one that explains concepts and how they are related, or, "how something works." Expository text comes in many forms: textbooks, journals, magazines, manuals, newspapers, and software. These forms can be either paper or computer based. A current trend in instruction is to supplement conventional textbooks with computer based modules which contain simulations, practice drills, diagnostic tests, and remedial exercises.

In all its forms, expository text plays a vital role in the instruction of elementary school students. In content areas such as science, mathematics, and social studies, students rely heavily on expository text for much of the knowledge they must learn.

Comprehending the concepts in an expository text can be difficult for an elementary school student. To facilitate students' meaningful comprehension of expository text, teachers and text authors must help students relate new concepts to concepts with which they are already familiar. If familiar concepts and new ones are related correctly, then the student will comprehend the text in a meaningful fashion. Otherwise, comprehension will break down and the student will not understand critical text concepts. Analogical reasoning is one of the most effective ways for students to integrate their existing knowledge with text knowledge (Sternberg, 1986).

Analogical Reasoning about Text Concepts

Frequent use of analogies to explain everyday events underscores their potential value as instructional tools. The following expressions are commonplace in casual conversation: "Let me give you an analogy...," "It's just like...," "It's the same as...," "It's no different than...." The process of relating concepts by means of analogy is a basic part of human thinking, and authors, teachers, and students are certain to use it. One way to ensure they use it effectively is to provide them with a model of analogical reasoning.

It is common for the teacher's edition of content area textbooks to point out, in the introduction, all of the special features incorporated into the design of the text to facilitate students' comprehension of text concepts. These features include: advance organizers; structured overviews; highlighted concept names; margin notes; introductory, adjunct, and review questions; illustrations; cartoons; boxed examples; concept summaries; lists of important terms; conceptual activities; and glossaries. These features, along with supplementary materials such as workbooks, resource books, videotapes, films, and software are promoted in the teacher's edition as valuable aids to comprehension.

Features such as these can be valuable aids to comprehension, *under certain conditions*, as many research studies have shown (Britton & Glynn, 1987; Britton et al., 1982; Glynn, 1978; Glynn, Andre, & Britton, 1986; Glynn & Britton, 1984; Glynn, Britton, & Muth, 1985; Glynn, Britton, & Tillman, 1985; Glynn & Di Vesta, 1977, 1979). Analogies rarely are mentioned in textbook introductions. This tends to be true even in textbooks in which authors make excellent use of analogies. In a number of research studies, analogical reasoning has been shown to facilitate comprehension and problem solving (Alexander et al., 1987; Alexander, White, & Magano, 1983; Bean, Singer, & Cowan, 1985; Brown & Clement, 1987; Gick & Holyoak, 1980, 1983; Halpern, 1987; Hayes, 1988; Vosniadou & Brewer, 1987). So, why not promote this valuable aid to comprehension in the introduction to the text?

One reason why analogies are not promoted, even in textbooks that make extensive use of them, is that the skill of writing good analogies is what psychologists call "procedural" rather than "declarative." Procedural knowledge is knowledge of "how to do something" rather than "how to explain it in words." Because teachers, authors, and publishers do not have guidelines or a model for what constitutes a good instructional analogy, the development and evaluation of analogies are fairly subjective, as they are more of an art than a science. Therefore, teachers, authors, and publishers may not feel comfortable about promoting them in textbooks as aids to comprehension until a model becomes available for designing and evaluating instructional analogies.

The following sections provide answers to the questions most commonly asked about instructional analogies by teachers and authors.

What Is an Analogy?

An *analogy* is a similarity in some respects between concepts otherwise dissimilar. An *analog*, a related term, is a concept from which we can draw an analogy to another concept. While the terms *analogy* and *metaphor* are frequently substituted for one another, analogy tends to be used more often in scientific and technical contexts. Metaphor is used more often in literary contexts (e.g., Her spectacular departure was the icing on the cake.). Since the examples presented in this chapter are from content area textbooks, analogy will be used rather than metaphor.

How Do Analogies Help Students Learn?

Meaningful learning has been defined by Wittrock (1985, pp. 261-262) as a "student generative process that entails construction of relations, either assimilative or accommodative, among experience, concepts, and higher order principles and frameworks. It is the construction of these relations between and within concepts that produces meaningful learning." When an analogy is drawn between concepts, a powerful relation is constructed that leads to the meaningful learning described by Wittrock. An analogical relationship is powerful because it comprises an entire set of associative relationships between features of the concepts being compared.

In content area texts, analogies are used in a relatively precise fashion to transfer ideas from a familiar concept to an unfamiliar one. We will call the familiar concept the analog and the unfamiliar one the target. Both the analog and the target have characteristics, or features. If the analog and the target share common or similar features, an analogy can be drawn between them. An abstract representation of an analogy, with its constituent parts, appears in Figure 2; note that the analog and the target are subordinate to a superordinate concept.

The target concept of an electric circuit, as discussed in the chapter introduction, will be used to illustrate the analogy representation in Figure 2. The water circuit will be the analog concept. Examine once again the table of electric and water circuit features constructed by the teacher. An analogy can be drawn between the electric and water circuits because they share the similar features mapped out in the table.

Note that the electric circuit and the water circuit are both circuits; that is, they are subordinate to the superordinate concept *Circuit*. There are other kinds of circuits that might be used to draw an analogy. For example, in a pinball machine, the pinballs (corresponding to electrons or water molecules) travel a circuit and are pushed by a plunger (corresponding to a battery or a pump). The

Figure 2
An Abstract Representation of an Analogy and Its Constituent Parts

Superordinate Concept, Principle, or Formula

Analog	compared with	Target
Feature	compared with	Feature
1	compared with	1
2	compared with	2
3	compared with	3
n	compared with	n

pinballs even meet "resistance" in the form of bumpers and funnels. Other analogies could be drawn by teachers who keep the abstract representation of an analogy and its constituent parts in mind when thinking about circuits.

Sometimes, there is no conventional name for the superordinate concept which subsumes an analog and a target. For example, authors of biology texts frequently draw an analogy between the camera and the human eye. Here are some of the similar features:

Camera	**Human Eye**
lens	lens
inverted image	inverted image
film	retina
lens cap	eyelid
focus	lens accommodation
aperture	pupil dilation

What is the name of the superordinate concept that subsumes the analog *camera* and the target *human eye? Visual Device* is one possibility, but it is certainly not as familiar a name as *Circuit* was in the previous example. General concepts that are not used often do not have labels. Nevertheless, the role of the superordinate concept in the representation of an analogy and its constituent parts is an important one. The identification and naming of the superordinate concept can suggest other analogies; it also can stimulate students to generalize what they have learned and apply their learning to other contexts. Therefore, although it might be difficult to identify and name the concept which subsumes an analog and its target, it is beneficial to do so for purposes of meaningful comprehension.

How Do Analogies and Examples Differ?

Sometimes students confuse an example of a concept with an analogy. An example is an instance of a concept, not a comparison between similar features of two concepts. Consider a science textbook which describes the relationship between an electric start and lightning. Lightning is not *like* a big spark, it *is* a big spark! So, lightning is an example of the concept electric spark.

An analogy also can be drawn between two examples of the same concept (or the same superordinate concept). Consider the analogy, "A whale is like a dolphin," used in a children's text by an author who wants to point out that both are examples of sea mammals.

How Do You Tell a Good Analogy from a Bad One?

How good an analogy is depends upon how well it achieves its purpose. In general, if an analogy is serving an explanatory purpose, the following three criteria can be used to judge its appropriateness: (1) **the number of features compared,** (2) **the similarity of the features compared,** and (3) **the conceptual significance of the features compared.**

The explanatory power of an analogy generally increases as the number of similar features shared by the analog and target increases. However, it is possible to draw a "good" analogy on the basis of a few (or even one) similar features, if those features are directly relevant to the specific goals of the teacher or author. For example, the following analogy is drawn on the basis of only one similar feature, but it is a very important one in terms of the teacher's goals: The moon acts like a mirror reflecting the light of the sun.

An analogy is considered "bad" if it is difficult to identify and map the important features shared by the analog and the target. For example, in the sixth grade Heath Science text (Barufaldi, Ladd, & Moses, 1981), three models of the atom appear in the drawing labeled "Billiard ball model; Plum pudding model; Rutherford's model: a nucleus surrounded by rapidly moving electrons" (p. 116). The titles of the first two models are historically accurate. Furthermore, they draw helpful analogies for readers who are familiar with billiard balls and plum pudding.

Unfortunately, few sixth graders are familiar with billiards and plum pudding. The titles should be maintained since they are historical; however, the text should explain billiards and plum pudding for the concepts and the associated analogies to be understood. Perhaps, an analogy could be used to explain plum pudding by comparing it to chocolate chip ice cream, a concept with which more sixth graders would be familiar.

A good analogy puts new ideas into terms with which students are already familiar. Analogies drawn by a teacher or author between concepts covered early in a text and those covered later (such as fractions and proportions in a math text) are particularly effective because there is assurance that the earlier concepts (which function here as analogs) are part of every student's knowledge base. Also, these analogies are particularly powerful because they prompt readers to connect related concepts and form conceptual systems.

Can Analogical Reasoning Hurt Comprehension?

The correspondence of features between two concepts is never identical; otherwise the corresponding concepts would be identical. When teachers, authors, or students intentionally or inadvertently compare features that do not correspond to one another, misunderstanding and misdirection result.

A careful examination of all aspects of an analogy is a prerequisite to using it effectively. An analogy easily can lead students down the wrong path. For example, students who believe that electricity in a wire is like water in a hose often conclude, erroneously, that if the wire is cut, the electricity will "leak out."

Teachers and authors should explain to students that analogies are double edged swords. An analog can be used to correctly explain and even predict some aspects of the target concept. At some point, however, every analogy breaks down. At that point, miscomprehension and misdirection can begin. Students must understand this.

Teaching with Analogies Model

The TWA model is based on a survey (Glynn & Britton, 1988; Glynn et al., in press) of forty-three content area textbooks in which the most effective analogies from the standpoint of instructional design were identified. The authors of these analogies performed certain key operations that have been incorporated into a model which can serve as a guide for authors and teachers. The TWA model contains the following six operations: (1) **introduce target concept,** (2) **recall analog concept,** (3) **identify similar features of concepts,** (4) **map similar features,** (5) **draw conclusions about concepts,** and (6) **indicate where analogy breaks down.** A well designed analogy performs each of these operations for the student, although not necessarily in the order listed. To illustrate these operations, recall the conversation between teacher and student used to introduce this chapter. In fact, you may want to reread that conversation before proceeding. Here are the six key TWA operations performed: (1) The target concept was introduced; (2) an analog concept was recalled; (3) similar features of the analog and target concepts were identified; (4) the similar features were graphically mapped; (5) conclusions were drawn about the target concept; (6) and the teacher indicated where the analogy breaks down.

In sum, the use of an analogy was good; all of the six operations in the TWA model were performed. If a teacher or an author were to leave some of the operations to the student, the technical quality of the analogy would be reduced because the student might fail to perform an operation or might perform it poorly.

In the aforementioned survey of content area textbooks, authors often suggested an analog to students, but then left the students to make sense (or nonsense) of it for themselves. Under these circumstances, the students could identify irrelevant features of the target and analog, map them, draw wrong conclusions about the target, and fail to realize where the analogy breaks down. In short, the students' understanding of the target concept could be both incomplete and incorrect.

The Elementary School Teacher's Use of the TWA Model

When new concepts are taught by a direct instruction method (cf. Rosenshine, 1983), it is absolutely essential that the children are provided with carefully planned, systematic explanations about the strategy the teacher is using. Winograd and Hare (1988) examined a variety of reading comprehension strategies and concluded that their effectiveness depends upon the teacher enlisting the children's active participation "through careful and complete explanation of the procedures and values of the strategy under question" (p. 123). Winograd and Hare identified five kinds of explanations that the teacher should give to students. For example, if a teacher repeatedly draws upon analogies during direct instruction, the teacher should be sure to describe to the children: "(1) what the strategy is, (2) why the strategy should be learned, (3) how to use the strategy, (4) when and where the strategy is to be used, and (5) how to evaluate use of the strategy" (Winograd & Hare, pp. 123-124).

Teachers who keep the TWA model in mind can interpret textbook analogies for their students. If the author fails to perform some of the operations specified in the model, the teacher can perform them. For example, suppose the author of a science text draws an analogy between electricity in a wire and water in a hose, but fails to point out where this analogy breaks down, namely, that electricity does not spill out if the wire is cut. The teacher can remedy this failure on the author's part by performing this essential operation for the students.

Teachers should familiarize students with this model so they will learn how to interpret, criticize, and extend an author's analogy on their own. When this model has been used in elementary school classes to dissect an author's analogy, the discussions that ensued between the teacher and students, and the students themselves, enabled the teacher to identify students' misconceptions and knowledge gaps that otherwise would have gone undetected. The discussion also prompted students to tie together concepts they previously viewed as unrelated.

Teachers and students also are encouraged to use the model as a guide when generating their own analogies. They may wish to do this when the textbook author has not provided an analogy. For example, a colleague who teaches biology to seventh grade students used the TWA model when explaining photosynthesis. She compared photosynthesis to the process of making a cake. Some excerpts from the lesson plan she developed (Sloan, 1988) appear in Tables 1 and 2.

Table 1
Pamela Sloan's Lesson:
What Happens during Photosynthesis?

Have you ever used a cake mix to bake a cake? When you bake a cake with a cake mix, you mix the cake mix together with some water and eggs, heat the batter in the oven, and thirty minutes later you have a cake. Scientists think about putting ingredients together and making something new by writing an equation. To a scientist, a cake equation might look like this:

$$\text{cake mix} + \text{water} + \text{eggs} \xrightarrow{\text{heat}} \text{cake}$$

You begin by mixing three raw materials together: cake mix, water, and eggs. Then you add heat from the oven, which is a kind of energy, and a cake is the end product.

The process of photosynthesis is similar to the process of making a cake. Plants need two raw materials: carbon dioxide gas and water. They also need a source of energy, which is sunlight. Using carbon dioxide and water, along with energy from sunlight, the plant is able to make its own food, sugar, and a waste product, oxygen. To a scientist, the photosynthesis equation looks like this:

$$\text{carbon dioxide} + \text{water} \xrightarrow{\text{sunlight}} \text{sugar} + \text{oxygen}$$

The raw materials in photosynthesis are carbon dioxide and water. Like the heat in the oven provided the energy for the cake batter to become cake, sunlight provides the energy the plant needs to change carbon dioxide and water to sugar and oxygen. The end products, or what the plant has after photosynthesis, are sugar and oxygen. The plant releases oxygen into the air and uses the sugar to obtain energy to carry out its body functions and grow.

You know from your experience with houseplants that if plants do not have sunlight, they will die. The plants actually starve to death since without sunlight they are unable to make food.

Chlorophyll: The Catalyst

Unlike making a cake, plants need a catalyst to change carbon dioxide and water into sugar and oxygen. A catalyst is a substance that helps a reaction to occur, but does not become part of the reaction.

Chlorophyll is the catalyst necessary for a plant to produce its own food through photosynthesis. Therefore, if a plant does not have any chlorophyll, photosynthesis will not occur even if the plant has carbon dioxide, water, and sunlight. The equation for photosynthesis now may be written like this:

$$\text{carbon dioxide} + \text{water} \xrightarrow[\text{chlorophyll}]{\text{sunlight}} \text{sugar} + \text{oxygen}$$

Table 2
Analogy between Making a Cake and Photosynthesis

Process	Making a Cake	Photosynthesis
Raw Materials	Cake Mix Water Eggs	Carbon Dioxide Water
Source of Energy	Heat from Oven	Sunlight
End Product	Cake	Sugar Oxygen

From P. Sloan, *Using research based considerations to develop a science textbook unit about photosynthesis,* University of Georgia, 1988.

Even if the text author has provided an analogy for a key concept, teachers and students may wish to generate another one so they can examine the concept from more than one perspective. For example, the author might use a "flowing water" analogy to explain the concept of electric current. The teacher and students, however, wishing to examine the concept from a different perspective, might generate a "moving crowd" analogy, in which electric current is compared to masses of people moving through tunnels.

The advantage of generating alternative analogies and viewing a concept from more than one perspective is that each perspective brings particular features of the concept into clearer focus. Thus, the teacher and the students who generate multiple analogies for a concept will have a more comprehensive understanding of that concept and its relationship to other concepts.

Although the focus in this chapter has been on the elementary school teacher's use of the TWA model, high school and college teachers also are encouraged to use it. Analogical reasoning can facilitate comprehension in students of all ages.

Conclusions

This chapter has shown that one of the most effective ways for students to integrate their existing knowledge with text content is by using analogical reasoning. Teachers and text authors can provide analogies for students, and students can be trained to generate their own analogies.

Analogies can put new concepts into familiar terms for students. Analogies can be used to transfer ideas from a familiar concept (the analog) to an unfamiliar one (the target).

In the representation of an analogy presented here, the analog and the target are subordinate to a superordinate concept. The identification and naming of the superordinate concept can suggest other analogies; it also can stimulate students to generalize what they have learned and apply their learning to other contexts.

An analogy should be used cautiously. An analog concept can be used to correctly explain and even predict some aspects of the target concept. At some point, however, every analogy breaks down. At that point, miscomprehension and misdirection can begin. Teachers and authors must make students aware of this.

Analogies drawn by a teacher or author between concepts covered early in a text and concepts covered later are particularly effective because there is some assurance that the earlier concepts (which function as analogs) are part of every student's knowledge base. These analogies prompt students to connect related text concepts and form conceptual systems.

Analogies which are effective from the standpoint of instructional design contain certain key features which have been incorporated into a model. The Teaching with Analogies model can serve as a guide for teachers and textbook authors. It can also serve as a guide for students who wish to interpret, criticize, and extend an instructional analogy or create one of their own.

References

Alexander, P., White, C., Haensly, P., and Crimmins-Jeanes, M. Training in analogical reasoning. *American Educational Research Journal*, 1987, *24*, 387-404.

Alexander, P., White, C., and Mangano, N. Examining the effects of direct comprehension in analogical reasoning on reading comprehension. In J. Niles and L. Harris (Eds.), *Searches for meaning in reading/language processing and instruction*. Rochester, NY: National Reading Conference, 1983, 36-41.

Barufaldi, J., Ladd, G., and Moses, A. *Heath science*. Lexington, MA: Heath, 1981.

Bean, T., Singer, H., and Cowan, S. Analogical study guides: Improving comprehension in science. *Journal of Reading*, 1985, *29*, 246-250.

Britton, B., and Glynn, S. (Eds.). *Executive control processes in reading*. Hillsdale, NJ: Erlbaum, 1987.

Britton, B., Glynn, S., Meyer, B., and Penland, M. Effects of text structure on use of cognitive capacity during reading. *Journal of Educational Psychology*, 1982, *74*, 51-61.

Brown, D., and Clement, J. *Overcoming misconceptions in mechanics: A comparison of two example based teaching strategies*. Paper presented at the American Educational Research Association meeting, Washington, DC, April 1987.

Gick, M., and Holyoak, K. Analogical problem solving. *Cognitive Psychology*, 1980, *12*, 306-355.

Gick, M., and Holyoak, K. Schema induction and analogical transfer. *Cognitive Psychology*, 1983, *75*, 1-38.

Glynn, S. Capturing readers' attention by means of typographical cuing strategies. *Educational Technology*, 1978, *18* (11), 7-12.

Glynn, S., Andre, T., and Britton, B. The design of instructional text: Introduction to the special issue. *Educational Psychologist*, 1986, *21*, 245-251.

Glynn, S., and Britton, B. *Explaining concepts in physics textbooks: A Teaching with Analogies* (TWA) *model*. Paper presented at the American Psychological Association meeting, Atlanta, August 1988.

Glynn, S., and Britton, B. Supporting readers' comprehension through effective text design. *Educational Technology*, 1984, *24* (10), 40-43.

Glynn, S., Britton, B., and Muth, K. Text comprehension strategies based on outlines: Immediate and long term effects. *Journal of Experimental Education*, 1985, *53*, 129-135.

Glynn, S., Britton, B., Semrud-Clikeman, M., and Muth, K. Analogical reasoning and problem solving in science textbooks. In J. Glover, R. Ronning, and C. Reynolds (Eds.), *Handbook of creativity: Assessment, research, and theory*. New York: Plenum, in press.

Glynn, S., Britton, B., and Tillman, M. Typographical cues in text: Management of the reader's attention. In D. Jonassen (Ed.), *The technology of text*, volume 2. Englewood Cliffs, NJ: Educational Technology Publications, 1985, 192-209.

Glynn, S., and Di Vesta, F. Control of prose processing via instructional and typographical cues. *Journal of Educational Psychology*, 1979, *71*, 595-603.

Glynn, S., and Di Vesta, F. Outline and hierarchical organization as aids for study and retrieval. *Journal of Educational Psychology*, 1977, *69*, 89-95.

Halpern, D. Analogies as a critical thinking skill. In D. Berger, K. Pezdek, and W. Banks (Eds.), *Applications of cognitive psychology*. Hillsdale, NJ: Erlbaum, 1987.

Hayes, D. *Directing prose learning with analogical study guides*. Paper presented at the American Educational Research Association meeting, Washington, DC, April 1987.

Rosenshine, B. Teaching functions in instructional programs. *The Elementary School Journal*, 1983, *83*, 335-351.

Sloan, P. *Using research-based considerations to develop a science textbook unit about photosynthesis*. Unpublished manuscript, University of Georgia, 1988.

Sternberg, R. *Intelligence applied*. New York: Harcourt Brace Jovanovich, 1985.

Vosniadou, S., and Brewer, W. Theories of knowledge restructuring in development. *Review of Educational Research*, 1987, *57*, 51-67.

Winograd, P., and Hare, V. C. Direct instruction of reading comprehension strategies: The nature of teacher explanation. In C. Weinstein, E. Goetz, and P. Alexander (Eds.), *Learning and study strategies*. San Diego, CA: Academic Press, 1988.

Wittrock, M. Learning science by generating new conceptions from old ideas. In L. West and A. Pines (Eds.), *Cognitive structure and conceptual change*. Orlando, FL: Academic Press, 1985.

9

Donna M. Ogle

The Know, Want to Know, Learn Strategy

> This chapter describes a strategy that helps teachers and students take an active role in reading and learning from expository text. The Know, Want to Know, Learn (KWL) strategy begins as the teacher leads students to brainstorm what they know about a topic and to categorize that information. Students then predict likely important categories and raise questions they want to have answered. During and after reading, students use personal worksheets to record what they are learning and what they want to know. A sample lesson is included to illustrate classroom use of the strategy.

A major requisite for school success is the ability to read and learn from expository text. Almost all school reading, beyond elementary basal instruction and literature classes, is filled with exposition. Teachers assume students know how to read and learn from these materials, yet seldom stop to inform students about how to do so successfully.

In addition to this school need to understand expository material, many students can be nurtured into developing lifelong reading habits if they are made aware of the wonderful world of nonfiction material that addresses their interests. This chapter describes a strategy designed to address these needs. The development of the KWL strategy is presented first, followed by a description of the steps in the strategy and a sample lesson.

Development of the Know, Want to Know, Learn Strategy

Few elementary reading experiences prepare students for expository text. Reading programs focus primarily on narrative text. When teachers use textbooks to teach social studies, science, and other content, they often fail to introduce good reading techniques.

In my ongoing classroom observations in several school districts, I find that the round robin oral reading and discussion format prevails when elementary teachers teach from textbooks and trade materials. In their defense, most say that the materials are too difficult for many of their students to understand independently, so for management purposes they have the whole class reading texts orally, paragraph by paragraph.

As I worked with teachers who were beginning to implement a more interactive approach to their teaching of reading with narrative text (see Fitzgerald, this volume), I challenged them to help me develop a way to build active, personal reading of expository text. The outgrowth is the KWL strategy, built around five criteria that the teachers considered important. As they defined it, the strategy should (1) be adaptable to whole class instruction since most content area work is done in large groups, (2) work with the textbooks and resource materials being used by the students, (3) include some means of involving all the students so that the passive one-third would be held accountable, (4) be flexible enough to be used with poorly structured texts (see Slater, this volume), and (5) model the kind of active reading students need to pursue when reading independently from similar materials.

Importance of Prior Knowledge

As the teachers and I explored options for strategic teaching, our awareness of the research on prior knowledge shaped our thinking and planning. We knew how important readers' prior knowledge is to their construction of meaning (Anderson, 1977; Slater, this volume; Steffensen, 1978). But most important, we knew that prior knowledge needs to be accessed in order to be useful to the reader (Bransford, 1983; Schuder, Clewell, & Jackson, this volume).

Recent work in science education (Anderson & Smith, 1984) has punctuated the need for instruction to begin with an assessment of students' prior knowledge, particularly when the concepts to be taught are counterintuitive. For example, if students think wolves are likely to kill humans, this assumption needs to be elicited so it can be refuted directly. If teachers ignore the assumptions of their students, little learning can be expected.

A related problem identified by Roth (1985) is that many elementary students don't even think of the reading they do in their science textbooks as interacting with their own real world knowledge. When Roth probed students' thinking about their reading, she found that few students even made an effort to connect ideas across sentence boundaries. Only when texts were rewritten to address prior knowledge misconceptions did students begin to compare and contrast ideas with their own assumptions and think about the sense that was possible from their reading.

Importance of Group Learning

Recent research concerning the nature of group learning (Johnson et al., 1984) led us to use the group process as a way of stimulating students' thinking and purpose setting. Vygotsky's (1978) concept of the social nature of learning leads to the challenge for teachers to help students move forward at their "zone of proximal development"—a possibility that can be realized only by watching and listening to students talk and explain their ideas.

Furthermore, Piaget's explication of the importance of conflict in stimulating thinking also made sense intuitively in terms of what we were trying to do in the classrooms. By engaging students as a group in predicting and positing alternate ideas and explanations, cognitive conflict can occur. Perrett-Clermont (1980) explains this concept of cognitive conflict:

> Of course, cognitive conflict of this kind does not create the form of operations, but it brings about the disequilibrium which makes cognitive elaboration necessary, and in this way cognitive conflict confers a special role on the social factor as one among other factors leading to mental growth. Social cognitive conflict may be figuratively likened to the catalyst in a chemical reaction: it is not present at all in the final product, but it is nevertheless indispensable if the reaction is to take place (p.178).

Importance of Engaging All Students through Writing

One of the concerns teachers expressed early in our work together was the need to involve as many students as possible in class learning. Oral discussion worked well for them in reading groups when the number of students was limited to about eight to twelve. However, in the content areas they generally had whole class instruction. In these situations, oral strategies like the traditional Directed Reading Activity (DRA) or even the Directed Reading - Thinking Activity (DRTA) often were not as satisfactory.

Teachers needed a structured way to engage students who didn't have an opportunity to share orally. This led to the development of the worksheet shown in Figure 1. This format allowed all students to write down their own ideas and questions. Teachers could move around the room and respond to written notes during silent reading times, thus making all contributions important. The writing also helped students focus their thinking and become more reflective (Murray, 1984).

As we experimented with various ways to use the worksheet for writing, we discovered that it served as a nice visual model of the steps teachers often engaged in orally but that many students had not previously understood as integral parts of learning. In most oral discussion lessons, teachers do not write down the ideas students suggest, and there is no way to retrieve them later. Through writing, the development of group and individual thinking becomes much more accessible. Yet, when we initially explored having children write as part of their prereading activity, we learned that many were hesitant to write any words they were not sure they could spell correctly. Therefore, we moved to having the teacher do the initial writing of brainstormed ideas and questions until students felt less inhibited.

The Teaching Model

KWL involves readers before, during, and after reading. The teacher models each step and then has students make personal commitments using a three column worksheet (see Figure 1). The first column is for listing what students think they know, the second for listing what students want to learn, and the third for recording what students do learn from their reading.

Figure 1
KWL Strategy Sheet

K – What we know	W – What we want to find out	L – What we learned/ still need to learn

Categories of information we expect to use

A.   E.
B.   F.
C.   G.
D.

From *The Reading Teacher,* February 1986, p. 565

Before Reading

Before the class actually reads the text, the teacher engages students in four steps: brainstorming, categorizing, anticipating, and questioning. Each of these steps is modeled by the teacher first and then transferred to student initiative through use of the worksheet.

Brainstorming. This process begins with the teacher asking students to brainstorm what they think they know about the topic of study. The teacher records all the thoughts on the board for the group to see. For example, one fourth grade class began a unit on the desert by brainstorming the following list of terms: sandy, hills, camels, few trees, cactus, snakes, lizards, peaceful, hot, sandstorms, Arizona, elephants, little water, quicksand, and toads.

Conflicts often ensue during this process, and the teacher can use these conflicts to help the group formulate questions for their reading. For example, students disagreed about what animals lived in the desert, so the teacher encouraged them to write questions: Do elephants live in the desert? What animals live in the desert? Do toads like the desert? These questions go in the "What we want to find out" column (see Figure 2). They provide specific purposes for reading.

Figure 2
KWL Strategy Sheet

What we know	What we want to find out	What we learned
Sandy camels live there cactus high hills hot weather lizards little water Indians live there dry - no water	Do elephants live there? What other animals live on the desert? How can something live without water? Where are deserts? Who lives on them?	

Next, all students make an individual learning preassessment record of what they think they know. Because the teacher has provided the spelling for all the ideas shared orally, even weaker students will be able to write on their own worksheets.

Categorizing. A second, more reflective level of thinking follows. The teacher asks students to look for ways to chunk or categorize the ideas they brainstormed. This step is similar to semantic mapping (Heimlich & Pittelman, 1986), except that students rather than teachers are asked to find categories or groups of ideas that fit together. This process comes after the initial brainstorming rather than as part of it.

For example, the teacher who had her fourth grade students brainstorm what they knew about deserts then helped them identify key categories, which included animals, descriptive words, and plants. In so doing, the basic categories or organizing structures of the topic could be anticipated.

When teachers first initiate this categorizing step into the prereading process, they may find that some students are weak at forming and naming categories. Two activities can help teachers model this categorizing step for their students. First, teachers can record similar ideas together on the board or paper (see Figure 3). The teacher then can ask, "Why did I put those ideas in the same area? What do they have in common?" As students determine the category, they can use the bottom of the KWL Strategy Sheet to list other categories of information they think an author might consider in writing an article on the topic. For example, students anticipated that their study of the desert would include information about animals, plants, climate, physical features, dangers, places, people, and transportation (see Figure 4).

A second way to model categorization from brainstorming is to do a think-aloud in front of the class. For example, the teacher might point to the words in the first column and say, "I see here four ideas about animals that live in the desert—toads, lizards, camels, and elephants. Those certainly are examples of an important topic, so I want to remember that category—animals. I will probably learn about some other animals as I read. What is another category that we already know something about? Can someone find two or three

Figure 3
Identifying Categories

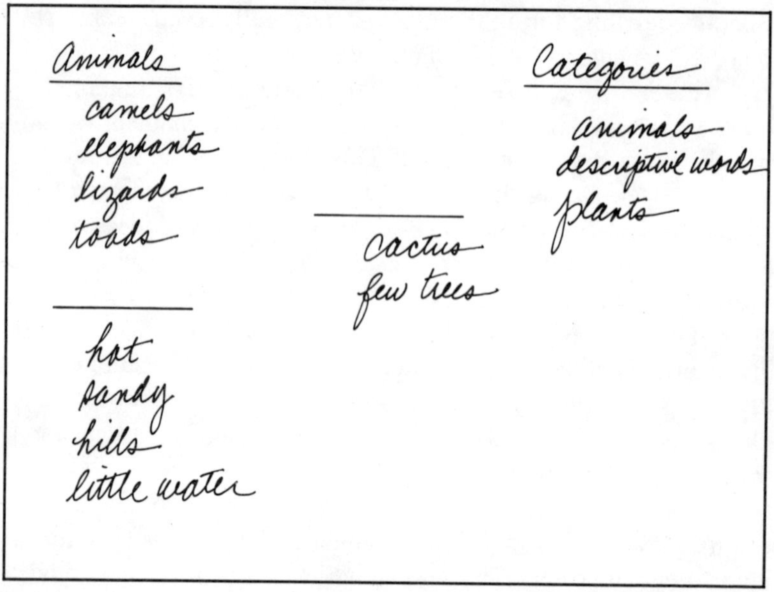

```
animals                                    Categories
  camels                                     animals
  elephants                                  descriptive words
  lizards                                    plants
  toads
                    cactus
                    few trees
  hot
  sandy
  hills
  little water
```

words that tell about the physical features of the desert? What are they? The teacher can write these categories on the board and have students list them on the bottom of their own worksheets. Then the group can identify each of the brainstormed list of items by the appropriate category. The students can then proceed to identify the appropriate categories for the information they wrote on their own worksheets by putting the correct letter of the category beside each item (see Figure 4).

Anticipating. Students also become proficient at reading expository text by anticipating the basic categories that should be included by authors. To initiate this process, the teacher might say, "Let's take a different perspective for a few minutes. If we were going to write an article on the desert, what topics or categories of information would we want to include for our readers? What would our audience need to know about deserts?"

Figure 4
KWL Strategy Sheet

What we know	What we want to find out	What we learned/ still need to learn
D - lots of sand A - camels A - lizards & toads C - hot & dry D - little water G - Indians F - Arizona F - Texas		

Categories of information we expect to use
A. Animals
B. Plants
C. Climate
D. Physical features
E. Dangers
F. Location
G. People
H. Transportation

In the elementary grades, many articles or chapters will be descriptive, telling about animals, events, or phenomena. Students should learn to anticipate the basic categories of information that are associated with the topic of study. For example, an article about an animal will generally include information about appearance, habitat, protective devices, enemies, raising young, family patterns, special characteristics, and eating habits.

By anticipating categories that authors should include on a certain topic, students approach reading already thinking of higher order categories and ways to organize the myriad of facts that so often drown young readers and kill their interest in expository text. Combined with the group discussion of the prior knowledge assumptions, the personal assessment of knowledge, and the generation of questions to guide reading, this additional "author or content" perspective establishes a rich framework for reading and learning.

Questioning. The teacher's role in identifying questions that will guide readers' search for knowledge is an extremely important one. As a class brainstorms and thinks of categorical structures, differences of opinion are nearly inevitable. The teacher should help articulate areas of partial knowledge and conflicting information and also help students focus on important questions. Asking probing questions such as "What do you mean by that?" or "Can you tell more about that?" can help students form their own questions and help develop interest in the topic.

A teacher should not initiate the reading of the text until some real questions to guide the reading have emerged from the group. Sometimes just asking "What do you want to find out?" is enough to get a group started. The teacher then writes the questions on the board so all can see. Before reading, students write on their own worksheets (see Figure 2) those questions that are most important to them. Again, the teacher has provided a model of questions with the words correctly spelled so students can make their own lists quickly. Initially, some students might feel bound to write everything on the teacher's list. However, the longer the group uses this process, the more individual the questions become.

During Reading

The teacher must determine the length of the teaching units. Depending on the difficulty of the material and the students' familiarity with the topic, some pieces can be read in their entirety before stopping to discuss and order ideas. Long pieces should be read in shorter units with discussion interspersed for clarifying and building a knowledge framework.

The students' task is to read actively, looking for new information and answers to their questions. Teachers need to make it clear that authors often provide new information that the class might

Figure 5
KWL Strategy Sheet

What we know	What we want to find out	What we learned
		many animals live on deserts - gila monsters, kangaroo rats, coyotes. Dunes are moving hills of sand. Navajo people live on the desert. They do dry farming There are deserts in Arizona & California

not have anticipated. As a result, there is always an exciting interaction of author and reader. The students should be instructed to jot down new information on their worksheets (see Figure 5) so they can recall it later.

After Reading

After reading each segment of text and again after the entire text is completed, the class needs to reflect on the "L" or Learned column. (See Figure 6 for an example of how one child, with a teacher's help, structured her learning.) At this time, the teacher can again create a class list of all that has been learned. From that list, students have another opportunity to clarify meaning and categorize the new knowledge by organizing what they have learned.

This is also an ideal time to help students reflect on the amount of learning that has occurred. If the teacher has kept the

Laura

Figure 6
KWL Strategy Sheet

What we know	What we want to find out	What we learned/ still need to learn
animals camels snakes ant eaters Weather hot Lots of sand dunes not lots of water Grows pecan trees Cactuses Has platues	What else grows? How animals servive? Does anyone live there? Were dessats are? How do plants servive? Where do people get water from when it's not raining	Plants servive because they have a thick leaves that don't vaporate easly. Desert plants cactus small low bushes Land formation flowers canyons from rain mountain dunes Animals 1. Ants, spiders, beatles and other insects 2. Gila monsters, Road runners, Kangaroo rat, owls, bats, foxes, bobcats, coyotes

Categories of information we expect to use
A. Animals
B. Plants
C. Weather
D. Land formations
E. Age
F. Size
G.

initial list of what students thought they knew, the misconceptions should have become apparent to students during the course of their study. Some teachers encourage students to keep revising that original list, deleting, adding, or changing parts as necessary. For example, on the class list about deserts, students learned that elephants are not really animals of the desert and crossed off that name. They also altered the information about camels to say "not native to America." Using different colored Magic Markers, students can revise, change, and add more precise information. This demonstrates the teacher's acceptance of students' incomplete entry knowledge and provides a process by which that knowledge can be accommodated. The revisions that students make help them focus on the process of learning and develop control of that process.

If there is a need to study and retain the new information, then extending the strategy to include semantic mapping (Heimlich & Pittelman, 1986) and summary writing (Carr & Ogle, 1987) can be valuable. By reorganizing the categories into a visual diagram, students make the new information their own. They then elaborate on that knowledge when they write a summary. By using the visual diagram with the categories and details clearly identified, summaries become fairly easy to write. Each category becomes one paragraph after the main topic has been identified and explained.

Sample Lesson

This classroom vignette took place as a teacher was introducing a new unit of study to her fourth grade students, who were somewhat familiar with the KWL process.

Before Reading Activities

Teacher: (Brainstorming begins) Today we are going to begin a unit about how animals and humans support one another. The first two articles and story deal with the relationships between wolves and people. Before we begin reading, let's think a little about what we know about wolves already and what we might learn. I'll record on the board what you think you know. You can brainstorm for a few minutes as a group.

Tom: I think they are related to dogs, but that they are wild and dangerous.

Danny: Yeah, I think they kill people when they are mad.

Suzanne: I remember seeing a movie of wolves in the mountains. They were hungry and looking for food. I think they were eating sheep.

Terry: They don't live in this part of the country. I don't even know if they still live out west.

Barbara: I thought they lived in the desert. If they eat sheep, they wouldn't be in the mountains.

Ann: They are big and gray.

Peter: And they make howling noises at night. I heard one on TV.

Terry: I think they have fangs and long ears.

AnnMarie: They are carnivorous; they eat meat. Any kind. And I think they live in Canada, not in the U.S.

Joshua: I think they are endangered. I remember a TV program about how few wolves are left. They are scarce.

Teacher: (Categorizing begins) Well, class. You do have some images of wolves. Look at the information listed on the board. Now write on your own strategy sheets whatever you think you personally know about wolves even before we start reading and studying. (pause)

Can we organize some of that information into chunks or categories? It seems to me that some of these ideas are about where the wolves live—their habitat. What words could we group together about habitat?

Sandra: Mountains, deserts, west, and Canada all fit together.

Teacher: Yes, they are all about the habitat of the wolf. Can you find other pieces of information that fit together in a category?

John: I think gray, fangs, and large ears all tell about the appearance of the wolf, what it looks like.

AnnMarie: Don't howl and carnivorous tell about their characteristics?

Peter: And scarce and endangered fit together because they tell about them now. They are animals that need protection.

Teacher: Good, class, you have found some important categories of information about wolves that we will want to expand on as we read. Let's list these and others that we think are important for our learning on our worksheets. I'll put them on the board first just as I did for what we brainstormed. Already we know something about their appearance, their characteristics, their habitat, and about their being endangered.

Teacher: (Anticipating begins) Are there other topics we can expect to learn about as we read about this animal and its relationship to people?

Peter: We didn't say anything about what kinds of homes they live in or what they eat.

Teacher: Yes, and those are both important categories of information that we should expect. Are there any others?

Sandra: We should find out how they protect themselves and who their enemies are.

John: And are people doing anything to protect them so they won't become extinct.

Teacher: Very good. I think you have included some of the most important categories we need to look for as we read. Get out your worksheets now and list on them the things you think you already know about wolves and the categories we are expecting to learn about.

Teacher: (Questioning begins) Now that you have done that, we should be ready with some specific questions for which we need answers. What do you want to find out about wolves? I will put your questions on the big paper, too, and when we find the answers you can write them for the whole class to see.

AnnMarie: I want to know if they really would kill people.

Teacher: Good concern. Just how dangerous are they to us?

Terry: I want to know where they really live.

Sandra: I want to know how they take care of their babies.

Teacher: Good thinking, Sandra. We didn't list family life as one of our categories, but we could. Let's put that question under "What we want to find out" and also add family life to our categories. (Discussion about specific questions continues)

The Know, Want to Know, Learn Strategy

Teacher: Now, record your own questions on your worksheets and then start reading.

During Reading

Teacher: Let's read the first two paragraphs silently. When you are finished, record on the worksheet what you have learned. Remember, you may find out that some of our initial ideas weren't quite right, and so we will have to revise what we wrote. I will do that on the big paper here, and you can do the same on your own worksheet.
(Class reads)

Teacher: What did we learn in these paragraphs? What topics or categories did the author start with? Which of your questions were answered?

John: I found out that wolves are endangered. There aren't many of them left.

Peter: Yeah, and there are some in the Rockies, but not many.

Suzanne: And they do kill animals—especially sheep.

Teacher: Yes, there was specific information about where some wolves live and why people kill them. Let's revise our original ideas now. What should we cross out as being inaccurate? What information does this author confirm? Let's put plus (+) marks by the ideas the author confirms. (And so discussion of the reading proceeds)

After Reading

After both articles had been read, the teacher had the students finish their strategy sheets and discuss all they had learned. They also identified some areas they had not learned about—specifically about how to protect wolves in the future. Then, as a way of visualizing their new knowledge, students worked together in pairs and created a chart of what they had learned. The basic categories that were generated before reading served as a framework for students' organization. Figure 7 contains a sample of one student's work.

Figure 7
KWL Strategy Sheet

Terry

What we know	What we want to find out	What we learned/ still need to learn
Wolves live in Canada. they like the woods They are dangerous & wild, gray & howl fangs & long ears eat meat-carnivorous dangerous to people	Do they attack people? Where do they live? Are they endangered? How do they care for their babies?	Wolves are endangered, People killed them because they eat sheep & horses. They don't attack humans They live mostly in Canada in the mountains They are intelligent. Wolf families live together and help each other.

Categories of information we expect to use
A. Habitat
B. Appearance
C. Characteristics
D. Endangered
E. Homes
F. Self-defense
G. Family life

Summary

Learning begins when students have a sense of disequilibrium in their own knowledge and are stimulated to want to learn. The KWL is a simple, teacher guided process that actively engages a class in learning. Brainstorming, categorizing, anticipating, and questioning all model the reality that the learning process begins with the learner. Using knowledge categories and searching for important information makes it clear that both the learner and the author need to be taken seriously. The reflection that goes on after reading is important as a clarification time for showing whether students have learned all that is important and whether misconceptions still remain.

Classroom research studies (Dewitz & Carr, 1987; Ogle & Jennings, 1987) have provided confirmation of the effectiveness of both KWL and KWL-Plus in enhancing students' learning in social studies. In addition, tests of students' ability to internalize the process for independent learning also have been demonstrated for elementary and remedial secondary students (Carr & Ogle, 1986).

Students can enjoy learning from content laden expository materials when we provide them with strategies that are adequate for the intellectual tasks they face. The KWL is one initial strategy that teachers can use as they work to meet that goal.

References

Anderson, R.C. The notion of schemata and the educational enterprise. In R.C. Anderson, R.J. Spiro, and W.E. Montaque (Eds.), *Schooling and the acquisition of knowledge.* Hillsdale, NJ: Erlbaum, 1977, 15-31.

Anderson, R.C., and Smith, E. Children's preconceptions and content area textbooks. In G. Duffy, L. Roehler, and J. Mason (Eds.), *Comprehension instruction: Perspectives and suggestions.* New York: Longman, 1984, 187-201.

Bransford, J. Schema activation—schema acquisition. In R.C. Anderson, J. Osborn, and R.J. Tierney (Eds.), *Learning to read in American schools.* Hillsdale, NJ: Erlbaum, 1983, 259-272.

Carr, E., and Ogle, D. *Improving disabled readers' summarization skills.* Paper presented at the annual meeting of the National Reading Conference, Austin, Texas, December 1986.

Carr, E., and Ogle, D. K-W-L Plus: A strategy for comprehension and summarization. *Journal of Reading,* 1987, *30,* 626-631.

Dewitz, P., & Carr, E.M. *Teaching comprehension as a student directed process.* Paper presented at the annual meeting of the National Reading Conference, St. Petersburg, Florida, December 1987.

Heimlich, J.E., & Pittelman, S.D. *Semantic mapping: Classroom applications.* Newark, DE: International Reading Association, 1986.

Johnson, D.W., Johnson, F., Holub, C.E., and Roy, P. *Circle of learning: cooperation in the classroom.* Alexandria, VA: Association for Supervision and Curriculum Development, 1984.

Murray, D. *Write to learn.* New York: Holt, Rinehart and Winston, 1984.

Ogle, D., & Jennings, J. *Teaching comprehension as a teacher directed process.* Paper presented at the annual meeting of the National Reading Conference, St. Petersburg, Florida, December 1987.

Perrett-Clermont, A.N. *Social interaction and cognitive development in children.* New York: Academic Press, 1980.

Roth, K. *Conceptual change learning and student processing of science texts.* Paper presented at the meeting of the American Educational Research Association, Chicago, April 1985.

Slavin, R.D. *Cooperative learning.* New York: Longman, 1983.

Steffenson, M., Jogded, C., and Anderson, C. *A cross-cultural perspective on reading comprehension*, 1978. (ED 159 660)

Vygotsky, L.S. *Mind in society: The development of higher psychological processes.* M. Cole, J.V. Steiner, S. Scribner, and E. Souberman (Eds.). Cambridge: Harvard University Press, 1978.

10

Ted Schuder
Suzanne F. Clewell
Nan Jackson

Getting the Gist of Expository Text

The strategy introduced in this chapter is a simple, highly motivating way to teach some basic reading comprehension processes in elementary school. It is made up of seven generic prompts which teachers can use to model and coach students through the process of constructing and evaluating an interpretation of expository text. The gist strategy is based on the common conceptualization of reading comprehension as hypothesis formation and evaluation, which is illustrated and discussed in the first section of this chapter. The second section describes the strategy and compares it with traditional reading practices. A sample lesson illustrates the use of the strategy with a social studies class in sixth grade, and the chapter ends with a discussion of that lesson and the use of the strategy in different contexts.

In 1979, John Bransford illustrated reading comprehension processes with three cartoon figures. The first frame showed what appeared to be a football player running downfield with arms outstretched. Based on a football game scenario, viewers expected the next frame to show him catching a pass or tackling an opposing player. Instead, the second frame revealed a woman in apparent flight from the football player. This frame caused viewers to reinterpret the situation as a damsel in distress or a cheerleader confused about her role in the game. Is he chasing her, or is she trying to catch the pass herself? These interpretations of the situation led to different expectations about the next frame, which were in turn thwarted by the appearance of a lion, jaws agape, in hot pursuit of the football player and the woman. At that point, viewers might impose a mascot gone amok interpretation on these events, sticking to their football game scenario, or perhaps some variation on the games in the Roman Coliseum, switching interpretations radically.

Their interpretations and predictions are limited only by their background knowledge, imaginations, and the data. That's reading. In fact, it's more than reading. It's hypothesis formation and evaluation.

Reading as Hypothesis Formation and Evaluation

An analogy between reading comprehension processes and hypothesis formation and evaluation is widely used throughout recent reading research literature (Afflerbach, 1987; Bruce & Rubin, 1984; Collins & Smith, 1982; Goodman, 1967, 1986; Johnston & Afflerbach, 1985; Orasanu & Penney, 1986; Smith, 1975, 1982; Spiro, Bruce, & Brewer, 1980; Stauffer, 1969). Collins and Smith make an important distinction between two kinds of hypotheses, both of which are essential to reading comprehension: (1) interpretations are hypotheses about what has *already happened* in a text, and (2) predictions are hypotheses about what is *going to happen* in a text.

Although teachers are more familiar with predictions in narration, predictions are equally appropriate to exposition, as we will illustrate in this chapter. In fact, the two kinds of hypotheses described by Collins and Smith and illustrated by responses to Bransford's cartoon figures seem to be appropriate to the interpretation of many kinds of information and codes (pictures, text, numbers). Strategies based on the hypothesis formation and evaluation analogy should, therefore, be generalizable across text types and across subject areas (e.g., reading and science instruction).

Reading Comprehension Processes

To get a full sense of the hypothesis formation and evaluation analogy, we can think of reading comprehension as a process of constructing and evaluating an interpretation of a text where the interpretation is understood to be a hypothesis about the meaning of the text. Hypotheses are both products (interpretations and predictions) and an essential part of the processes of reading comprehension, as we will illustrate.

Assuming that someone is reading for gist (the overall sense of the text), a common purpose in exposition, reading as hypothesis formation and evaluation could be illustrated as a set of Venn diagrams organized by prereading, reading, and postreading stages as in Figure 1. The top circle on the left represents background knowledge that becomes specific schemata when activated by contact with the text (Rumelhart, 1980). For example, given some information about a cherry tree chopping episode, the reader might activate an organized body of knowledge including an instrument (ax or hatchet), an agent (George Washington), and some of the attributes of that agent ("I cannot tell a lie"). The circle on the right represents the text, which reveals itself chunk by chunk as the reader moves through it. The activation of text and background knowledge is indicated by the movement from dashes to solid lines on the circles.

Figure 1 shows that background knowledge is activated well before text knowledge. This means that more information is coming from the head than from the text, especially in early stages of the reading process. Collins, Brown, and Larkin (1980), Rumelhart (1980), Johnston and Afflerbach (1985), and Afflerbach (1987) provide clear evidence for this phenomenon in interviews with skilled readers. Given mere scraps of information such as a title, an illustration, or a few sentences of text, expert readers often advance tentative hypotheses about what is going on (interpretations) and what is probably going to happen next (predictions). These tentative hypotheses are based on activated schemata, highly organized sets of information which make inferences and hypotheses possible (Rumelhart, 1980).

The third circle in the middle on Figure 1 represents the hypothesis. It is a function of the interactions between text and background knowledge, and those interactions are driven by the reader's purpose(s). In the case of reading exposition for gist, the hypothesis first emerges as a topic—what the text is going to be about in terms of general or specific subject matter. By step 3 in Figure 1, with very little contact with the text, skillful readers have already made a tentative hypothesis, more or less consciously, about the gist (topic and comment) from clues such as the title and pictures. Hypotheses in narration generally center on events, whereas hypotheses in exposition generally center on topics and comments about them.

The text in Figure 1 is thought of as a cue system activating responses in the reader (steps 2 through 4) and used to verify the appropriateness of those responses (step 5). In step 6, which may recur several times as the reader progresses through the text, enough evidence accumulates to allow the reader to confirm the hypothesis, revise the hypothesis, or disconfirm the hypothesis and generate a new one. In that decision making process, the hypothesis is evaluated against activated background knowledge and an organized set of cues in the text—in effect, two separate but related bodies of information against which the hypothesis is matched for "goodness of fit" (Rumelhart, 1980). The hypothesis has to make sense in light of the reader's knowledge of the world and must be supported by the cues and their organization in the text.

A Gist Strategy*

The easiest way to get from Figure 1, which helps to clarify the process, to materials for students is to translate the steps in the process into prompts. If the prompts work, we can eliminate the gap between what we ask as teachers and what we expect the students to do when we are not around. The teacher uses the prompts to model and think aloud (Davey, 1983) through the reading comprehension process and then coaches students in asking themselves the same questions while reading. Students consciously use the prompts to guide reading processes until they become the internalized, rapid, and automated processes of independent readers.

Prereading

Figure 2 is a simple series of seven prompts that picks up the reading comprehension process where readers first meet the text (step 2, Figure 1). The first direction on the left of Figure 2 is

---

*Cunningham's (1982) strategy was also dubbed the GIST procedure (Generating Interactions between Schema and Text). His teacher directed procedure emphasizes the written construction of text summaries from memory and is very different from the more informal, naturalistic, on line reading comprehension processes illustrated in this chapter.

Figure 1
An Illustration of the Role of Schema and Text in Constructing and Evaluating an Interpretation of Text

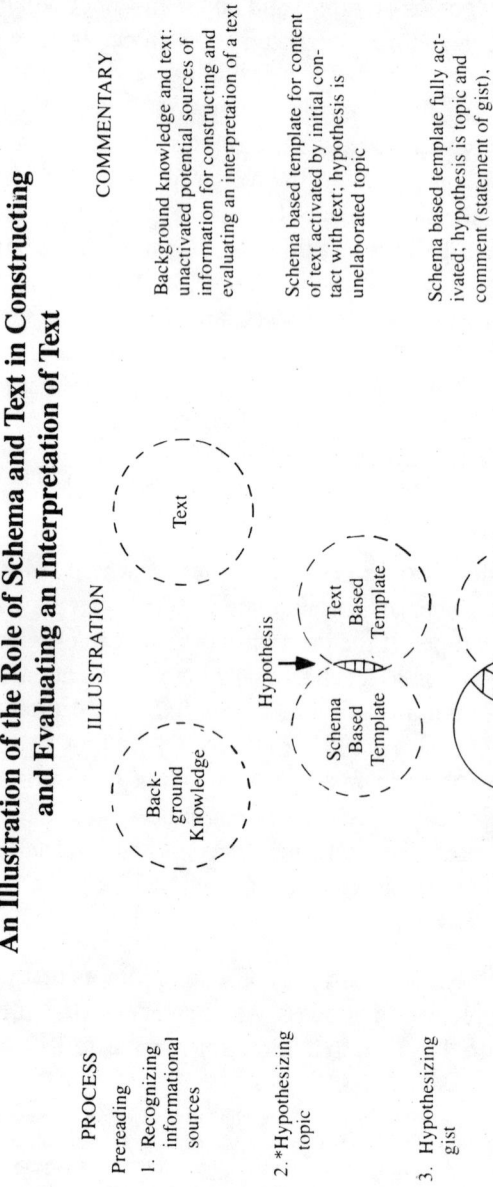

PROCESS	ILLUSTRATION	COMMENTARY
Prereading		
1. Recognizing informational sources	Background Knowledge / Text	Background knowledge and text: unactivated potential sources of information for constructing and evaluating an interpretation of a text
2. *Hypothesizing topic	Hypothesis → Text Based Template / Schema Based Template	Schema based template for content of text activated by initial contact with text; hypothesis is unelaborated topic
3. Hypothesizing gist	TBT / SBT	Schema based template fully activated: hypothesis is topic and comment (statement of gist), driven by schema

Reading

4. Elaborating hypothesis — Adding detail to the hypothesis; hypothesis is evolving, driven by schema; asymmetry is inferences

5. Verifying hypothesis — Exploring the goodness of fit between schema and text based templates; text driven process

6. Evaluating hypothesis — Hypothesis evaluated against schema and text based templates; decision making on status of hypothesis

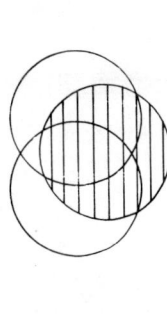

Postreading

7. Consolidating and evaluating hypothesis — Interpretation of text emerges as construct constrained by but independent of both schema and text

*Steps 2 through 6 are recursive as reader entertains multiple hypotheses and encounters new "chunks" of text.

Note: Discontinuous lines on the perimeters of the circles indicate unactivated informational sources. Continuous lines indicate fully activated schema and text read so far.

Getting the Gist of Expository Text

Figure 2
Directions and Prompts for Helping Students Get the Gist of Exposition

	Direction	Prompt
Prereading	In the next (two) minutes, scan the ...(page, chapter, unit) to see what it is going to be about. Record predictions about topic and gist on board, chart paper, or overhead.	1. What do you think this...(chapter, unit, page) is going to be about? What makes you think so? 2. What do you think...(the text) is going to tell you about...(predicted topic)? What makes you think so?
During reading	Read the first/next...(paragraph or larger chunk) to find out if it supports your prediction. List and/or diagram relationships between evidence and statements of gist on the board, chart paper, or overhead. Record changes, if any, in statements of predicted gist.	3. Did you find evidence that supports your prediction? What was it? 4. Did you find evidence that does not support your prediction? What was it? 5. Do you want to change your prediction at this point? If not, why not? If you do, how do you want to change it?
Postreading	Think about what you have just read. Make a final revision of the statement about the gist. Record final changes, if any. Discuss.	6. Do you want to make any changes in your statement of what this is about? If yes, what changes do you want to make? Why do you want to make those changes? 7. What did you learn that you did not know before reading?

Questions may be omitted if the students supply the information prior to prompting. Note: Prompts are recursive as the students entertain multiple hypotheses and/or move to new chunks of text or read other texts on the same topic.

intended to limit readers' first sight of the text so they are forced to attend to highlighted features such as titles, pictures, and boldfaced words, rather than reading the text line by line. These textual features are important signals from the author to readers in exposition. The teacher can control students' access to the text by asking them to open and close their textbooks or other print material or displaying the text briefly on an overhead projector.

The first prompt, "What do you think this material is going to be about?" is traditional and elicits a general or specific prediction of the topic of the text. The second part of Prompt 1, "What makes you think so?" is less traditional. It requires students to verify the prediction by citing the textual evidence that engendered it. This increases the quality of the predicted topics in comparison with simply accepting students' predictions. The teacher is nonjudgmental, encouraging students of all ability levels to cite supporting evidence. As students learn to do this, the quality of that evidence can be increased by brief follow up comments and questions encouraging student reasoning processes. For example, the teacher might cite evidence to support students' hypotheses or elaborate on students' evidence (modeling), ask where the students' evidence comes from (raising consciousness of informational sources and their use), or cite conflicting evidence and ask the students how to respond to the (apparent) conflict. Palincsar and Brown (1986) showed how explicit attention to mental processes is effective as early as grade one.

The second prompt in Figure 2, "What do you think the... (text) is going to tell you about...(the predicted topic)?" breaks sharply with traditional practice by asking the students to predict not only the topic, but the commentary on it prior to reading. The rationale is that the prereading prompts are designed to activate relevant background knowledge and to motivate students to look for evidence in support of a knowledge based prediction. Merely predicting topic fails to engage students fully. Some predictions are silly, irrelevant, or otherwise not worth evaluating. Citing evidence helps to improve the quality of the predictions, but predicted topics are still too text based to motivate students to read. The second prompt forces students to fully activate relevant background knowledge by requiring them to state something about the topic. The response has to be a complete statement, and the only information available to elaborate on the topic comes from background knowledge. The follow up question, "What makes you think so?" makes the informational source and reasoning processes explicit.

Drawing a complete statement of gist out of students without bogging down requires skill, persistence, and sensitivity to timing and pacing. Students familiar with traditional practices will often elaborate on the topic without saying anything substantive about it. For example, predictions about "toads" become predictions about "chartreuse spotted dwarf toads." The teacher must prod students into formulating a complete statement of predicted gist: "So you think the text is about toads, but what will it *tell you* about those toads?"

The differences are dramatic between reading behavior based on a predicted topic and that based on predicted gist with supporting evidence. In traditional practices, there is a certain amount of fidgeting, looking around, questioning, or pencil sharpening between making a prediction and reading to evaluate it. In this gist strategy, the students fairly leap upon the text "like hungry wolves" (Jackson, 1985). Full activation of relevant background knowledge in direct response to textual cues is highly motivating. The student has committed personal resources to the reading activity and is not likely to take that commitment lightly. Richek, List, and Learner (in press) confirm the consistent motivational power of the gist strategy with remedial readers.

In this strategy, neither background knowledge nor vocabulary is developed prior to encountering the text. Instead, relevant background knowledge is activated in direct response to attempts to make sense of the text. This practice avoids overgeneralized background knowledge (noise) created by having students cite everything they know about a topic prior to reading. The gist strategy also increases the direct attention to reading comprehension processes and the actual time spent reading. Vocabulary is first encountered in the context of a fully activated semantic network and a student motivated to get the gist of the text. Vocabulary and key concepts can be revisited for more focused attention following an initial reading for gist. Students need multiple encounters with the same text to develop fluency (Allington, 1983) and learn new concepts.

During Reading

Prompts 3 and 4 on Figure 2, "Did you find evidence that supports or does not support your prediction?" require students to cite evidence for and/or against their hypotheses as they proceed through each chunk of the text. In these prompts, the teacher is leading students to make decisions about the quality of that evidence. This nonjudgmental response on the part of the teacher is critical to participation by students with a history of failure in school. There is also an important distinction between citing supporting evidence and proving an assertion. Proof is much too rigorous a criterion for this process, just as acceptance of any response without evidence was much too loose a criterion for reading instruction.

As evidence accumulates for and/or against any hypothesis, the teacher encourages students in Prompt 5 to begin to decide whether or not the hypothesis is still tenable. There are several possibilities: confirm the hypothesis as stated, revise the hypothesis to better conform with the evidence, or reject the hypothesis and formulate a new one in light of the evidence.

This point in the gist strategy is quite diagnostic. Jackson (1985) found several revealing response patterns. One group of fourth grade students tended to resist any change in their hypotheses in spite of overwhelming textual evidence to the contrary. These students tended to rely excessively on background knowledge at the expense of textual cues. At the other extreme, another group of fourth graders tended to abandon their hypotheses in the face of the first piece of conflicting evidence from the text. These students relied excessively on text at the expense of background knowledge. This latter group is easily confused by the many textbooks with introductions, sophisticated heads, and transitional pieces written as if the audience were adults.

The instructional implications are clear for both groups. The inflexible readers must be encouraged to change their hypotheses in response to evidence, and the other group must be taught to persist a little longer with their knowledge based predictions. Suspending judgment temporarily while evidence accrues is an important problem solving strategy.

Prompts 1 through 5 are recursive as the teacher proceeds through the text with the students. In the beginning, the teacher "chunks" the text for the students. As students become more proficient, they should begin to segment the text themselves, moving toward independence. This can be monitored and encouraged by asking students to indicate when they are ready to confirm, disconfirm, or revise their hypotheses and when they want to make additional predictions.

Postreading

The postreading stage (Prompts 6 and 7) produces a final hypothesis about the meaning of the text and a better understanding of how the text, background knowledge, and the readers' purpose(s) contributed to that understanding. It has been our experience that student statements of gist or main idea produced with the gist strategy often are superior to those written in the text itself or in the teacher's edition of the text. Students also become critical of text characteristics such as misleading heads, insufficient transitional markers and supporting detail, or subsections that contribute little or nothing to the gist. They are then less likely to be victimized by less than perfect text. It is a liberating experience for weak readers to discover that the textbooks themselves often cause misunderstandings.

The Gist Strategy and the DRTA

The foregoing description of the gist strategy may bring to mind Stauffer's (1969) Directed Reading-Thinking Activity (DRTA). Like the DRTA, the gist strategy emphasizes reading as a thinking process and the conscious interactions between reader and text. Both strategies emphasize hypothesizing and the use of evidence to confirm or disconfirm predictions, and both avoid preteaching vocabulary, opting instead to return to vocabulary and "skills" following initial reading for meaning.

There are, however, some important differences between the gist strategy and the DRTA. The DRTA entertains possible new purposes (questions) and perhaps new hypotheses with each new chunk of the text. In sharp contrast, the gist strategy is driven by only one compelling purpose—to get the gist of the text. To continue or not to continue with any given hypothesis across each successive chunk of text is inconsequential in the DRTA; in the gist strategy, it is the major decision facing the reader. The gist strategy forces the reader to integrate information from background knowledge and text and across chunks of text. It focuses on coherence of text, background knowledge, and interpretation. The principal source of evidence in the DRTA is the text itself, whereas the gist strategy gives equal play to text and background knowledge. The product of the gist strategy is a single, highly honed statement of the gist of the text, whereas the DRTA focuses on the process of predicting-reading-proving as an end in itself. Finally, the gist strategy comprises a simple set of prompts intended to be internalized by the student. The DRTA is much more complex and open-ended in its verbalization and teacher directed in practice.

Despite these differences, teachers who are familiar with the DRTA can add the gist strategy to their repertoire easily.

Sample Lesson

The Context

The lesson discussed here was taught to a heterogeneous class of twenty-six sixth graders in midyear in the context of a social studies unit on ancient Greece. Under the guidance of their regular classroom teacher, the students had been experimenting with the gist strategy once or twice a week over a period of two months. This particular lesson took about forty-five minutes to teach.

The Text

The lesson focused on a section entitled "Women of Ancient Greece" (Abramovitz & Job, 1981) in the students' social studies textbook (a copy of the text is reproduced at the end of this chapter). The text begins with a fairly typical introductory paragraph on the role of men in Greek society and contrasts the role of Greek women with that of Greek men by asking a rhetorical question. The main body of the text starts in the second paragraph with two sentences that amount to the main idea of the text: "Women were not regarded [as] equal to men. However, not all Greek women were treated the same in all parts of Greece." The rest of the text elaborates on that point, using Spartan and Athenian societies as examples.

Thus, the overall structure of this deceptively simple looking text is illustration by example of an assertion about the status of women in ancient Greece. Embedded within that macrostructure is description by comparison and contrast on three levels: men versus women, Spartan versus Athenian women, and upper versus lower-class Athenian women. Finally, imposed over all of that is a functional structure of an introduction and a main body. (For a discussion of these structures, see Calfee & Curley, 1984, and Slater & Graves, this volume.)

In addition to the title, the text is accompanied by two photographs (not included here)—one of a woman holding a bird and the other of an urn showing a standing figure holding a container in front of a seated woman. The photographs have no bylines, and they are not referred to in the text.

Prereading

Previous lessons had already established the significance of the gist strategy for the students, so the teacher immediately described the purposes of this lesson: to gain information about Greek society to use later in comparing ancient civilizations, and to practice using the gist strategy to get the gist of expository text. Students then were directed to open their textbooks and to spend two minutes scanning the two pages of text to see if they could predict the topic. The teacher then asked, "What do you think these two pages will be about?" One student responded, "Women in ancient Greece," and the class quickly concurred. The prompt, "What makes you think so?" elicited references to the title and illustrations.

Prompt 2, "What do you think it's going to tell you about women in ancient Greece?" forced students to predict the gist of the text: the topic and the commentary on it. They predicted, "It will tell us that the women of Greece lived well." The teacher asked, "What makes you think it's going to tell you that the women of Greece lived well?" The students referred to the photograph of a woman holding a bird and conjectured that it could be a pigeon or a pet dove. They thought the photograph showing a servant pouring a drink for a woman indicated that Greek women were well off.

During Reading

Students were directed to read silently the first paragraph to see if it supported their prediction. Then the teacher asked, "Did you find evidence that supports your prediction?" The students replied with drooping intonation, "It's about men. Most of the sentences are about men. Only the last sentence says anything about women." In response to the question, "Did you find evidence that does not support your prediction?" the answer was, "Yes, it told about Greek men as warriors and rulers of the Greek city-states." The teacher responded, "Do you want to change your prediction at this point?" The students decided not to expand their prediction to include men because the title mentioned only women, and there were no men in the pictures.

Students went through the next three paragraphs in the same manner, citing evidence in support of their prediction: "It told how Spartan women were treated. The women were educated. They were honored. They didn't have to fight in the war. They gave advice to their husbands." The teacher jotted their evidence on the chalkboard. For conflicting evidence, the students doubted whether having women give up their husbands and children to war was an example of being well treated. Although noting that the text was only about Spartan women so far, they decided not to reduce their statement of gist from Greek women in general to Spartan women in particular. Instead, they decided to read on, watching for examples of how other Greek women were treated.

The teacher assigned the last four paragraphs for silent reading, and the students pored over the text. They found what they were looking for—evidence that Athenian women were treated well. But they found some conflicting evidence, too, and said, "Upper class women could not make decisions even though their life was easy; men had control and told the women what to do."

Students matched what they found in the text with their prediction. They confirmed that most sections did tell them how ancient Greek women were treated because the text described what women's lives were like in Sparta and Athens. The sections on Greek men told "how women stood compared to men."

Postreading

The students then were ready to evaluate their original hypothesis about the gist of the text. The teacher prompted, "Do you want to make any final changes in your statement of what this is about?" The students maintained that the text confirmed their prediction that Greek women were treated well, but they concluded that the way women were treated depended on riches and where they lived. "It tells how their jobs affected their lives." When asked, "What did you learn that you did not know before reading?" the students replied that Greek women were not as well treated as they originally thought. "We changed our minds about that," they said.

Discussion

There are several interesting features of this lesson. One of them is how the students dealt with the structural complexity of the text and its lack of useful structural markers for them. It is clear that they failed to recognize the function of the introductory paragraph. Beginning a discussion of women in Greece with the role of men mystified these sixth grade students. But their response to this apparent contradiction is more interesting; they would not abandon their hypothesis. Instead, they suspended judgment on the role of men in this text until they had read more, a response reflecting prior experience with the gist strategy and the mysteries of textbooks.

The students' reasoning is also revealing. For them, titles and pictures are much more reliable sources of information for predicting the gist of exposition than introductory paragraphs. By the end of the lesson, they had resolved this apparent topic shift by subordinating the discussion of the role of men to that of women, noting that the sections on Greek men told "how women stood compared to men." Thus, by focusing their attention on the gist of the text, they were able to find their way through a complex text with poor markers.

This lesson might well be followed by explicit instruction in the functional structure of exposition—introduction, main body, and, sometimes, conclusion. The gist strategy is a good diagnostic device, even in whole class instruction.

In this lesson, the students failed to recognize an explicit statement of main idea and its structural implications for the rest of the text: "Women were not regarded equal to men. However, not all Greek women were treated the same in all parts of Greece." "Not...equal" and "not...the same" are typical markers for comparison and contrast structure in exposition. But the students relied almost exclusively on the title and pictures. In spite of that, their final statement of the gist is better than that in the text because it incorporates more of the substantive content of the text: "The way women were treated depended on riches and where they lived." They confirmed their prediction of topic and revised their prediction on the commentary.

Excessive reliance on pictures and titles as informational sources might be unfortunate for these students in the long run. Titles and pictures in textbooks can be very misleading. This lesson seems to have established the need and created an opportune moment for explicit instruction in a specific expository text structure (comparison and contrast) as illustrated in Richgels, McGee, and Slaton (this volume).

We are suggesting that students read the text first for its gist, attending to a generic and simple level of structure—topic and comment. They then can return to the text for concept and vocabulary development and attention to more complex text structure as the need is established. In effect, attention to text structure per se becomes a study strategy as opposed to an on-line comprehension strategy.

Finally, the lesson is interesting in the satisfaction in learning it created, even from a dull text. "We changed our minds about that," the students said at the end of the lesson. Changing one's mind in light of compelling evidence to the contrary is vital to learning. Consciously and explicitly addressing differences in concepts and world view between learners and the body of evidence accumulated in the natural and social sciences is also at the center of learning in the content areas (Eaton, Anderson, & Smith, 1984). These kinds of learning habits are beginning to emerge in this lesson.

Toward Independence

All students participated successfully in these lessons in both small and large (whole class) groups. In this particular lesson, the class developed a single, consensus hypothesis. There is much security in this kind of noncompetitive learning. In other lessons, multiple hypotheses were entertained. While whole class settings identified clear group needs, smaller groups and multiple hypotheses were much more diagnostic for individuals.

This particular lesson was largely teacher directed for demonstration purposes. The teacher voiced the prompts, decided how to segment the text, and recorded student generated evidence for and against the hypothesis. After a few lessons, these students began to respond to the next prompt without being asked, indicating internalization of the prompts. Next, students took on the roles of prompter and recorder. The final stages of this movement toward independence would be internalization of the entire process in reading exposition and transfer to other information processing activities in social studies and science.

Women of Ancient Greece

Ancient Greece is often thought of as a "man's world." Men were the warriors, law makers, and rulers of the Greek city-states. It is often not clear what part women had in the Greek civilization. Were they limited to being wives, mothers, and housekeepers?

In Ancient Greece, as in almost all the ancient societies, women were not regarded equal to men. However, not all Greek women were treated the same in all parts of Greece. The women of Sparta were highly honored, even though there was a military type of society. Girls were educated at home and received a very athletic training. They were taught to run, wrestle, and perform in athletic contests. Spartan women were expected to be strong and brave, even though they were not soldiers.

The Spartans expected their sisters, wives, and mothers to be ready to give up everything in time of war. Spartan women were not expected to fight and die for their city-state, but they had to offer their husbands and sons. A Spartan soldier who lacked courage might suffer more from being shamed by the women than from the actions of other Spartan men.

Spartan women often were asked for advice on important matters. This was not done in a formal way and the women did not serve as government officials. Sparta was too much a part of the "man's world" to admit it needed the advice of women. But the women of Sparta were looked upon as special people by other Greek women. A lady from one of the city-states is supposed to have said that "Spartan women are the only women in the world who can rule men." This was true, to a degree, even though they "ruled" in an informal way.

The women of Athens held a different place in Greek life than that held by Spartan women. In fact, the women of Athens were divided into several groups. Each group lived a very different kind of life. The largest group of Athenian women were the members of the working class. These working class women had a much different life than the women of the upper class.

The working class women very often worked side by side with their fathers, husbands and sons. This was true in Greek cities and on the farms. Women did not do much of the planting of crops, but they were important workers at harvest time. Also, many working class women often spent hours each day spinning and weaving wool to make cloth.

Working class women in the villages and cities held a great number of jobs. Many women kept inns, worked at baking bread, and were crafts workers. Some women even worked at making shoes, a job usually thought of as "man's work." Great numbers of Greek women worked in the marketplaces. They ran small shops and stalls that sold wine, vegetables, honey, perfumes, and dozens of other items. These Athenian merchant women were well known for being sharp business people and were important to Greek life. In addition to their work in the fields and city marketplaces, Athenian women did the housework and raised their children. Life was not easy for the working class women in Athens.

Upper class Athenian women led easier lives than did the lower class women. However, the upper class women had much less freedom. Their marriages were arranged by their parents, and few women had any say in the choice of husbands. Women were treated like children in many ways. They were always considered to be in the care of some man, either a father, a husband, or a son. Men signed contracts and controlled all property.

References

Afflerbach P. How are main idea statements constructed? Watch the experts. *Journal of Reading,* 1987, *30* (6), 512-518.

Abramovitz, J., and Job, K. Women of ancient Greece. In *Civilizations of the past: Peoples and cultures.* Cleveland, Ohio: Modern Curriculum Press, 1981, 106-107.

Allington, R. The reading instruction provided readers of differing reading abilities. *Elementary School Journal,* 1983, *83,* 548-559.

Bransford, J. *Human cognition: Learning, understanding, and remembering.* Belmont, CA: Wadsworth, 1979.

Bruce, B., and Rubin, A. Strategies for controlling hypothesis formation in reading. In J. Flood (Ed.), *Promoting reading comprehension.* Newark, DE: International Reading Association, 1984.

Calfee, R., and Curley, R. The structure of prose in the content areas. In J. Flood (Ed.), *Understanding reading comprehension.* Newark, DE: International Reading Association, 1984, 161-180.

Collins, A., Brown, J., and Larkin, K. Inference in text understanding. In R. Spiro, B. Bruce, and W. Brewer (Eds.), *Theoretical issues in reading comprehension.* Hillsdale, NJ: Erlbaum, 1980, 385-407.

Collins, A., and Smith, E. Teaching the process of reading comprehension. In D. Detterman and R. Sternberg (Eds.), *How and how much can intelligence be increased?* Norwood, NJ: Ablex, 1982, 173-185.

Cunningham, J. Generating interactions between schema and text. In J. Niles and L. Harris (Eds.), *New inquiries in reading research and instruction.* Rochester, NY: National Reading Conference, 1982, 42-47.

Davey, B. Think aloud: Modeling the cognitive processes of reading comprehension. *Journal of Reading,* 1983, *27* (1), 44-47.

Eaton, J., Anderson, D., and Smith, E. Students' misconceptions interfere with science learning: Case studies of fifth grade students. *Elementary School Journal,* 1984, *84 (4),* 365-379.

Goodman, K. Reading: A psycholinguistic guessing game. *Journal of the Reading Specialist,* 1967, *6,* 126-135.

Goodman, K. *What's whole in whole language?* Portsmouth, NH: Heinemann, 1986.

Jackson, N. *Through the labyrinth: An exploration of student, text, and teacher interactions.* Paper presented at the annual International Reading Association Convention, New Orleans, May 1985.

Johnston, P., and Afflerbach, P. The process of constructing main ideas from text. *Cognition and Instruction,* 1985, *2,* 207-232.

Orasanu, J., and Penney, M. Introduction: Comprehension theory and how it grew. In J. Orasanu (Ed.), *Reading comprehension: From research to practice.* Hillsdale, NJ: Erlbaum, 1986, 1-9.

Palincsar, A., and Brown, A. Interactive teaching to promote independent learning. *The Reading Teacher,* 1986, *39,* 771-777.

Richek, M., List, L., and Learner, J. *Reading problems: Assessment and teaching strategies,* second edition. Englewood Cliffs, NJ: Prentice Hall, in press.

Rumelhart, D. Schemata: The building blocks of cognition. In R. Spiro, B. Bruce, and W. Brewer (Eds.), *Theoretical issues in reading comprehension.* Hillsdale, NJ: Erlbaum, 1980, 33-58.

Smith, F. *Comprehension and learning: A conceptual framework for teachers.* New York: Holt, 1975.

Smith, F. *Understanding reading,* third edition. New York: Holt, 1982.

Spiro, R., Bruce, B., and Brewer, W. Introduction. In R. Spiro, B. Bruce, and W. Brewer (Eds.), *Theoretical issues in reading comprehension.* Hillsdale, NJ: Erlbaum, 1980, 1-5.

Stauffer, R.G. *Teaching reading as a thinking process.* New York: Harper & Row, 1969.

Part Three
Summary

11

James H. Mosenthal

The Comprehension Experience

> This chapter discusses comprehension instruction in terms of the reader's experience of the text. The author distinguishes between the abstraction of a comprehension process and the concrete experience of the reader comprehending text. He argues that reading strategies used to teach comprehension derive their form from the theory of a comprehension process, but function primarily in instruction to cultivate the reader's experience of the sense of the text as a whole. The comprehension experience is discussed in terms of textual moments and the movement of the text. The author describes how strategies for reading such as experience-text-relationship (ETR) and reciprocal teaching are based on the definition of moments and on the cultivation of the experience of movement. The article concludes with a discussion of how and why teachers and students should adapt and develop strategies.

If we ask what happens when a reader comprehends a text, we are asking about the reader's experience comprehending it. In instruction, we want to cultivate the quality of that experience. We strive to achieve that cultivation by studying the comprehension process and designing strategies for reading (and writing) that stimulate comprehension processes. But the comprehension process and readers' experience comprehending are different issues. The former deals with theory and the latter with personal experience. It seems that, as a result of our bridges constructed between research and practice, we understand the experience in terms of the theory. But we don't talk much about the experience per se and the relationship of theory to it. This chapter tries to place the comprehension experience in the foreground and discuss it against the background of a theory based approach to reading comprehension instruction using reading strategies.

Stauffer's (1969) Directed Reading-Thinking Activity (DRTA) and Manzo's (1968) ReQuest procedure are forms of instruction that use a reading strategy to promote comprehension. These strategies consist of a questioning pattern applied to portions of text encountered during reading. The DRTA and ReQuest are precursors to the more recent development of reading strategies to promote comprehension. Au's (1979) experience-text-relationship strategy (ETR) and Palincsar and Brown's (1986) procedure for the reciprocal teaching of comprehension monitoring activities are exemplars of the type of strategy format developed by Stauffer and Manzo. Considerable research has documented the efficacy of these latter strategies in improving comprehension performance. (See Au & Kawakami, 1984; Au & Mason, 1981; and Tharp, 1982 on the benefits of instruction based on the ETR. See Brown, Palincsar, & Armbruster, 1984; and Palincsar & Brown, 1984 on the benefits of instruction based on the reciprocal teaching of comprehension monitoring activities.)

Part of the power and appeal of these strategies is that they are based on the theoretical delineation of a comprehension process. This delineation typically identifies the component, interactive processes of accessing prior knowledge, inferring, and monitoring. (See Pearson, 1984 for a discussion of these processes and a review of the research pertaining to them.) The ETR and the reciprocal teaching procedure are based on this concept of component, interactive processes. They are theory based guides to discussion meant to promote students' capacity to process and comprehend text. At one level, these strategies teach the delineation upon which they are based.

At another level, the use of a reading strategy helps a reader experience the sense of a text and learn what it means to make sense of text. A reading strategy is a means for cultivating this experience, but it is not a means for directly teaching the experience. What is directly taught is the use of the strategy. The effective use of strategies over time helps the student learn to experience the sense of text.

The Comprehension Experience

What does it mean to experience the sense of text? It is tempting to talk about the comprehension experience in terms of comprehending and something comprehended. However useful it might be to separate out such components for analytic purposes, they probably have no independent existence. There is no comprehending without a thing comprehended; there is nothing comprehended without the comprehending of it. At a basic level, to experience the sense of text is to experience, simultaneously, a part of the text and the developing whole to which it contributes.

Moments

To experience the sense of text is to see the relevance of a moment in the movement of the text. It is as if, while we read, we are always stopped, yet always moving. Much text analytic work can be thought of as characterizing moments of text. This includes the work of Mandler and Johnson (1977) with respect to narration, and Meyer (1975) with respect to exposition. (See chapters by Fitzgerald and by Slater & Graves, this volume.) Comprehension is characterized in terms of text parts and the basic structural relationships that exist between them: initiating event, goal, attempt, and outcome in the case of narration; and problem/solution, compare/contrast, and others in the case of exposition. All propositional information of a text is represented in terms of such structural relationships. In a map of the content of a text, such analysis defines the moments in a text as well as the relationship of each moment to other moments. In the system of the analysis, there is no uncertainty. There is no movement or change. There is only the structurally complete text.

The representation of a structurally complete text is an ideal, and therein lies its power as a way of getting at the comprehension experience. These representations set as a goal of reading the moment of a complete text, something comprehended as a whole. Intuitively, the wholeness or coherence of the text is basic to the comprehension experience. However, such a representation explains something comprehended as a whole, but it tends to ignore the temporal aspect of reading, making the text whole—the comprehending. We cannot always make sense of what we read, much less predict the sense of information we have not read. We read with uncertainty. We read for the satisfaction of achieving certainty. It could not be otherwise. In the reading of any text, it is assumed that there is a purposeful chronology or sequence of information. As a result, we are drawn into the movement of the text. For any moment or part of the text, there is a tension born out of its identity and the movement from the past into the future of the text.

This tension between a moment of information and the movement of the whole is characteristic of the comprehension experience. I am reminded of a scene in the movie *The Graduate* when Benjamin is running along the sidewalk to a church where Elaine is to be married to someone else. In the movement of that text, I identify with Benjamin's love for Elaine, and I want him to get to the church on time. I am also aware of the moment of his running. I believe he will succeed because I know he is a collegiate cross country runner, and this is a movie, etc.

Although I never abandon the movement of the film's text—I am thoroughly absorbed in the action of that scene and of the movie as a whole—somehow, I simultaneously stop the text, step outside it, and see the moment of Benjamin running and recognize it as part of the plot. Minimally, I comprehend Benjamin's attempt to get Elaine back. Associated with it is knowledge of Benjamin's cross country running, his relationship with Elaine's mother, his status as a graduate, the year 1967, my status as a student, and my status as a viewer of *The Graduate*. These events, associations, circumstances, and concerns for the whole story enable me to be both in and outside the film. I am vulnerable to Benjamin's passion as he runs, and sensitive to the significance of what is portrayed at that moment.

The text I read and the situation in which I read provokes me to do that. I am at once in the text and outside of it. This is my experience as a comprehender. It is as if in the reading of text we comprehend as we are drawn into the movement of the whole, which we see as a series of significant moments.

The above discussion recalls that in reading there is investment. If certainty is a motive in reading, it is a source of investment. A text's structure means to represent wholeness and certainty. But structure is not what wholeness and certainty is. Certainty is a function of the satisfaction of working well in a text to achieve something whole.

Movement

The terms *prior knowledge, inference,* and *monitoring* are related, basic components of the representation of comprehension as a cognitive process. For our purposes, they can be thought of as a way of representing a reader's movement through text.

It is not prior knowledge per se that is important in comprehending, but accessing prior knowledge relevant to the text read. A story grammar, or story schema, is a form of relevant prior knowledge that the reader accesses in making sense of stories, as the rhetorical predicates described by Meyer (1975) are for reading exposition. Such schemata help in experiencing something as a whole. There is also the prior knowledge relevant to the world depicted in the text. While watching *The Graduate*, I make sense of the world of the graduate in terms of my own experiences.

It is important to remember that the reader brings prior knowledge to the text. I access my experiences, my schemata, as reference is made to a world. I access this knowledge to make sense of the reference. Sense does not exist as a coded part of the text. I am not controlled or passive in accessing prior knowledge. Specific knowledge or memories are not activated by an equation formulated by the author. In accessing prior knowledge, I continually flesh out a world that is familiar and understandable to me but at the same time is grounded in the writer's continuing reference to a world.

Another way of saying this is that I access my prior knowledge in order to help infer the implications of the world the writer refers to. A reader's inferring is triggered by the assumption that there is a purposeful chronology of information, a design, and that inferring is the effort to see that intent, that design, that world. My movement through the text is the movement of inferring. As I read, I make inferences about the coherence of the world referred to by the author. I access prior knowledge to facilitate the inferring, for relevant prior knowledge reduces friction in the movement of the text by making the movement happen over familiar territory.

Inferring and accessing prior knowledge describe my movement through a text, but there is a check on that movement. If the satisfaction of achieving certainty is a goal, then it must be convincing. So I monitor its achievement. By strict definition, monitoring refers to the process of checking for comprehension failure (Baker & Brown, 1984). Generally, monitoring refers to checking out how sensible things are. It is not just a concern for failure; it is also a concern for success.

With respect to failure, when I misidentify a word or overlook a transition, an inference is not made or a misinference is made. I say to myself, "That didn't make any sense." It is not the lost or misguided inference that brings me to my senses, but the awareness that no sense is being made. This awareness is healthy, for it is the result of a desire to achieve certainty. It may prompt reaction, depending on how uncertain I am about the direction of my movement in the text. I may stop to contemplate the significance of a word or section of text. In so doing, I strive to make strong the mesh of relationships that connects me to what has gone before and that guides me into what lies ahead.

My monitoring is as much a concern for comprehension success as it is for comprehension failure. With respect to success, my monitoring looks for strong implications: moments perceived as beginnings, middles, and ends and movement perceived as beginning, continuing, and ending. As reading continues, moments and movement take on new aspects. New moments become old moments, and what is perceived as beginning, continuing, and ending changes. Strong implication is like the proliferation of roots seeking to anchor themselves in a stable perception of the whole. My experience reading is like an organic growing where beginnings are rooted in ends and vice versa.

Think of the image of Benjamin in his scuba gear in the backyard pool and the image of Benjamin running to the church. These two images have the potential to be related; the significance of one is experienced in the significance of the other. This is not an example of simple sequencing, but an indication of a world's dense mesh of implication grown forward and backward between moments identified in the reading of the text. This fleshing out of a world that is whole is what I mean to do—it is what I monitor—and to the extent that I succeed, I derive satisfaction. Things make sense.

Teaching to the Comprehension Experience

Identifying and Attending to Moments

Instruction in the use of reading strategies can teach to this experience of moments, movement, and sense. The standard use of a strategy might legitimately have readers look at the title prior to reading a text and speculate what the text will be about. The reader is asked to look forward to text before reading it. In this effort, the reader is asked to deal explicitly with incompleteness and uncertainty. Reading strategies emphasize addressing moments as they are identified and, hence, in their uncertainty. Readers are uncertain about the relevance of these moments because the whole is as yet unencountered and hypothetical. As readers are shown how to use the strategy, they learn a heuristic for finding a fit for the moment in question.

The claim to directly engage the reader in the process of making sense through the use of reading strategies is a false one. In strategy instruction, the teacher and students stop to discuss a chunk of information in the context of the text being read. They identify a moment in the movement of the text. It is impossible in discussion not to be stopped. Therefore, reading strategies concern moments; they cannot deal directly with movement, and as a result, they are artificial. This is not bad, but it is misconceived to think that in strategy use, comprehension is taught directly.

Reading strategies force the reader to be attentive to various aspects of moments identified in reading the text: their status as moments, and their relationship to moments past and to come. In other words, reading strategies that attend to moments as they are identified force the question of the moment's role in a whole. The belief is that this attention to the moments of the text heightens the reader's sensitivity to the movement toward an ending and something whole. A primary purpose of reading strategies is to have teacher and student identify different types of moments and discuss their relevance in the text as a whole.

Three types of moments surface in the description of reading strategies. They can be characterized as book defined, discourse defined, or reader defined.

Book defined moments. These moments are defined by the physical characteristics of the book, and they exist without uncertainty. They can be the moment of the word, sentence, paragraph, page, chapter, etc. In using a strategy, adherence to a book defined moment means discussing each word, sentence, or paragraph, whichever is the moment of interest in the strategy. Titles and headings are used in this way since they automatically define sections that are often dealt with as moments. The ReQuest procedure (Manzo, 1968) progresses sentence by sentence. The reciprocal teaching strategy suggests a paragraph by paragraph reading of non-fiction texts (Palincsar & Brown, 1986).

There is one obvious weakness in basing a strategy on such moments. These moments, stopping points or discussion breaks in the reading of a text, can be arbitrary and identify information less relevant to the text as a whole. A related, potential weakness is that the student will not see past the moments and may understand text in terms of parts, not a whole.

A great strength of such strategies, however, is that book defined moments, in instruction, are unambiguous for the teacher and students. The focus on unambiguous, valid moments relieves the reader of the responsibility of identifying a moment while reading. With legitimate, book defined break points, the reader learns that there is something, usually, to make sense of within the boundaries of the moment and that the reader's responsibility is to do just that.

In most contemporary reading strategies, making sense of a moment in the text entails questioning strategies meant to cultivate the processes of accessing prior knowledge, inferring, and monitoring. The reciprocal teaching strategy epitomizes this attempt to cultivate the basic cognitive processes of comprehension. After reading a paragraph of text, students identify and discuss points of comprehension failure (monitoring), question and summarize main points of the paragraph (interpretive inferring), and predict what type of information might be covered in the following paragraph (predictive inferring). (The distinction between interpretive and predictive inferring is one borrowed from Collins & Smith, 1982.) If there are titles and headings, students discuss what they know about the topics identified in the title and headings (accessing prior knowledge).

It is important to note that much of the rigor of this strategy is a consequence of the adherence to book defined paragraph boundaries and strategy defined questions. Such rigor takes the ambiguity out of the instructional task. The strategy does not make simpler the fleshing out of a moment's relevance in the text, but it identifies clearly what the moment is (the paragraph) and what it means to make sense of it (responding to the tasks of the strategy). As a result, as students become familiar with the use of the strategy, they gain independent control of a way to read, or process, expository text. In reciprocal teaching, this possibility is theoretically key to the development of self-regulated comprehension. (See Brown, Palincsar, & Armbruster, 1984, and Palincsar & Brown, 1984.)

Discourse defined moments. Since book defined moments may become ends in themselves, the task of comprehension may become one of fleshing out moments rather than making sense of the whole text. Discourse defined moments avoid this problem by defining in advance the nature of the whole text constituted by the moments identified for discussion. Here, moments are not defined by physical characteristics of the text, but by a text's modal characteristics, for example, the characteristics which define the text as a type of discourse.

In reading instruction, two basic types of discourse are recognized: nonfiction and fiction. This is similar to Fitzgerald's discourse types (this volume): narrative, descriptive, and expository. Text analytic research in nonfiction (Slater, this volume) and fiction (Fitzgerald, this volume) has led to applied work in reading strategies based on these types of discourse. The majority of the strategies presented in this volume are based on discourse defined moments. (See the narrative strategies discussed by Morrow, Tompkins and McGee, and Gordon, and the expository strategy presented by Richgels, McGee, & Slaton, all this volume.)

As an aside, the distinction between fiction and nonfiction appears more useful than the distinction between expository and narrative. Applied work on the reading of narrative usually entails strategies for reading and discussing fictional narrative. Drawing a distinction between fictional and historical narrative and refining strategies as a result has not been a major concern. Similarly, with exposition, applied work in the use of strategies based on rhetorical predicates and the concept of top level structure does not clearly distinguish what is characteristic about the texts of a discipline. What is a problem/solution rhetorical structure in a social studies text is potentially as appropriate a structure for characterizing a science text and even a fictional text. The generic quality of reading strategies seems natural, given their source in a concern for the basic processes of comprehension. It should be noted, though, that despite the practical and instructional relevance of strategic reading and reading strategies, the student's experience of reading literature, science, or history is not generic. Our strategies only lightly distinguish between these experiences.

As stated, in strategies based on discourse defined moments, the modal characteristics of the type of discourse determine what a moment is. These moments correspond to superordinate nodes in psychological schemata for processing text.

For example, Meyer (1975) characterizes text in terms of text level rhetorical predicates, which are organizational schemata for text content (Slater, this volume). They represent a form of prior knowledge of text that can be accessed in reading. Any instance of a predicate type (such as compare-contrast, attributive) results in a top level structure that serves to organize and set expectations for the general content of the text. Bartlett (1978) has developed a reading strategy wherein students learn to identify the top level structure of texts.

In the case of fictional text, instead of discourse level rhetorical predicates, there is a generalized story schema (Fitzgerald, this volume). In the example of Mandler and Johnson (1977), the schema is defined in terms of a set of interrelated parts which constitute the whole of the story schema: setting, initiating event, reaction, goal, attempt, outcome, and resolution. As with the concept of rhetorical predicates, a story schema represents a form of prior knowledge of the structure of fictional text that is accessed in reading fictional text. This knowledge serves to organize and set expectations for the general content.

The intent of strategies based on discourse defined moments is to have students develop an awareness of the structural integrity of texts, as that integrity is defined by the relationship of story parts in a general schema for stories, or the relationship of the components of rhetorical predicates in a general schema for nonfiction text. Since the intent of such strategies is to strengthen students' schemata for processing text, students learn that a moment in the reading of a text may not correspond with types of physical boundaries in the book. A discourse defined moment is a moment determined by the type of text being read. In other words, a text's modal characteristics (the story parts of a story schema, or the components of a rhetorical predicate) define significant moments for discussion.

Reader defined moments. Reader defined moments are those identified by the reader, whether the reader be a teacher or a student. Obviously, the identification of these moments is influenced by book characteristics, such as paragraphs. The identification is also influenced by discourse characteristics, for we read the text as a story or as coherent nonfiction and are sensitive to the development of the text as a type of discourse.

In strategies based on the reader's identification of moments, however, those moments are freely defined. A reader is not required to stop at every word, paragraph, or page, or at all discourse defined moments. In other words, in instruction the reader is not required to process certain units of print in a text, nor is the reader required to map the text's discourse parts. Rather, reader defined moments are those perceived by the reader (whether the reader is the teacher or the student) to have relevance to the text as a whole. The relevance is fleshed out by the questions used in the strategy. (Ogle's KWL strategy and Schuder, Clewell, & Jackson's gist strategy, both discussed in this volume, appear to be based on reader defined moments.)

Consider the example of the experience-text-relationship ETR strategy (Au, 1979). The moments of the *T* phase are defined by breaks in the reading of a story where discussion takes place. These are moments identified by the teacher as reader to discuss what is happening and what inferring can be done. The relevance of the moment is fleshed out by the inferring provoked in discussion. (See Wong & Au, 1985 for a strategy similar in principle to the ETR but designed for nonfiction text.)

The ETR is a strategy based on reader defined moments. Intuition helps determine the best places to stop and make inferences. To the extent that such artificially stimulated processing provokes an appreciation of movement in text, it does so by provoking an appreciation of the whole in which the moment is a part. Thus, good moments are relevant not because they are good places to practice inferring. They are good places because they are relevant to the reader in appreciating the whole text. This is what is to be learned.

In most strategies based on reader defined moments, the teacher plays the part of the reader and defines the moments that will be fleshed out. The advantage of such teacher direction is that the teacher can control the subtlety with which a strategy is applied, based on the subtlety of the moment in the whole of the text. For example, any word or phrase, such as a metaphor, can be identified as a moment to be dealt with.

Generally, the noninvolvement of the student in the choice and identification of significant book, discourse, or reader defined moments is curious. The use of reading strategies makes moments of comprehension concrete by having break points in the reading and discussion of text. This is done to approximate movement in text and so influence comprehension of subsequent text. If the relevant moment is central to the instructional use of reading strategies, it would seem appropriate to involve the student in the choice and identification of these moments. It would not be difficult to ask, "Where is a good place to predict?" "Where is a place you get lost?" "Where is a good place to ask questions?"

This is not a pitch for a new strategy. Rather, I only want to reiterate that basic to the comprehension experience and a strategy approach to reading comprehension instruction is the perception of moments and their relevance in the movement of the text. It seems legitimate to try to cultivate the reader's capacity to identify relevant moments in order to complement instruction in fleshing them out. The involvement of students in the identification of relevant moments is half the battle in cultivating self-regulated comprehension, as opposed to a dependency on book characteristics or a teacher's knowledge. In this volume, the strategies that involve composing text are necessarily based on kids' identification of moments just because the moments are theirs to define when writing. (See Gordon; Richgels, McGee, & Slaton; Tompkins & McGee, this volume.) Perhaps this is another aspect of the connection between reading and writing and a reason for teaching them in a complementary fashion.

Adapting Strategies

Previously, I described the reading experience in terms of satisfaction in achieving coherence. Instruction is committed to cultivating this satisfaction. The nature of satisfaction is complicated, but its principle is simple—things make sense. My son may derive satisfaction from a picture of a rumpus when I read him Sendak's *Where the Wild Things Are* (1963), without knowing it is a dream of Max's, or the result of being punished. The satisfaction is in the experience of the moment of Max's rumpus. For my son, this moment is a whole. It is a comprehension experience.

In book defined fashion, I may, with my son, look at and talk about the pictures in the order they appear in the book. This may help him make explicit in his own mind lots of moments and maybe even a sequence. Here the moments start to blur, and the movement of the story of Max is an experience from which my son derives satisfaction. More sense is made while incorporating the sense made of the picture of the rumpus.

In discourse defined fashion, I may stop at those moments in the text where Max fades in and out of his imaginary world in order to help my son see the story of Max and to see the episode of Max's dream in the context of the episode of Max's mischievousness and the resolution of the conflict. Perhaps my son will experience the story's plot and derive satisfaction from the sense made of the story—still appreciating the sense of sequence and moments.

Or, in reader defined fashion, I may ask my son to pick out the pictures he likes best, tell me why he likes them, and say why he thinks Sendak likes them and put them in the book. Here my son gets satisfaction in owning and determining the sense of the text.

In the three scenarios depicted, I teach my son, sensitive to his satisfaction. His satisfaction is mine. The fact that there are things that engage him in the story and that he can identify and expound upon is a freedom and a capacity he was not aware of before. Schooled in specific book, discourse, and/or reader based strategies, he has the potential to pursue the satisfaction of making sense out of text. What has been telescoped here is something played out over long periods of time and with lots of text. It is important, therefore, to consider an intent and a direction for a strategy approach to reading comprehension instruction over long periods of time.

Satisfaction derives from the reader's capacity to make sense of the text as a whole. As teacher and students learn to use a strategy effectively, they learn to make reasoned and insightful predictions, to ask questions probing the central content of the text, and to bring up relevant personal experiences. Reason, insight, perception of centrality, and relevance are part of the satisfaction inherent in making sense out of text. For example, at one time in instruction a student may predict based solely on free association, thinking that the task is only to predict and not to flesh out a moment of information. With continued practice in predicting, within the structure of the strategy, the reader learns that predictions are confirmable and that free association is not the basis upon which one makes a prediction. Rather, the reader learns that a good prediction is one that makes sense in terms of what she or he understands the whole text to be about. At this point, the activity of predicting is a means for achieving insight into the text as a whole, and the reader's experience of insight is satisfying.

Over time, such capacity develops in a strategy approach to reading comprehension instruction. I assume that more than one strategy is used over the course of a year. It would be simplistic to think that strategy instruction consisted of only one strategy, or that writers' texts could be accessed and their meaning exhausted in a discussion based solely on a questioning pattern reiteratively applied to stipulated parts of the text. This does not undercut the importance of the use of a strategy.

The point is, we compromise the experience of making sense of text if we isolate the individual strategy. The rigor and understanding that a strategy promotes are limited. If the use of a strategy brings teacher and students to a level of expertise, then some adaptation or change in strategy use should follow, for the level of expertise attained is defined in terms of the strategy. The experience of the sense of text is much more multifaceted than what one strategy can reveal. Teacher and students must lead themselves in directions that build from the levels of expertise established in prior instruction.

In order to see where these reading strategies might lead the teacher and the students, we need to go back to our initial description of the content of reading comprehension instruction. We said that the goal is to convey what it means to make sense of text by helping readers experience the sense of texts. The experience of the sense of text is the experience of seeing information as moments in the movement of text. With respect to the reader's perception of moments, we discussed book, discourse, and reader defined units of information. With respect to movement, we discussed the operations of monitoring, inferring, and accessing prior knowledge applied to those units of information. These moments and this movement are our content.

It is clear that strategies are simply part of a repertoire from which a teacher can draw to cultivate students' sensitivity to moments in text and the movement they reveal. Teachers can choose and sequence the types of moments and operations students confront by choosing, sequencing, and adapting the strategies to be used. In this context, the boundaries of individual strategies merge over time.

How does this happen? It is not simply a matter of jumping from one strategy to another based on some perceived logic. If we remind ourselves that the content of comprehension instruction has to do with units of information, operations, and something whole, then it is in and around those concepts that we ought to play. There is not a scope and sequence and a program of instruction to match. Rather, there is instruction using and adapting strategies to teach toward an understanding of moments, movement, and sense.

For example, imagine a class that has used reciprocal teaching for an extended period of time, and the teacher feels that the students use the strategy effectively. The teacher chooses to adapt the strategy so that instead of relying on book defined moments, she or he determines what might be characterized as discourse defined moments that are coherent and complete dealings with a topic or subtopic. The teacher defines moments that bind units of information relevant to the discourse and that are not perfunctorily based on the physical characteristics of the book. The reason for doing this is that the tasks of reciprocal teaching (and any strategy) are more appropriately applied to moments coherent in the discourse.

Instead of focusing on single paragraphs, if a four paragraph section of a text about insect eating plants describes how a Venus's-flytrap captures insects, then the teacher can have the students ask questions and make summaries of that section. The teacher makes the change to help students become sophisticated in their sensitivity to a text's moments. Such an adaptation of reciprocal teaching assumes that the teacher and students have learned to use the strategy well at the paragraph level. It assumes that the jump from book to discourse defined moments is feasible given the complexity of the texts and the abilities of the teacher and students.

At some point, the teacher and students should have developed the capacity to apply the steps of the reciprocal teaching strategy to the type of discourse defined moments described above. At that point, the teacher may decide to turn over responsibility for identifying moments to the students so that they are made to think about moments in a text that are relevant to the text as a whole. In other words, the teacher decides to move from discourse defined moments to a form of reader defined moment, and so regain the potential for self-regulation that was key in the original formulation of the strategy.

Consider another example. Imagine a teacher and students using the ETR. The teacher challenges the students to construct a scenario for a story based on their prior knowledge of the type of issue a current story is dealing with. For example, in a story about a girl who disobeys her mother, the teacher, during the E phase, challenges the students to predict the action of the story based on their own knowledge and experience of disobedience. In this case, the teacher would challenge the students to consider how someone can be disobedient, the usual consequences, and how disobedience is resolved. This challenge is an adaptation of the E phase of the ETR.

The resultant disobedience schema sets a purpose for reading the whole story that goes beyond just setting a purpose such as "Let's read to find out how the girl disobeys her mother." In addition, the disobedience schema doubles as a schema for the story and puts students in the position of being able to define, in reader defined fashion, relevant moments of the text to discuss in the T phase. Pursuing such connections between the E and T phases of the strategy also places the reader in the position of being able, in the R phase, to discuss the specialness of the story by noting the identities and deviations with the students' own concept of disobedience. In this example, to the extent that the story has depth (think of the story of Antigone's disobedience), discussion may provoke the experience of the more profound reason, insight, and relevance associated with the reading of literature.

The reader who participates in such a discussion is confronted with the task of making sense of text. The ETR is an instructional heuristic that the teacher, in the example, has adapted for the purpose of making sense of text.

As a final example, consider the question of monitoring. Imagine a teacher who, familiar with the concept of monitoring for comprehension failure, tries to get students to identify and discuss what is unclear in their reading of fictional texts. The teacher finds that the students' use of the strategy is restricted primarily to vocabulary, and that besides recognizing that they don't know a word, the readers learn to do little else than consider context for the meaning of a word. This in itself is not insignificant reading behavior. The teacher may, however, feel that the students do not have a true sense of monitoring and how it aids in the recognition of subtlety and ambiguity in fiction, aspects that may cause readers to fail to comprehend them.

As a result, the teacher adapts the monitoring strategy based on the notion of a moment's relevance. As before, the strategy is simply to read a portion of text (this moment is reader defined but at first, is most likely defined by the teacher as reader) and to identify smaller moments or units of information that are the source of confusion (these also can be identified by teacher or students). But the teacher adds the task of discussing such moments in the context of the text as a whole. It is a monitoring strategy with two parts: "What does this mean?" and "So what?" or "How is this important to the story?" By adding the second question, the teacher introduces as a possible source of confusion the idea of relevance to a whole.

Consider the following scenario. At a point in a story about a boy who is sad because he is too poor to have a costume for the carnival, he and his friends discuss costumes. At this point, neither the friends nor the readers know that the boy does not have a costume. It is only known that he is sad. When asked about his costume, the boy makes up a response after "thinking fast." The teacher, or a student, identifies the moment and asks, "What does 'thinking fast' mean?" The strategy then requires the followup question of "So what?" or "Why does he have to think fast?" In the story, the boy thinks fast because he doesn't have a costume and has to say something. The story is about how the friends help the boy get a costume. Here, fleshing out the meaning and significance of thinking fast leads to a prediction (an insight) about what's at issue in the story.

A class adept at various strategies and adaptations of strategies may end up without distinctive strategies, but with an awareness of units of information, operations, and the whole text. Over time, a legitimate teacher directive might be, in ultimate reciprocal fashion, "Discuss this text as you think it needs to be discussed." At this point, students have an understanding of what it means to make sense of text and derive satisfaction from doing so. Their awareness of units of information, operations, and the whole text is a legitimate means to moments, movement, and sense. But then, at that point, they are ready for more strategy and the greater satisfaction it cultivates.

References

Au, K.H. Using the experience-text-relationship method with minority children. *The Reading Teacher,* 1979, *32* (6), 677-679.

Au, K.H., and Kawakami, A.J. Vygotskian perspectives on discussion processes in small group reading lessons. In P.L. Peterson, L.C. Wilkinson, and M. Hallinan (Eds.), *The social context of instruction: Group organization and group processes.* Orlando, FL: Academic Press, 1984, 209-225.

Au, K.H., and Mason, J.M. Social organizational factors in learning to read: The balance of rights hypothesis. *Reading Research Quarterly,* 1981, *17* (1), 115-152.

Baker, L., and Brown, A.L. Metacognitive skills and reading. In P.D. Pearson (Ed.), *Handbook of reading research.* New York: Longman, 1984, 353-394.

Bartlett, B.J. *Top level structure as an organizational strategy for recall of classroom text.* Unpublished doctoral dissertation, Arizona State University, 1978.

Brown, A.L., Palincsar, A.S., and Armbruster, B.B. Instructing comprehension fostering activities in interactive learning situations. In H. Mandl, N.L. Stein, and T. Trabasso (Eds.), *Learning and comprehension of text.* Hillsdale, NJ: Erlbaum, 1984, 255-286.

Collins, A., and Smith, E.E. Teaching the process of reading comprehension. In D.K. Detterman, and P.F. Sternberg (Eds.), *How and how much can intelligence be increased.* Norwood, NJ: Ablex (1982), 173-185.

Mandler, J.M., and Johnson, N.S. Remembrance of things parsed: Story structure and recall. *Cognitive Psychology,* 1977, *9,* 111-151.

Manzo, A.V. *Improving reading comprehension through reciprocal questioning.* Unpublished doctoral dissertation, Syracuse University, 1968.

Meyer, B.J.F. *The organization of prose and its effects on memory.* Amsterdam: North Holland Publishing, 1975.

Palincsar, A.S., and Brown, A.L. Interactive teaching to promote independent learning from text. *The Reading Teacher,* 1986, *39* (8), 771-776.

Palincsar, A.S., and Brown, A.L. Reciprocal teaching of comprehension fostering and comprehension monitoring activities. *Cognition and Instruction,* 1984, *1* (2), 117-175.

Pearson, P.D. *Handbook of reading research.* New York: Longman, 1984.

Sendak, M. *Where the wild things are.* New York: Harper & Row, 1963.

Stauffer, R.G. *Directing reading maturity as a cognitive process.* New York: Harper & Row, 1969.

Tharp, R.G. The effective instruction of comprehension: Results and description of the Kamehameha early education program. *Reading Research Quarterly,* 1982, *17* (4), 503-527.

Wong, J.A., and Au, K.H. The concept-text-application approach: Helping elementary students comprehend expository text. *The Reading Teacher,* 1985, *38* (7), 612-618.

12

Joan Nelson-Herber
Carolyn S. Johnston

Questions and Concerns about Teaching Narrative and Expository Text

> In this chapter, the authors answer common questions related to teaching narrative and expository text. Providing research support as needed, they attempt to help teachers apply the research and models to their own teaching practices. They also call attention to other similar strategies that teachers may wish to explore.

The purpose of this chapter is to respond to questions and concerns about research on narrative and expository text and about strategies designed to enhance reading comprehension. The chapter is divided into three parts: (1) questions relating to narrative text, (2) questions relating to expository text, and (3) more general questions.

Narrative Text

Q. *How does prior knowledge fit with the teaching of story parts?*

A. The critical role of prior knowledge in reading comprehension has been amply demonstrated in recent research. Prior knowledge includes what people know about the way that text is organized and structured, as well as what they know about the subject matter of the text.

Story grammars are based on the premise that stories have a predictable structure and sequence and that readers use prior knowledge of story structure to aid in comprehension. This knowledge is held in memory as a story schema that helps them understand, predict, recall, and create stories. Rand (1984) describes the effect of story schema on the reader: "The schema helps the reader attend to certain aspects of the incoming material while keeping track of what has gone on before. The schema lets the reader know when a part of the story is complete and can be stored in memory, or whether the information should be held until more is added" (p.377).

Most children come to school with a schema for stories (Stein & Glenn, 1979), but a significant number appear to lack this story sense (Fitzgerald & Spiegel, 1983). Given the growing body of evidence that teaching story structure can improve students' comprehension of stories, it seems prudent for teachers to make children aware of story structure by teaching story parts and relating them to the text to enhance comprehension. Even children who already have a sense of story structure can benefit from being given labels for their knowledge. Knowledge of story structure empowers students in monitoring their own reading comprehension to determine whether what they are reading sounds right and makes sense.

Q. *How do we decide which story parts to teach?*

A. Several story grammars have been described and used in research (Mandler & Johnson, 1977; Rumelhart, 1978; Stein & Glenn, 1979; Thorndyke, 1977). They are based on simple stories such as folktales and fables. Although they use different terminology, they all include character, setting, a problem, one or more attempts to overcome the problem, a resolution, and an ending. Some include other elements such as motives, goals, and consequences. To avoid confusing children with varying terms, teachers should try to be consistent in the use of descriptors.

The teacher may wish to begin instruction with primary children even more simply by calling attention to what usually takes place in the beginning, the middle, and the ending of a story. As children recognize the predictability, the teacher may use one of the story grammars to label the various story parts. When the children recognize story parts, the teacher may begin to use strategies that require the students to apply their knowledge in various ways.

The sensitive teacher will recognize that some children have a well developed story schema, whereas others need patient instruction to develop or refine their story sense. If students lack a sense of time and place in a story, the teacher can discuss *setting*. If students don't understand a character's behavior, elements of *characterization* can be highlighted. If students lack the ability to pick out the events of a story and the character's reactions to them, the teacher can focus on *plot episodes*. If students have difficulty in finding how a character solves the problem or attains the goal, the teacher will emphasize *resolution*.

As children become more skillful in the use of simple story structures to enhance comprehension and recall, a more analytic process begins, and the children learn to understand characters' motives and goals.

Q. *What strategies can be used for teaching story parts?*

A. "While there is considerable agreement that it is useful for children to acquire knowledge of story features, there is some debate about whether and how features should be taught" (Fitzgerald, this volume). A variety of strategies have been proposed for teaching story comprehension. Some excellent ones are described elsewhere in this book. Additional strategies, some with research support, may be found in the recent literature.

1. Spiegel and Fitzgerald (1986) describe direct instruction of the elements of a story. Using the story grammar described by Mandler and Johnson (1977), intensive instruction was given in the setting, the beginning, the reaction, the attempt, the outcome, and the ending of a story. The researchers taught the students to think about the story parts while they were listening to and reading stories.

   The lessons included story production, sequencing with story parts, macrocloze activities, group inquiry, and story organization questioning. *Story production* activities involved writing group and individual stories. The stories were then cut up according to story parts, and the children were asked to put the parts back in proper order. *Sequencing* activities had the children put selected stories into correct order and then justify their ordering. *Macrocloze* activities involved eliminating a whole part of a story and then asking the children to read the story with the part missing and supply the missing part in their own words.

The researchers checked to see if the student supplied the right story part and if it fit the entire story. For *group inquiry,* the children were separated into three groups, each group receiving an incomplete story. Through a series of questions to other groups, the children had to find the missing information and complete the story. *Story organization* activities involved six questions used to guide the children through the retelling of any story part. The questions were as follows: How did _____ feel? What did _____ want (or decide)? What did _____ do? What did _____ do next? How did it turn out? How did _____ feel about this after it was all over? (Spiegel & Fitzgerald, 1986, p.681). The researchers found that these methods of teaching had a powerful effect on students' comprehension.

2. Smith and Bean (1983) describe four strategies to help children in the primary grades predict events and outcomes in stories: circle stories, story patterns, story pictures, and story makers. *Circle stories* are pictorial representations of a story where a circle is sectioned into pie shapes representing the important events of the story. After the children read the story, they and the teacher decide together which events should be pictured, and in what sequence. This is a beginning strategy to help primary children get a sense of story grammar. *Story patterns* use repetition to help children see a pattern emerge from a story and to use the same pattern to write their own stories. *Story pictures,* modeled after the story grammar of Mandler and Johnson (1977), are pictures drawn for each of the story elements: setting, initiating event, reaction or consequence, attempt to solve the problem or reach a goal, the outcome of the attempt, and the ending. The shape is a rectangle divided into six parts labeled one through six. Children draw pictures of each of the story elements to represent their understanding of the story and its parts. Finally, *story maker* is a tree shaped diagram designed to take primary children through the story parts. It is also used to help organize the writing process.

3. Piccolo (1986) describes a writing method derived from using the story grammar models of Stein and Glenn (1979) and Thorndyke (1977). She presents a series of questions that the teacher can use to help a student organize a written story. The questions relate to the setting (time, place, location, characters, problem), the plot episodes (initiating event, response, attempt, outcome, reaction), and the resolution. Piccolo also gives a chart for analyzing student stories according to a story grammar model.
4. Olson (1984) suggests a way to support children in writing book reports using story grammar elements. Like Piccolo, she uses a series of questions: Where and when did the story occur? What is the initiating event; what got the story started? What was the goal of the hero/heroine? What were the major events in the story? What finally happened in the story; how did it end? What did you learn from this story? These major questions are elaborated with subquestions to help students understand what is required. For example, the elaborative questions related to the goal are: What is the hero/heroine's problem? What does the hero/heroine need to do?
5. Nessel (1985) describes six steps a teacher can use to support children's story sense by becoming a storyteller in the classroom. In condensed form, they are
   - Choose a story you like and want to tell.
   - Read and reread the story to make it familiar.
   - Study the story structure.
   - Put the book aside and visualize the story.
   - Go back to the book and read the story aloud.
   - Tell the story in your own words.

   While telling the story, the teacher may give children opportunities to anticipate or predict what will come next on the basis of their knowledge of story grammar.
6. Moldofsky (1983) uses the following clue questions to help children find the central story problem.
   - Who is the main character?
   - What does he or she want, need, feel, or think?

- Check: Does this fit all the important things that happen in the story?
- Statement: The central story problem is that (who?) _____ (pick one) wants/ needs/ feels/ thinks (what?) _____ (pick one) but/ because _____ (p.741).

Moldofsky notes that children began using the strategy to find the central point independently, but only after eight to ten guided practice stories.

7. Moss and Oden (1983) developed a "Friendship Unit" with a wide range of stories relating to friendship and peer relationships. They used questions about characters, settings, and plot to assist primary children in acquiring story schema and comprehension of social interactions. Subsequently, students began to "internalize questions about the story structure and themes as they initiated their own story analysis as the basis for discussion" (p.787).
8. Fowler (1982) suggests the use of *story frames* to help primary children with story comprehension. "A story frame is a sequence of spaces hooked together by key language elements" (p.176). It is designed to support young students in their understanding and expression of story elements. An example of a story frame for a setting follows.

Setting

This story takes place _____ .

I know this because the author uses the words " _____

_____ ." Other clues that show when the story takes place are _____

_____ (p.177).

Fowler lists story frames to help with story summary, plot, character analysis, and character comparison.

The strategies listed here are not meant to be all inclusive. They represent a starting place for teachers seeking ideas about how to enhance their students' comprehension of stories through story grammar.

Q. *Which is more important, teaching story schema or teaching for meaning and understanding of the story?*

A. A growing body of evidence suggests that understanding story parts aids a child's ability to comprehend a story (Fitzgerald & Spiegel, 1983; Mandler & Johnson, 1977; Stein & Glenn, 1979). Recognizing story elements can help children to anticipate, predict, and recall story events and to understand characters' motives, goals, actions, and feelings.

Think about the last time you tried to learn how to do something, such as make a skirt. If you have never sewn a skirt, you would have difficulty applying the instructions until you recognized that there were certain preparations you complete in the beginning, middle, and end. Once you have mastered the steps and the sequence, however, all sewing becomes easier because you apply what you have learned to the next sewing task. Your sewing schema is developed. Teaching story parts to a child is similar in that what is learned about one story helps to develop a child's schema for understanding the next story.

Q. *How do we avoid overanalyzing stories so as not to spoil story reading for children?*

A. We must remember that we teach reading skills and strategies as an aid to comprehension and enjoyment of literature. All children should have access to whatever skills they may need to help them understand and enjoy stories. Our mistake in teaching is that we sometimes focus so hard on the skills and strategies that we (and the children) lose sight of the goal. Perhaps we need to remind ourselves that one way children learn to read better is by reading more. There needs to be a time for teaching and a time for reading for pleasure.

Lessons on story structure can begin with the usual preparation for reading—discussing background knowledge and setting purposes. The story then can be read for sheer enjoyment. Following the reading, the teacher may ask students to read aloud the part that tells the time and place of the story, the part that introduces the characters, and the part that starts the action. In later lessons using other stories, the story parts may be labeled, with some parts left out for the children to complete in their own words, or part of the story may be read and the children asked to predict consequences or resolutions. A variety of strategies may be used for guided practice to help students internalize information about story structure and use this information to enhance both their comprehension and enjoyment.

Some cautions for the teacher:
- Not every story needs to be analyzed. Children should be encouraged to read some stories purely for pleasure.
- Not every story part needs to be addressed. Some stories are notable for characterization, others for setting, and others for action.
- Not every story will adhere to story grammar. Some stories vary from normal structure for effect.

Children also should have plenty of time in school to read stories for enjoyment, to discuss stories with classmates, to write their own stories, and to read their stories to classmates.

Expository Text

Q. *How does prior knowledge fit with the teaching of expository text?*

A. As mentioned earlier, the research has indicated clearly that what the reader already knows about the *content* of the text determines to a large extent what is comprehended from the text. However, we often ignore the fact that readers also bring to the text a knowledge of *structure*. Just as prior knowledge of story structure can support comprehension and recall of stories, knowledge of the way expository text is structured supports comprehension and recall of information. Studies by McGee (1982), Meyer, Brandt, and Bluth (1980), and Taylor (1980, 1985) have demonstrated the importance of readers' sensitivity to the organization of ideas in recognizing the relative importance of information in the text and in recalling that information.

Equally important, studies such as those of Armbruster, Anderson, and Ostertag (1987), Bartlett (1978), and Mosenthal

(1983) suggest that students can be taught to identify and use text structures in comprehending and recalling information. To put it simply, we have evidence that students who have prior knowledge of text structure use it in understanding and recalling information. Furthermore, the research suggests that teaching students to be aware of the ways that ideas are organized will aid them in comprehending expository text. Thus, it is important for teachers to use strategies that show students how to use their background knowledge of both content *and* structure to support their comprehension of expository text.

Q. *How do we decide what strategies to use in teaching content and structure?*

A. Many good strategies for teaching students to comprehend expository text are described elsewhere in this book. Other strategies may be found in the professional literature relating to content area reading instruction. Indeed, many of the techniques that are affirmed by recent research have been suggested earlier by authors such as Herber (1970, 1978), Niles (1964), Robinson (1975), and Vacca (1980, 1986). The research has shown that the same kinds of techniques that have been successful in helping secondary students to use their knowledge of content and structure to support their reading comprehension can be used in simpler form with younger students.

It may be helpful to consider a framework for instruction that includes preparation for reading, guidance of the reading process, and development of independence. During the preparation phase, teachers use strategies that (1) activate prior knowledge relating to or analogous to the content of the reading material; (2) preview key concepts and vocabulary; (3) give a sense of the organization of the material; and (4) create curiosity and expectation, set purposes, and feed forward to the content of the text (Nelson-Herber, 1985).

As an example, for a reading selection on *pollution,* the teacher may activate students' experiences relating to the topic by having them list all the words they can think of relating to *pollution.* The teacher then shows students how to organize the words into a structured overview (or semantic map) that depicts types of pollution, causes and effects of pollution, laws relating to pollution, and agencies that address the problem. Before students begin to read, they are asked to predict from the overview what the author might say in the text. The students are learning to use their own knowledge of content and sense of structure to make predictions, and they have the built-in motivation of wanting to confirm their predictions as they read.

The teacher then guides the reading process by instructing students to read the selection to confirm or reject their predictions. Students monitor their own reading comprehension to detect dissonance or conflict with what they already know. When what they read doesn't sound right or doesn't make sense, they either reread the material to correct their understanding or resolve the conflict by learning the new knowledge or elaborating on old knowledge (Nelson-Herber, 1985). Finally, the teacher guides students in creating a graphic organizer that uses the material from the original overview, corrects it, and adds relevant information. Students gain independence when they internalize these strategies and apply them to new materials. In other words, they use prior knowledge of content and structure as a base for reconstructing meaning from text and for constructing new knowledge from text.

Q. *Should we be more concerned with the content or the process in teaching text structures? How do we avoid overanalyzing texts and isolating the structure from the content?*

A. Herber (1978) advises that content and process be taught simultaneously. The focus of concern should be on understanding the content of the text. The processes taught should be those that support the student's comprehension of the content.

For example, a science textbook chapter usually has section headings, subheadings, illustrations, pictures, and captions. Probably the chapter contains a heavy load of technical vocabulary and builds on material from previous chapters. Teaching students to read this material calls for activating their knowledge of both content and structure acquired in earlier chapters and helping them relate it to the new material, perhaps with a structured overview. New technical vocabulary would be presented in the overview and reinforced with discussion. Students might be asked to predict what they will learn from the chapter on the basis of what they already know from earlier chapters.

On the other hand, if the material is about the Declaration of Independence, the problem is to understand the feelings, concerns, needs, and desires of the people who wrote it. Teaching students to read this material calls for activating their knowledge about human rights, representation, voting, and taxes, perhaps with an anticipation guide (Nelson-Herber, 1985). The guide might present the student with items such as, "How would you feel if your country was ruled by a king in a distant land?" or "How would you feel if the king sent soldiers to live in your house without your permission?" Each item would paraphrase one of the problems the founding fathers faced in terms of the students' own feelings. After discussing each item, the students would read the material to determine how the founding fathers dealt with these problems.

As students internalize these processes, they learn that their own experiences are valuable in understanding text, and they learn to apply these strategies to new materials to enhance comprehension.

General Questions

Q. *Haven't good teachers been using many of these strategies for years to teach text comprehension?*

A. Although research related to story schema and text structure is currently an active topic in reading and psychology, reading educators have been intuitively aware of the importance of text structure for many years. Articles and textbooks written over the past three decades contain strategies directed at teaching students to use story and text structure to support comprehension.

For example, as early as 1947, Gates recognized the importance of story sense in comprehension. Reading textbooks in the 1950s and 1960s encouraged teachers to make students aware of setting, plot episodes, rising action, denouement, and falling action. Though the new story grammars are more detailed and probably more accurate in describing story structure, the related research simply affirms what reading educators have been aware of for many years.

Robinson's SQ3R technique (1962) required students to actively survey expository text and note the structure by using organizational factors such as headings, subheadings, charts, graphs, and topic sentences in order to ask self-directed questions to anticipate content within that structure. SQ3R was originally offered as a study technique, but it was a precursor of more recent similar strategies that promote both text structure awareness and metacognitive skills.

The use of structured overviews and graphic organizers (Barron, 1969; Barron & Earle, 1973; Barron & Stone, 1973; Herber, 1970, 1978) to depict the structure of text and/or content has been recommended for almost two decades. Structured overviews were originally intended to show relationships among the ideas in a selection by placing vocabulary relating to the selection in a framework showing superordinate, coordinate, and subordinate concepts. Graphic postorganizers were used by Herber (1970) and Barron and Stone (1973) to promote recall of the content according to the way it was structured. These strategies were precursors of more recent strategies such as mapping and networking.

Niles (1964) recommended teaching patterns of organization in text, such as cause and effect, comparison and contrast, time order, and simple listing as a strategy for improving comprehension and recall. This technique was a precursor of more recent and similar strategies recommended for teaching macrostructure.

It should be no surprise, then, that for years good teachers have been using techniques to make students aware of text structure. That's part of what makes them good teachers. It may be confusing to teachers, however, when certain strategies are promoted as new, and yet are similar to strategies they already use. Part of the answer is that some of these earlier strategies were considered study techniques and deemed more appropriate for middle and secondary schools. With the new research on schema theory, story grammars, and expository text structure, elementary school teachers are being encouraged to use similar but simpler techniques for the improvement of general comprehension. The recent rash of new ideas for teaching structure in text is based on the current research that confirms the relationship of knowledge of text structure and reading comprehension and affirms the practice of teaching text structure.

It probably would be helpful if young authors would trace the roots of their ideas to their origins so that teachers could recognize the development and improvement of teaching techniques over time and on the basis of new research. They would also recognize the magnificent heritage of reading education on which both the new research and the new strategies are based.

Q. *Is the research on narrative and expository text reflected in the current reading tests we use?*

A. No. Most standardized reading comprehension tests are still based on literal and inferential questions about the content of a series of unrelated paragraphs. Although questions may require knowledge of story elements such as characters and events, or in the case of expository text, knowledge of cause and effect, sequence, or comparisons and contrasts, they are not specifically designed to measure awareness or use of text structure in comprehending. Reading skills tests still focus on vocabulary and word recognition. The newer tests of reading comprehension based on the cloze process may be more promising, but they have not been designed to test students' use of prior knowledge, story schema, or text structure in comprehending.

Some new approaches to research on testing seek to expand the range of behaviors assessed by reading tests. Tests are being developed to include measures of background knowledge, reading comprehension, reading strategies, and reading attitudes (Wixson & Peters, 1984).

Until the new tests appear, teachers may use a variety of informal procedures to assess their students' use of background knowledge, story schema, and text structure to enhance comprehension. During preparation for reading, teachers can use brainstorming and discussion to assess students' background knowledge. Some of the same techniques that have been suggested for teaching story grammar and text structure can be used to assess their use. For example, a structured overview may be used both to introduce new content and as a graphic organizer to support reproduction of the content to assess both comprehension and the use of text structure. Retelling of stories by students also can yield a great deal of information.

One of the best assessment procedures is for the teacher to listen to a group of children discussing a story they have read in terms of setting, characterization, plot, and resolution. With minimal teacher questioning, the discussion can reveal all the teacher needs to know about students' use of text structure. Students' writing also can be an excellent source of information about their use of story elements and organizations of text. With instruction on the structure of text, writing improves along with reading. The reading-writing connection is very strong.

In any testing, the focus should be on measuring comprehension. Skills and strategies should be measured only in terms of how they enhance comprehension and how they affect attitudes toward reading. It would be tragic if all the products of the new research were used only to impose new sets of skills to be mastered and new obstacles for children to overcome. The goal is to make children competent and enthusiastic readers, not to make them skilled nonreaders.

Q. *How should staff development programs on these issues be conducted?*

A. In a review of research relating to inservice and staff development, Joyce and Showers (1980) identified several components of training:

- Presentation of theory or description of skill or strategy
- Modeling or demonstration of skills or models of teaching
- Practice in simulated or classrooom settings
- Structured and open-ended feedback (provision of information about performance)
- Coaching for application (hands-on assistance with the transfer of skills and strategies to the classroom).

Research evidence suggests that when these components are combined in a comprehensive training sequence, each has much greater power than when used alone. It is estimated that when presentation is used alone, only 5 percent of the teachers hearing the presentation make any effort to implement the new strategy.

It seems clear then that, depending on its size and organization, a school system must be willing to commit to a long range plan for school improvement. First, teachers need access to information about research based teaching skills and strategies. Then, they need time and support to assimilate new ideas, to learn new instructional strategies, to practice these in the classroom, to integrate the new behaviors into their teaching repertoires, to help students adapt to the new approaches, and to fine tune and consolidate for teaching confidence. Furthermore, teachers need the support and commitment of the school administrative and supervisory personnel to do all this. According to Samuels,

> Current research suggests that significant innovation requires two years of planning and incubation time, two years for implementation, and two years to produce a stable effect on student achievement. Those projects which were unsuccessful rushed forward too soon and often failed to create the necessary climate for district support and commitment (1981, p.271).

The use of a multiplier model can sometimes speed the process (Nelson-Herber, 1982). In a multiplier model, a core group of volunteer teachers receives training as described above, and they become facilitators for other teachers in a school. They provide information, demonstrate the innovation in their own classroom or school settings, and coach other teachers in its use.

Volunteerism is important because it is the best teachers in a district who are likely to volunteer for a program that meets the needs of their students. These teachers usually have enough teaching experience to have developed their own teaching styles and sufficient comfort with their styles to consider theory based alternatives. This builds a success factor into the early stages of the program. Because they are respected as competent professionals, their enthusiasm and success persuade others to learn and implement research based innovations (Nelson-Herber, 1982).

Whenever possible, teachers should be encouraged to attend professional meetings and conferences to keep current on new topics of research and to renew enthusiasm and energy for the educational enterprise.

Q. *How do all these strategies relate to independence in reading, the real goal of reading instruction?*

A. Young children are not passive receivers of language instruction. They have a capacity for recognizing the rules of their language and internalizing them. Indeed, they internalize the complex rules of the spoken language almost entirely without formal instruction. They learn to talk because they need to talk. They are constantly constructing meaning from all their experiences. Children learn what they need to know to make sense of their world and control it, not necessarily what we want them to know.

We, as teachers, must constantly remind ourselves of two factors relating to reading. The first is that no sequence of reading skills has been verified on the basis of research. All skill sequences are based on armchair speculation and common sense considerations. To require mastery of reading skills in linear fashion, as if we had evidence that one were prerequisite to another, is to place barriers in the way of learning. Reading is not simply an accumulation of skills. It is an active, constructive process in which the reader uses background knowledge, language knowledge, and skill knowledge interactively to make meaning from text.

The second is that all language skills—listening, reading, writing, and speaking—are interrelated. What is learned about language in one mode supports learning in other modes. Children need a rich variety of language experiences to support them in learning about the world and about their language.

None of this is to suggest that skill development is not important. All children should have access to good skills instruction, but they should not spend large chunks of their time practicing discrete skills in workbooks and on ditto sheets. They should be provided with many and varied opportunities to integrate their skills, knowledge, and experience in real reading and language activities. They should spend a good portion of their instructional time listening to stories; talking about characters, settings, and plot episodes; reading stories; discussing stories with their classmates; writing their own stories; reading their stories to classmates; critiquing their own stories and those of classmates; reading, writing, and producing plays; reading for information to solve problems and to complete group projects or reports; and reading to carry on investigative activities for science, mathematics, and social studies.

Skills are learned best when they are needed to be successful in real life activities. Children will gain independence in reading as we provide them with the kinds of school activities that model real life situations requiring reading and language skills. They will read for pleasure, for information, and to solve their own problems both in school and in their lives.

References

Armbruster, B.B., Anderson, T., and Ostertag, J. Does text structure/summarization instruction facilitate learning from expository text? *Reading Research Quarterly,* 1987, *22,* 331-346.

Barron, R.F. The use of vocabulary as an advance organizer. In H.L. Herber and P.L. Sanders (Eds.), *Research in reading in the content areas: First year report.* Syracuse, NY: Syracuse University, Reading and Language Arts Center, 1969.

Barron, R.F., and Earle, R. An approach for vocabulary development. In H.L. Herber and R.F. Barron (Eds.), *Research in reading in the content areas: Second report.* Syracuse, NY: Syracuse University, Reading and Language Arts Center, 1973.

Barron, R.F., and Stone, F. *The effect of student constructed graphic postorganizers upon learning of vocabulary relationships from a passage of social studies content.* Paper presented at the National Reading Conference, Houston, Texas, 1973.

Bartlett, B.J. *Top level structure as an organizational strategy for recall of classroom text.* Unpublished doctoral dissertation, Arizona State University, 1978.

Fitzgerald, J., and Spiegel, D.L. Enhancing children's reading comprehension through instruction in narrative structure. *Journal of Reading Behavior,* 1983, *15,* 1-17.

Fowler, G.L. Developing comprehension skills in primary students through the use of story frames. *The Reading Teacher,* 1982, *36,* 176-179.

Gates, A.L. *The improvement of reading.* New York: Macmillan, 1947.

Herber, H. *Teaching reading in content areas.* Englewood Cliffs, NJ: Prentice Hall, 1970, 1978.

Joyce, B., and Showers, B. Improving inservice training: The messages of research. *Educational Leadership,* February 1980.

Mandler, J.M., and Johnson, M.S. Remembrance of things parsed: Story structure and recall. *Cognitive Psychology,* 1977, *9,* 111-115.

McGee, L.M. Awareness of text structure: Effects on children's recall of expository text. *Reading Research Quarterly,* 1982, *17,* 581-590.

Meyer, B.J.F., Brandt, D.M., and Bluth, G.J. Use of top level structure in text: Key for reading comprehension of ninth grade students. *Reading Research Quarterly,* 1980, *16,* 72-103.

Moldofsky, P.B. Teaching students to determine the central story problem: A practical application of schema theory. *The Reading Teacher,* 1983, *36,* 740-745.

Mosenthal, J. *Instruction in the interpretation of a writer's argument: A training study.* Unpublished doctoral dissertation, University of Illinois, 1983.

Moss, J.F., and Oden, S. Children's story comprehension and social learning. *The Reading Teacher,* 1983, *36,* 784-789.

Nelson-Herber, J. *A staff development program for teaching reading in content areas.* Network Report #2. Binghamton, NY: Network of Demonstration Centers for Teaching Reading in Content Areas, 1982. (ED 282 176)

Nelson-Herber, J. Anticipation and prediction in reading comprehension. In T. Harris and E. Cooper (Eds.), *Reading, thinking, and concept development.* New York: The College Board, 1985.

Nessel, D.D. Storytelling in the reading program. *The Reading Teacher,* 1985, *38,* 378-381.

Niles, O. Organization perceived. In H.L. Herber (Ed.), *Developing study skills in secondary schools.* Newark, DE: International Reading Association, 1964.

Olson, M.W. A dash of story grammar and...presto! A book report. *The Reading Teacher,* 1984, *37,* 458-461.

Piccolo, J.A. Writing a no-fault narrative: Every teacher's dream. *The Reading Teacher,* 1986, *40,* 136-142.

Rand, M.K. Story schema: Theory, research, and practice. *The Reading Teacher,* 1984, *37,* 377-382.

Robinson, H.A. *Teaching reading and study strategies.* Boston: Allyn and Bacon, 1975.

Robinson, P.R. *Effective reading,* New York: Harper & Row, 1962.

Rumelhart, D.E. Notes on a schema for stories. In D.G. Bobrow and A.M. Collins (Eds.), *Representation and understanding.* New York: Academic Press, 1975.

Samuels, S.J. Characteristics of exemplary reading programs. In J. Guthrie (Ed.), *Comprehension and teaching: Research reviews.* Newark, DE: International Reading Association, 1981.

Smith, M., and Bean, T. Four strategies that develop children's story comprehension and writing. *The Reading Teacher,* 1983, *37,* 295-301.

Spiegel, D.L., and Fitzgerald, J. Improving reading comprehension through instruction about story parts. *The Reading Teacher,* 1986, *39,* 676-688.

Stein, N.L., and Glenn, C.G. An analysis of story comprehension in elementary school children. In R.O. Freedle (Ed.), *New directions in discourse processing.* Norwood, NJ: Ablex, 1979.

Taylor, B.M. Children's memory for expository text after reading. *Reading Research Quarterly,* 1980, *15,* 399-411.

Taylor, B.M. Toward an understanding of factors contributing to children's difficulty summarizing textbook material. In J.A. Niles (Ed.), *Issues in literacy: A research perspective.* Rochester, NY: National Reading Conference, 1985, 125-131.

Thorndyke, P.W. Cognitive structures in comprehension and memory of narrative discourse. *Cognitive Psychology,* 1977, *9,* 77-110.

Vacca, R., and Vacca, J. *Content area reading.* Boston: Little, Brown, 1980, 1986.

Wixson, K.K., and Peters, C.W. Reading redefined: A Michigan Reading Association position paper. *Michigan Reading Journal,* 1984, *17,* 4-7.